EVANSTON
WYOMING

Also available by Dennis J Ottley

Remembering (Korea: 1950-1953)

IZZARD INK PUBLISHING COMPANY
PO Box 522251
Salt Lake City, Utah 84152
www.izzardink.com

LIBRARY OF CONGRESS CONTROL NUMBER: 2018960342

Designed by Alissa Rose Theodor
Cover Design by Andrea Ho
Cover Photograph by Shelly & Deann Horne of Creative Ink Images
Cover Images: Robert Castillo/Shutterstock.com ivangal/Shutterstock.com monofaction/Shutterstock.com

First Edition January 28, 2019

Contact the author at djottleybooks@gmail.com

Hardback ISBN: 978-1-64228-023-4
Softback ISBN: 978-1-64228-024-1
eBook ISBN: 978-1-64228-025-8

1967 TO 1995

EVANSTON
WYOMING

VOLUME FIVE

BOOM-BUST-POLITICS

"IN THE EYES OF A MAYOR"

DENNIS J OTTLEY

IZZARD INK
PUBLISHING

CHAPTER 27

1993....The first Evanston City Council meeting for the year of 1993 was held on January 13th. Roll call was taken by City Clerk Don Welling who declared that there was a quorum present.

Before consideration of any agenda items I recognized another group of Boy Scouts who were in attendance. I introduced Scoutmaster Richard Black from Troop 9 and had him introduce the following scouts: Chris Warner, Tygh Hutchinson, David Munoz, Justin Keyes, C. J. Revelli and Alex Black.

Scoutmaster Black explained that attending a public meeting was one of their requirements in receiving their Citizenship Badge. I thanked them all for coming to the meeting and told them they would be more than welcome to attend any future city meetings. I also wished them the best in completing their other requirements and success in earning their badge.

We followed up by acting on the approval of minutes of all previous meetings in December, approval to pay the outstanding bills, and acknowledging and accepting department reports. This business was passed and approved by a council motion and a second, with 7 votes in favor, including Evanston's newly appointed city council member, Ron Barnard, who was sworn in by oath during last month's meeting.

In giving my State of the City address, I started out by thanking the members of the Evanston City Council, the city staff, commissions and boards, the Evanston Chamber of Commerce, and all committees and anyone else who was involved in making 1992 another successful year. I thanked them all for their cooperation throughout the year in getting things done.

I spoke of the same programs and projects as I did in my talk at the last meeting in December of last year. I spoke of the goals and the programs we accomplished during the year. I spoke of the election, the property that the U.P.R.C. deeded to the city, and the possibility of receiving more property west of the Roundhouse.

I mentioned the possibility of getting enough land to enlarge the golf course and creating another industrial park, enticing other companies to build in Evanston. I spoke of the heavy snowfall we were having this winter. I said that this winter of 1992 had come in like a lion, giving the city a very expensive snow removal problem, and if it kept up into 1993 we might have to make some budget changes, because snow removal could exceed its budget .

I mentioned that we must continue to plan and set goals, and try to complete our ongoing goals. And that we should all be concerned with the future of our community, and we must continue to work hard and strive to continue to retain and improve Evanston's lifestyle and economy.

We must continue to work closely with the Evanston Chamber of Commerce, the Elks Club and all service organizations to encourage them to continue with their programs. We must work closely with the Uinta County Commissioners and the Uinta County School District No. 1 Board of Trustees. We can only make things work by cooperating with others, and by learning to disagree without being disagreeable.

We must make changes where needed. I once heard someone say that the most dangerous phrase in the language is "We've always done it this way." That is probably the time when changes need to be made.

I spoke with boldness on the economy, cooperation, and said that if we don't or can't work together, nothing will get done. I thanked everyone again and ended my State of the City address by saying, *Evanston is a great community and I love it. The people are great and may God bless you all.*

After I finished my talk each of the city council members expressed themselves, thanking the staff for their cooperation, and a special thanks to each other and the public for placing their confidence in them as representatives. They stated that 1992 was a good year and each council member said they were optimistic for a good year in 1993.

I turned the meeting over to City Clerk Welling to administer the Oath of Office to the three city council members who were re-elected during the past November election; Clarence Vranish of Ward 1, Jerry Wall of Ward 2, and Tom Hutchinson of Ward 3. After being sworn in they each signed the Oath of Office and returned them to the city clerk.

A public hearing was held, conducted by City Attorney Dennis Boal on a new application for a restaurant liquor license applied for by Bonnie Bell, dba Red Chili Pepper. The hearing was recorded and the tape would be on file at City Hall. Blair Bell was in attendance to represent the applicant. There was no one present in opposition. Therefore, Councilman Nelson made a motion to approve the Red Chili Pepper application for a restaurant liquor license, seconded by Wall, with all voting in favor.

I read a letter from Ruth Dahlman resigning from the Evanston Planning and Zoning Commission. Motion was made by Councilman Davis to accept Dahlman's resignation, seconded by Nelson with all voting in favor. I expressed the city's appreciation to Ruth for her service to the city and wished her and her husband well in the future.

I reported that Keith Cerny wished to resign from the Uinta County Economic Development Commission. Motion was made by Council Hutchinson to accept Cerny's resignation, seconded by Davis, with all voting in favor. I thanked Keith for his service to the commission, and I thanked him for his cooperation with the city in getting local news to the folks in the *Uinta County Herald*, and wished him well in his new ventures.

Cerny had been Publisher for the *Herald* for years, but had recently been replaced by Mike Jensen, *Uinta County Herald's* new publisher.

The next order of business was the assignment of my appointed staff as follows: Chief of Police, Dennis Harvey; Community Development Director/City Planner, Paul Knopf; City Clerk/Assistant City Treasurer, Don Welling; City Treasurer/Assistant City Clerk, Steve Widmer; City Engineer/Director of Public Works, Brian

Honey; City Court Judge, John Phillips; Assistant Court Judge, Greg Phillips; Assistant Court Judge, Bruce Barnard; City Attorney, Dennis Boal; and Assistant City Attorney, Rick Lavery.

Motion was made by Councilman Nelson to confirm the above appointments, seconded by Davis. Motion passed with 6 votes in favor. I had to abstain because, by law, I am not able to vote on my own appointments.

I announced, although it is not an appointed position, that Allan "Oop" Hansen would remain as Operations Superintendent, under the supervision of the City Engineer, Brian Honey.

I made the appointment of all personnel of the Evanston Police Department which by law is required. All in all there were 26: patrolmen, detectives, training personnel, animal control personnel, parking control officer, and others. Motion was made by Councilman Vranish to confirm all the Police Department personnel named, seconded by Hutchinson with 6 votes in favor.

I then made my appointments to the following boards and commissions: Planning and Zoning Commission, Board of Adjustments, Beautification Committee, Urban Renewal Agency, Evanston Tourism (Lodging Tax) Board, Evanston Housing Authority, Airport Joint Powers Board, Human Services Joint Powers Board, and the Uinta County Economic Development Commission. All appointments were passed unanimously by motions and seconds by the city council members.

Every two years following elections, the Evanston City Council must vote on the President of the City Council. At this time Councilmen Clarence Vranish and Councilman Will Davis were nominated. Voting was by secret ballot, under the supervision of City Attorney Boal. Councilman Vranish was elected.

Under public participation, Evanston's First Lady Sandy Ottley made a request for two parades to be held in January: a Torchlight Parade on Friday, January 22nd at 6:00 p.m., and a Dragon Parade on Saturday, January 23rd at 12:00 noon to celebrate the Year of the Rooster during Evanston's fourth annual Chinese New Year: *Gung Hay Fat Choy,* which translates to *Happy New Year.*

Councilman Vranish made a motion to allow both parades as requested and to notify the police department of the times and route, seconded by Nelson, with all voting in favor.

Urban Renewal Director Jim Davis made a report to the city council concerning the 1992 Renewal Ball and that the event generated enough money that $26,000 had been donated to the Urban Renewal Agency by the Renewal Ball Committee, to be used for improvements and projects at Depot Square. Jim reported that approximately 75 volunteers worked on the Ball, and that Lynn Fox had been elected Chairperson of the Renewal Ball for the 1993 event, and Lori Alexander was elected to Chair the 1994 event, both of which would be in June.

The council and I expressed our thanks and appreciation for all the efforts and hard work given to the City of Evanston by the Urban Renewal Agency and its committees, the Renewal Ball and Beautification Committees. I said to Jim Davis, *You have done a terrific job in getting local folks involved, this makes for a great and healthy community.*

With the heavy snowfall, and with the new development throughout the city, we had been having a hard time locating vacant properties where the city street department could dump the snow removed from the streets, alleys and public parking lots.

I wrote a letter to the Union Pacific Railroad to get their permission to use some of their vacant property. It was necessary to pinpoint certain areas so the street crews wouldn't have so far to haul and dispose of the snow. This made it possible to remove the snow much faster from streets and other areas.

I reported to the council that the U.P.R.R. had given us permission to use the vacant property near the Bear River Commercial area and other locations which would give the city many more places to dump snow.

Prior to adjournment I called for a work session to be held on January 20th at 5:00 p.m.

The *Uinta County Herald* of January 26th printed a headline article by Reporter Ann Curtis titled, CENTURY CABLE PAYS CITY $12,000, *Company says mistakes discovered during internal audit.*

The article continued: *Century Cable Company's local representative Bob George delivered a $12,725.46 check to the city, said the company would be adding two more channels and issued a 10-page letter in response to a study on their services.*

City Attorney Dennis Boal reported at the next regular meeting on January 27th, that having the meetings about the cable TV company had been very fruitful and productive to both the company and the city. It seems through these meetings the TV franchise had been straightened out, complaints from the public had come to a stop and the cable company was giving much better service, and in some areas expanding. Boal stated that their next TV committee meeting would be held on February 11th at 5:00 p.m.

The *Herald* of January 26th also reported on the recent Chinese New Year's event. The article was also written by Reporter Ann Curtis and stated the following:

Evanston's Year of the Rooster celebration had a rocky beginning on Friday evening, but progressed into a spectacular climax with a cheering crowd at the rickshaw races on Saturday.

Friday's blowing snow and bitter cold had organizers debating whether to hold the evening's event—but being hearty Wyoming folks, the festivities went on.

The article continued: *The torchlight parade began at the Uinta County Library with approximately 30 participants, who moved at a brisk pace to fend off the cold.*

The article mentioned all other activities during the two-day event, but concluded by mentioning a new program added to the Chinese New Year celebration:

The Uinta County Amateur Radio Club had advertised the event in four national magazines and was set up to speak to "ham operators" all over the world.

Clarence Vranish, club member, reported that over 1,000 calls were received from all around the United States, Canada and England.

"People were just waiting to talk to us," he said.

The club will send parchment certificates commemorating Evanston's Chinese New Year celebration to those operators who requested them.

But according to Curtis's article, the highlight of the event was the rickshaw race.

During the January 27th city council meeting I recognized some Cub Scouts and their leaders from Pack 2 Den 1. Leaders Scott Robinson and Mark Cox introduced their Cub Scouts, Rory McDonald, Zane Stahl, Jaush Francis and Nathan Greer. I commended the scouts and their leaders for attending the meeting and invited them to participate in the meeting if they desired.

Evanston Mayor Dennis Ottley was surprised at Wednesday evening's city council meeting when his staff came marching in singing "Happy Birthday" and carrying a cake to celebrate his 61st birthday which took place Thursday. Ottley was completely surprised and pleased at the gesture.

Uinta County Herald, January 29, 1993.

After the initial business was acted on, a public hearing was held with City Attorney Boal conducting, concerning vacating a part of the Overthrust Meadows Subdivision. The hearing was recorded and the tape would be on file at City Hall.

There was no one in opposition to vacating that portion of Overthrust Meadows. Therefore, action was taken on the issue by ordinance at later meetings.

About that time several staff members from the city hall office entered the City Council Chambers and sang, "Happy Birthday" to me and presented me with a birthday cake and a gift.

Actually it would not be my birthday until the next day, January 28th, but the staff really surprised and embarrassed me by presenting me with birthday wishes during this meeting. But it was well appreciated and turned out to be a lot of fun.

The subject of the high "ham operator" antennas had previously come up, which a number of citizens had concerns with, especially the pole height, size, support structures and location. The city had spoken, in previous meetings, of some process to permit ham amateur radio operators to be able to legally construct their antennas. There were already dozens of antennas in place in various areas of the city.

Councilman Clarence Vranish was a radio ham operator and he had previously suggested an ordinance controlling high antennas. During a previous meeting he had sponsored and introduced Ordinance 92-19, regulating amateur radio operators, to provide an application process and permit system for the construction of antenna support structures within the City of Evanston.

During this meeting of January 27th Ordinance 92-19, which had already been passed unanimously by the council on first and second readings, was now up for third and final reading and passed, once again unanimously, by the council.

In other action taking place during the meeting, Councilman Vranish made a motion that City Engineer Brian Honey be directed to replace yield signs at 10th and Lombard with stop signs and make Lombard a through street, seconded by Davis with all voting in favor.

The police department had reported three recent accidents on Lombard because of the yield sign and suggested that Lombard be a through street. By passing the motion it had made Lombard a much safer street.

City Engineer Honey reported on a successful meeting he had recently attended in Cheyenne with the Farm Loan Board, resulting in obtaining funding in the amount of $64,000, one half of the cost to repair the roof on the water storage tanks.

I congratulated Brian for his success in receiving the funds and told the council that we needed to keep close contact with those in Cheyenne so that they realize that Evanston is still in Wyoming.

I took a moment to express the city's thanks and appreciation for all the publicity gained throughout the country with the annual Chinese New Year event—the Year of the Rooster. I thanked Councilmember Jerry Wall who chaired the event and thanked Councilmember Clarence Vranish for his part in promoting it beyond the United States through his Ham Operator Club advertising.

I thanked them all for another great and successful event, and mentioned that I was amazed that the event went off as well as it did, as snowy and bitter cold as it was.

I adjourned the meeting with the announcement that there would be a work session on February 3rd at 5:00 p.m.

The Annual Agri-Business Banquet wasn't scheduled until March 16th and would be held at the Elks Lodge, but I announced early in February that the city was starting to ask for nominations for Citizen of the Year, to be voted on by the mayor and city council, and the winner would be announced during the Agri-Business Banquet.

In the February 9th issue of the *Uinta County Herald*, an article was published announcing Hillcrest Chevron, owned by Dave Madia, officially became Evanston's and the State of Wyoming's first retail gasoline outlet to dispense natural gas for gas operated vehicles.

Madia, who also owned Evanston Motor Company (presently the Rocky Mountain Yeti car dealership), spoke to the crowd about his excitement having the new natural gas service available and the potential for natural gas as the fuel of the future.

Although after all the effort to set up Hillcrest Chevron as a retail outlet for natural gas, there is no longer any such outlet in Evanston providing natural gas for vehicles. Natural gas as the fuel of the future for vehicles never materialized and Hillcrest Chevron had some time ago removed their natural gas dispenser.

In opening up the first regular city council meeting on February 10th, I first recognized a single Boy Scout, Mark Cutler. I thanked him for his attendance at the meeting and presented him with one of Evanston's promotional pins (Fresh Air, Freedom and Fun), and invited him to stay at the meeting as long as he wished.

Scouts and school students were always welcome to the city meetings. It made me feel good to see Evanston's young folks interested enough to attend the meetings. However, I realize that the scouts were attending the meetings for merit badge purposes, but nevertheless it still makes a person feel good to see them in attendance.

Mr. Jeff Shaffer had previously been appointed to the Evanston Lodging Tax Tourism Board, but never showed any interest and often missed meetings; therefore, the Board requested that I write him a letter asking for his resignation, in which I did.

Due to the fact that he had never responded, I requested a motion from the city council to vacate Shaffer's position. Councilman Nelson made the motion to vacate Shaffer's position on the Board as of February 1, 1993, because of his lack of interest and his lack of response to any correspondence, seconded by Wall, with all voting in favor.

I made more appointments to the various boards and commissions as follows: Councilman Will Davis to the Tourism Board in place Jeff Shaffer who resigned; Councilmen Tom Hutchinson and Ron Barnard, to assist me as Police Commissioner on the Evanston Police Commission; Councilmen Clarence Vranish and Ron Barnard, city employees Sue Norman, Arvel "Bud" Eastman and Officer Jake Williams to the Personnel Board; Don Bodine to the Fire Department and City Planner Paul Knopf to Uinta County Emergency Management; Councilmen Ron Barnard and Clarence Vranish to the Joint Powers Human Service Board; Councilman Craig Nelson to the Uinta County Economic Development Commission; Councilman Tom Hutchinson, replacing former Councilmember Julie Lehman, to serve on the Rural Conservation District; Councilman Ron Barnard as liaison to the Evanston Housing Authority; Councilwoman Wall as liaison to the Urban Renewal Agency; Councilman Will Davis as liaison to recycling; and myself as liaison to the Planning and Zoning Commission.

Councilman Davis made a motion to confirm all the above appointments, seconded by Barnard. The motion carried with 5 yes votes and 1 no vote (Vranish). I'm unaware why Vranish voted no.

I appointed the following to the Historical Preservation Commission: Janice Bodine, Cheryl Lowham, Sandy Ottley, Georgia Harvey, Gary Cazin, Gale Curtis, John Clements, Urban Renewal Director Jim Davis, and Councilwoman Jerry Wall.

Councilman Hutchinson made a motion to confirm the appointments to the Historical Preservation Commission, seconded by Nelson, with all council members voting in favor.

Ordinance 93-1, which had passed by a unanimous vote on first and second readings, was up for passage on third and final reading. This ordinance made <u>Disturbing the Peace</u> in the City of Evanston a misdemeanor crime. It would be unlawful for anyone within the city to disturb the peace of another. The motion to pass Ordinance 93-1 was made by Councilman Vranish, seconded by Barnard, with all voting in favor.

Hillcrest Chevron owner Dave Madia, Mountain Fuel President D.N. "Nick" Rose, members of the Evanston Chamber of Commerce Red Carpet Committee and Mountain Fuel representatives cut the red ribbon during ceremonies marking the official opening of the natural gas refueling station at Hillcrest Chevron in Evanston.

Evanston Mayor Dennis Ottley, Hillcrest Chevron owner Dave Madia and Mountain Fuel President D.N. "Nick" Rose unveil a sign showing the price of natural gas for vehicles - 65.7 cents per equivalent gallon.

Uinta County Herald, February 9, 1993.

After a ten-minute recess, I called the meeting back to order and congratulated Allan "Oop" Hansen for being chosen as a recipient of a management scholarship in the amount of $2,000 from the American Water Works Association. This was the first time a scholarship for an operator had ever been offered.

Oop was chosen over candidates from Colorado, New Mexico and Wyoming, and had a choice of 5 universities to attend for the specialized management training. I told Oop that we were very proud of him and to let us know which university he would be attending.

I announced that the second Annual Railroad Days event would be held on July 17th and 18th, and that the committee chaired by Denice Wheeler was starting to make plans. The committee had received a letter from Union Tank Car Company that the old U.P. roundhouse and machine shop would be open for tours at that time. U.T.C.C. General Manager Gilbert Olson, City Planner Paul Knopf and Urban Renewal Director Jim Davis would be conducting the tours.

Prior to adjournment, I announced that there would be a work session on February 17th at 5:00 p.m.

Surprisingly, early in February, Sandy and I had received a special invitation, with tickets enclosed to the Governor's Prayer Breakfast in Cheyenne on Friday, February 26, 1993. It was held at Little America in Cheyenne from 7:00 to 8:30 a.m.

The Governor's Prayer Breakfast was a state version of the National Prayer Breakfast held in Washington, D.C., much as the Mayor's Prayer Breakfast in Evanston was a version of the National and the State Prayer Breakfasts.

State and City Prayer Breakfasts had been held in every State of the Union and by the mayors of many cities and towns at that time. The breakfasts, whether national, state or local had always been entirely nondenominational and nonpartisan. They included people from all walks of life, and it had always been a very successfully event in Evanston with outstanding speakers.

I had returned notice to the Governor's office that Sandy and I would not be able to attend the Prayer Breakfast, as we had in the past, because of prior commitments. But I thanked them for the invitation and said that we were very honored to have been invited.

I was also invited to the Drug Abuse Resistance Education (D.A.R.E.) graduation exercises at Davis Middle School on Friday, February 12th to speak. The D.A.R.E. Program is law enforcement's approach to the nation's drug problem. It was felt that by educating our children, the nation could reduce the demand for drugs. The program had been started in the 1980s by a small group of officers teaching a small number of students in Los Angeles, California. D.A.R.E. is now taught in all 50 states and some foreign countries.

D.A.R.E. is a proactive program designed to educate the youth in our community with cooperation between parents, schools, and local law enforcement. A D.A.R.E. officer spends one hour during one day a week in each 6th grade classrooms, teaching skills to the youth of our community to help them resist the pressure to use drugs. "Just say no" is the slogan kids were encouraged to say.

I attended the D.A.R.E. graduation exercises and spoke about how great and important the D.A.R.E. Program had been over the years, and congratulated those graduating for their hard-earned awards. I thanked them for having the honor to speak at their graduating exercises.

In opening the second regular city council meeting of the month on February 24th, under unfinished business we acted on the third and final reading of Ordinance 93-2 to repeal, amend and re-enact a section of the present ordinance to prohibit hunting within the City of Evanston. This ordinance had been introduced and sponsored by a member of the city council and had passed on first and second readings unanimously.

We had a few incidents where some hunters had killed deer within the city limits; therefore, the Evanston City Council felt it was necessary to enact a no hunting section in the city code.

Councilman Nelson made a motion to pass Ordinance 93-2 on third and final meeting, seconded by Barnard. The motion passed with 6 votes in favor and 1 absent (Wall).

At this time there was a request by the Union Pacific Resources Company to re-open two natural gas wells that were within the half-mile limits of City of Evanston jurisdiction. These two wells were named the Harry Moon #1 well, and the Bradbury B #1 well. Resolutions to re-open both wells were brought up under new business and introduced by members of the council as Resolution 93-8 for the Moon well and Resolution 93-9 for the Bradbury well.

Motions on Resolutions 93-8 and 93-9 were made for adoption and approval of the U.P.R.C. applications to re-open the wells and put them in operation. Permits would be for a period of one year from the date of issuance, at which time they would expire. Motions to adopt the resolution were made by members of the council and seconded with 6 votes in favor on both and 1 absent (Wall).

It looked like the county was going to get some more natural gas production, which should be a boost in Evanston's economy.

Previously John and Jim Bowns had requested the City of Evanston's support in their desire to promote tourism within the community by increasing the use of the Uinta County Fairgrounds, which is located within the City of Evanston. Since that time Jim Bowns had passed away, leaving his brother John to continue with the project.

Jim's passing was a big loss to his family and also to the City of Evanston, because Jim had been very active in the community and had plans to help the economy of the area.

At this time Resolution 93-10 was introduced by Councilman Davis with the following title:

RESOLUTION 93-10
RESOLUTION AUTHORIZING THE CITY OF EVANSTON, WYOMING TO ENTER INTO A MEMORANDUM OF UNDERSTANDING WITH THE UINTA COUNTY COMMISSIONERS TO PROMOTE THE USE OF THE UINTA COUNTY FAIRGROUNDS WITHIN THE CITY OF EVANSTON.

This resolution requested the use of the fairgrounds for the Evanston Rodeo Series, a program that would carry on through the summer months on weekends and would be promoted and managed by John Bowns, and would feature various cowboy type events.

Although there were no costs to the city mentioned in the resolution, it did demonstrate that the City of Evanston was 100% behind the Rodeo Series programs, and by passing the resolution it made the Uinta County Commissioners more receptive to the programs. Councilman Nelson made the motion to adopt Resolution 93-10, seconded by Hutchinson. The motion passed with 6 votes in favor and 1 absent (Wall).

After 25 years the Evanston Rodeo Series is still operating and John Bowns is still overseeing the program with a very active and hardworking committee in support of the program. They are all volunteers and very much concerned with Evanston's economic future. I give folks like this a lot of credit for their service.

We next acted on Resolution 93-11, introduced by Councilman Davis, to enter into an agreement with John H. Bowns for professional services to basically promote the Evanston Rodeo Series within the city. A motion to adopt Resolution 93-11 was made by Councilman Nelson, seconded by Barnard. The motion passed with the same vote.

All expenses and costs for the Evanston Rodeo Series would come from what the committee raised through gate receipts, concession sales, donations and other means. The program was to be self-sustaining.

During the February 24th meeting Councilman Vranish made a motion to authorize City Clerk Don Welling to provide written approval for Brent Bateman, dba Spirits of Red Mountain, for a catering permit at the Elks Club for February 27th. The Elks Club is located outside the city limits of Evanston, but still within the one-half mile jurisdiction. The motion was seconded by Barnard, and passed unanimously with 1 absent.

City Planner Paul Knopf presented Urban Renewal Director Jim Davis a check from the Wyoming Game and Fish Department in the amount of $55,200 to be used for the BEAR Project as Wetland Mitigation because there was a lot of wetland within the BEAR Project area, including the ponds. the Game and Fish Department were demanding that those areas be preserved for fishing, boating and other recreation uses.

I expressed the city's thanks and appreciation to Wyoming Fish and Game for their interest and contribution, and expressed the city's appreciation to Knopf and Davis for their success in obtaining the funds and for their absolute involvement in the BEAR Project as well as other city programs that have been so successful.

Knopf gave a report on the Evanston 2000 Project, stating that it is almost complete and should be ready for city council to act on it soon. The Evanston 2000 Project was the comprehensive plan that had been in the making for the past year, and it was very important that the city proceed to get the project approved by the city for the sake of growth and the economy.

On behalf of the city I thanked Paul and his neighborhood committees for the time and hard work spent on the project, but I stated that we need to get this completed for the sake of the community.

I once again called for a work session and announced that it would be held on March 3rd at 5:00 p.m. prior to adjournment.

I don't know why, but about this time I got the feeling that one or more of the council members were conspiring against me as mayor. I know that Councilwoman Wall was upset with me for running against her for mayor in 1992, and also because I hadn't appreciated that she was trying to manipulate the new W.A.M. Executive Director Carl Classen and bringing politics into the organization.

The Wyoming Association of Municipalities was supposed to be a nonpartisan organization, but when Wall and Classen started making sly remarks about Governor Mike Sullivan and other state officials only because, most of them were of the Democratic Party, and both Wall and Classen were Republicans.

I wondered, at that time, just how W.A.M. could have hired someone like him as executive director. As far as I was concerned Classen had shown himself to be the worst executive director W.A.M. had ever had, at least during the time I had been a member of the city council and mayor. I had been well acquainted with a few, and this was the first time I had seen the association getting into partisan politics.

Governor Mike Sullivan, Kathy Karpan and other members of the Wyoming State Farm Loan Board, had done nothing but support Evanston. We all had been very successful in getting grants and loans, and other funding through the Farm Loan Board and other State agencies. I always got outstanding cooperation from Governor Sullivan, who had already visited Evanston a dozen or more times.

During my time as mayor of Evanston I worked with two Democrat Governors; Ed Herschler and Mike Sullivan, both of whom have worked closely with me to achieve assistance from the State of Wyoming. Neither of them ever refused any of the help and assistance that we requested. Leno Menghini, Superintendent of the Wyoming State Highway Department, went out of his way to give Evanston all the help we needed. Some of it we didn't even request; they just made suggestions based on their studies of Evanston streets where we most needed to improve, at the State's cost.

I couldn't understand what kind of game Wall and Classen were playing, but during some of the meetings during W.A.M. conferences, I noticed that they would make little sly and cunning remarks about Governor Sullivan and others. I don't know whether anyone else noticed it or not, but no one ever mentioned it to me, and a few years later W.A.M. did get rid of Classen.

During one of our work sessions the council requested that they have an office in the administrative part of City Hall to use as a visiting room or meeting room, and have the city clerk and secretary fix up separate boxes to put their mail and other information in.

We chose the corner office in the back that had been used for numerous things over the years as an office for the city council members. It was located in the far left corner of the area as you walk in past the reception desk and past my Mayor's office, which was the first enclosed office after you pass the reception desk.

I guess I wasn't thinking right at that time, but I found out later the main reason they wanted the office was to have their own little secret and underhanded meetings that didn't involve me: meetings where they could discuss issues away from everyone else, including staff, so no one knew what they were talking about.

At first it was only Jerry Wall that I thought was against me, but in the next months she manipulated four of the city council members to be against me as well, and help her undermine my goals. The next two years would be hell for me, but I still had Councilman Hutchinson working with me, and most of the staff helping me get things done, especially City Attorney Boal and my secretary, Sharon Constantine.

⤜⟁⟁⤛

During the many times in the past few years that I had met with George Peters, the General Superintendent for this area of the Union Pacific Resources Company (U.P.R.C.), aka Upland Industries, I talked about the possibility of obtaining some or all of the property west of the roundhouse, including the 75+ acres west of the railroad tracks toward Almy. In total, the U.P.R.C. still owned approximately 265 acres of undeveloped land extending from the roundhouse property west to Constitutional Avenue, as well as approximately 75 acres on the west side of the railroad tracks.

During our conversations, he told me that he was working with the head office in Omaha, Nebraska to donate all of the land to the city. I explained that city was having problems trying to work with those in Evanston that wanted to take the roundhouse property back from the Union Tank Car Company and break the lease agreement to use the property for historic purposes. I told him that some of the locals, even if it meant losing the employment, didn't care. They just wanted to get the Roundhouse property back to the City of Evanston. I said to Peters, *There's no way Evanston can afford to lose the jobs provided by the company, not to mention losing the taxes that they pay, and if those folks are successful in pushing the Tank Car Company out of Evanston, then the city will lose both the employment and the tax base.*

I told him that even some of the city council members were against trying to keep them in Evanston. As he already knew, the council turned down the Union Tank Car Company's request for an extension on their lease.

The company explained that their plans were to add a $4 million expansion to the plant, which would add dozens more employees, but they needed an extension on the lease to do this.

I explained to him that the council had been unable to approve their request for an extension because of a close split vote; some of the public had showed that they didn't really want them. I told George that though there were people speaking against the company, I knew that a large majority wanted them to stay, even if it meant remaining on the roundhouse property.

But after several local meetings with Union Tank Car officials in attendance, those in opposition to the lease extension were so noisy, I got word that the Union Tank Car Company would be withdrawing their request for the extension of the lease and that they would be looking to move their operations to Utah.

City receives 73-acre gift

At a Thursday afternoon donation ceremony and press conference Union Pacific Resources Company donated a 73-acre tract of land to the City of Evanston to expand its industrial land base.

The land is located just west of the historic roundhouse which is now leased by Union Tank Car.

Evanston's Mayor Dennis Ottley stated, "We are very excited to have this land transfer completed and to have the opportunity to work with Union Pacific Resources Company on this donation. We certainly thank Resources for their cooperation and generosity. We also appreciate the help that Governor Mike Sullivan gave this project."

According to Ottley, the land transfer will allow Union Tank Car to expand its operation.

He noted the expansion of the tank care company should create new jobs and will also boost the local economy.

"This will be the first real break that Evanston and Uinta County have had in a long time to help diversify their economies. We're anxious to get on-line with the expansion because this is a big opportunity to expand our local industries and to attract new industry to our area," he explained.

UPRC officials thanked the city, county and state officials for their work and cooperation in making the land donation a reality. "We especially appreciate Mayor Ottley's hard work on this project," said Dale Bossert, Vice President for UPRC.

He stated, "It's our hope that this donation will enable the city to prosper in the future. We look forward to a long and friendly relationship with the city and the people of Uinta County."

Both parties noted that a second phase of land conveyance from UPRC to the city is in the works. The remaining adjacent property has been identified by the city for future industrial development and expansion of the Purple Sage Golf Course.

UINTA COUNTY HERALD

April 17, 1993

UP Resources vice president Dale Bossert presents map of 73 acre land gift to mayor Dennis Ottley.

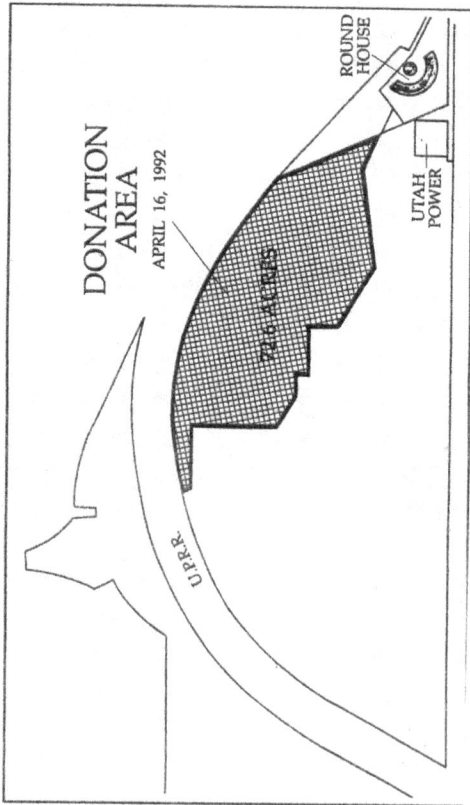

DONATION AREA

APRIL 16, 1992

73.6 ACRES

U.P.R.R.

ROUND HOUSE

UTAH POWER

I mentioned that U.T.C.C. had indicated to me that they were looking at a location in the American Fork and Ogden areas, and that's why I wanted to get some additional property from Union Pacific Resources (U.P.R.C.) adjacent to the Roundhouse property. They could relocate their operation from the Roundhouse and machine shop to the property that the city hoped to get from the U.P.R.C., even if the city had to buy it. I said, "We do not want to lose them."

I told him that Evanston could not afford to lose a company like that and that they would probably need about 70 to 100 acres where they could run railroad spurs off the Union Pacific main line.

Reporting back to me, Peters said that there was a very good chance that the U.P.R.C. would be willing to donate some of the land west of the roundhouse to the city so that the City of Evanston could make a deal with U.T.C.C., providing enough land for them to construct a new operation in Evanston and keeping them here.

During the process, George Peters met with me and asked if I had any problem with them selling the 75+ acres west of the main line to someone who had made a bid on it. I told him that I wouldn't have any problem with that. I said to him, *Hell, George, I wouldn't have any problem if you had someone in mind to sell the entire property to them. I'm not one to blame anyone if they get a chance to sell their property,* but he assured me that the city would get all of the rest of the property.

I asked if he would mind telling me who had put the bid in for the property? He said, *No I don't mind, it's one of your city council members.* Then he said it was Tom Hutchinson, surprisingly. I just said *Good for Tom.*

But he did assure me that we would be getting the remaining 265 acres owned by Union Pacific Resources located on the east side of the tracks adjacent to the roundhouse property and the golf course, and he said that his company was planning to donate 70+ acres to the city soon, and they did.

During one of our work sessions I told the city council about my visits with George Peters. I mentioned that he had indicated to me that Union Pacific Resources Company planned to donate the

265 acres to the city, but they would be donating 70 acres of it very soon so that we could go ahead and make a deal with Union Tank Car Company and try to keep them in Evanston. I said I was going to go to Chicago to meet with the CEO and the board, after we were sure we had the 70 acres deeded to us.

At one of the work sessions when I spoke of the property being donated to the city Councilman Vranish made a sly remark, *We don't want any of that contaminated property. The U.P. just wants to get rid of it so they don't have to clean it up.* Councilman Nelson, as usual, bobbed his head in agreement with Vranish.

My answer to Vranish was, *Hell, if someone is willing to give me 265 acres of property, I sure as hell would be willing to clean it up.* No comment was made by Vranish; he just turned to Nelson and whispered something to him. More discussion was held and a suggestion was made that the city should have a study done on the property for contamination. And we did.

We completed a study and I just happened to receive the results on a day when we were having a regular council meeting. At this meeting the city council was going to vote on accepting the U.P. Resources Company donation or not.

The contamination study did indicate some contamination. This would be the first time I had ever kept information from the members of the council with the intent of getting something passed, but in receiving the information I told Sharon, my secretary to keep it quiet until I had a chance to talk to the city attorney.

I immediately got a hold of Dennis Boal to discuss the results of the study. The study indicated there was some mild contamination of the property, and Boal and I decided to keep the letter from the council members until the next day, because we didn't want to give them any ammunition to try to kill the deal with the U.P.R.C. donating the land to the city.

There were some council members who would have used any means to argue against accepting the property, no matter how serious economic conditions were. I felt bad about withholding information, but during the meeting they passed a motion to accept all or part of the property offered to the city by the resource company. After they found out about the letter the next day I caught all kinds of hell, but it was a good move.

During the first meeting of the month on March 10th, I opened the meeting up with just four members: Councilmen Vranish, Hutchinson and Davis, plus me, giving us a quorum. Councilmembers Wall, Nelson and Barnard arrived later.

After the usual business I went right into public participation and introduced Bruce McLean, Chairman of the Evanston Cowboy Days committee. He expressed his committee's concerns about the agreement the city had recently made with John Bowns to sponsor other events during the summer at the rodeo and fairgrounds. He was mainly speaking of Bowns Evanston Rodeo Series that would take place on weekends through the summer until September. McLain was afraid that the Bowns Rodeo Series would be a detriment to the Labor Day celebration.

I assured McLean that the Evanston Cowboy Days program had always had my support, as well as the city council's support. I told him that I thought the Rodeo Series would do nothing but help the Labor Day celebration of Cowboy Days. I said I thought it would create more interest in the western cowboy tradition and might just bring more folks to the Cowboy Days celebration, and make our young cowboys more interested in maybe becoming a rodeo cowboy.

It appeared that McLean was satisfied with the council and my comments and left the council chambers feeling a lot better about it. Neither the city council nor I heard anymore from the Cowboy Days committee about it, so we never heard whether it helped or it hurt the Labor Day celebration.

Next, I recognized more Boy Scouts from Troop 75. I introduced Scout Master Brent Hatch and had him introduce his scouts Randy Haider, Brad Taylor, Jeremiah Dobare, David Bennett, Paul Denson, and Brandon Bowcut.

In addition, I introduced Scout Master Dean Bowen, also of Troop 75, and had him introduce his scouts Jason Denson, Kris Hatch, Thayne Jasperson, Clint Erickson, and Aaron Thomson.

As the scouts were introduced they were instructed to approach the Mayor's bench, where I shook hands with each of them and presented them with Evanston's "Fresh Air, Freedom and Fun" promotional pin, and I thanked each one for attending the meeting and wished them luck in achieving their merit badges.

After acting on some pending old business, we went into New Business with Resolution 93-12 being introduced by Councilman Davis, amending the Joint Powers Agreement with Uinta County relating to the budgeting and financing of the Evanston/Uinta County Airport (Burns Field).

However, because only three council members were present (plus me), Councilman Vranish made a motion to table any action taken on Resolution 93-12 until the next regular meeting on March 24th, seconded by Davis, with all 4 votes in favor.

Councilman Hutchinson introduced Resolution 93-13 authorizing a Letter of Support to the Evanston Housing Authority (EHA) for a grant of Home Funds in the sum of $128,300 for the Ortega Court Housing Project. This letter would be in support of the Evanston Housing Authority receiving a grant from the Wyoming Community Development Authority (W.C.D.A.).

At that time city council members Jerry Wall and Craig Nelson arrived at the meeting. They had just returned from attending a National League of Cities Convention in Washington D. C.

After a short discussion, Councilman Vranish made the motion to adopt Resolution 93-13, seconded by Davis with 6 votes in favor and 1 absent (Barnard). The motion passed.

I called a 10-minute recess at this time to allow Councilmembers Wall and Nelson to pick up their packets concerning the meeting in progress, and having a little time to look the packets over.

After I opened the meeting back up, Councilman Davis introduced Resolution 93-14, authorizing the city to enter into a Memorandum of Understanding with the Evanston Urban Renewal Agency as the same relating to the management, preservation and development of Depot Square in the City of Evanston. Motion was made by Councilman Nelson to adopt Resolution 93-14, seconded by Vranish, with all voting in favor.

After acting on a few other resolutions, Councilman Vranish introduced Resolution 93-17, to authorize the city to enter into a Mutual Assistance Agreement with Uinta County to coordinate the use of manpower and equipment to benefit the citizens of both city and county.

This resolution would legally allow both the county and the city to use manpower and equipment from both entities involving joint projects. Councilman Nelson made a motion to adopt Resolution 93-17, seconded by Davis, with all voting in favor.

When I called for comments from the council members before adjournment, Councilman Vranish made a motion to support the Uinta County Commissioners' opposition to the Forest Service Environmental Impact Study and to direct the mayor to write a letter opposing the E.I.S. on behalf of the City of Evanston, seconded by Davis with all voting in favor.

The National Forest Service was trying to limit the public's use of the National Forests. In writing the letter to the Forest Service I also sent copies to each of Wyoming's Congressional Members.

I received a letter back from United States Senator Malcolm Wallop thanking the City of Evanston for their decision in taking a stand to support Uinta County Commissioners' opposition to the Forest Service E.I.S., because each of Wyoming's Congressional Group were also in opposition to the E.I.S. This made me feel much better taking the stand we did, writing to the Forest Service and County Commissioners in support of the Commissioners' opposition to the study.

I reminded everyone of the Annual Agri-Business Banquet on March 16th at the Elks Lodge. The meeting was adjourned at 9:20 p.m.

The Annual Agri-Business Banquet came off as scheduled and was another big success. Those nominated for Citizen of the Year were all very deserving folks:

Gerda Robison had worked for 20 years in many capacities, such as Chairman of Evanston Chapter of the American Heart Association, Vice President of the Evanston Council of Catholic Women, President and Vice President of the Evanston League of Voters, President of the Evanston Ladies Literary Club, Charter President of the First Evanston Memorial Hospital Auxiliary, and Co-Chairperson of Evanston's Annual Renewal Ball in 1990. She had also accepted the Vice Presidency of the Uinta County Teen Pregnancy Task Force, moving to the Presidency in 1991, a position she still held at that time. She was also recognized in 1975 as an Outstanding Young Women of America.

Bird "Rip" Bruce served the youth of his community by giving a lot of his time and finding projects for them to do; he was very active in his church and assisted anyone in need; as a Boy Scout Leader he helped countless boys to help them achieve their goals and believe in a higher degree of appreciation for their future and for their consideration for others. Rip had been a lifetime resident and had always been well respected.

Kay Gruber had years ago, almost single-handedly, started a food distribution program which she named the Lord's Storehouse, after Evanston's "boom" period was over and the city came into a "bust" period. The "Lord's Storehouse" is still in operation today. She also worked with some government agencies, the United Way, and churches in the community. She often purchased food with her own money to feed those in need.

These were three great nominations and any one of them, through their dedication and love for the people of Evanston would be well deserving of the honor of being named Evanston's Citizen of the Year, but Bird "Rip" Bruce received the honors.

During the previous meeting, the city council and I voted by secret ballot, after receiving the three nominations. The vote was very close, with a three-way split.

I was a little disappointed at who got it, but was glad for Rip. I had known Rip a long time. When he was employed by Woolley's Automotive Supply, he had serviced the Evanston Frontier/Husky

Truck Stop with auto parts for years, while I managed and was part owner of the truck stop between 1955 and 1974. However, I voted for Gerda Robison because of how active she had been in the community through the many years she had lived in Evanston and because of the diversity of programs she had been active in that helped Evanston so much, especially when the City of Evanston had such a soft economy.

But it took people like the three mentioned above to make the community of Evanston a worthwhile place to live and raise children. All three deserved to be mentioned, and I, for one, appreciated them all very much.

During the second city council meeting of the month held on March 24th I again recognized more Boy Scouts. I introduced Scoutmaster Robin Conk from Troop 30 and had him introduce his scouts, Loran Pace, Nick Lancaster, Calob Taylor, and Jeremy Conk.

I shook hands with each scout and gave them an Evanston "Fresh Air, Freedom and Fun" promotional pin, thanked them for attending the meeting and wished them well in their future achievements.

Under public participation Joni Loxterman and Delana Albrecht requested support from the City of Evanston for the annual March of Dimes Walk America program and asked for the same route they used the previous years. They stated that the event would be held on April 24th.

Councilwoman Wall made a motion to support the Walk America Program and allow the requested route, seconded by Barnard, with all voting in favor.

Under new business Councilwoman Wall introduced Resolution 93-19 as follows:

RESOLUTION 93-19

RESOLUTION OF THE CITY OF EVANSTON, WYOMING, SETTING FORTH THE REQUIREMENTS THAT AN INDIVIDUAL OR GROUP MUST FULFILL IN ORDER TO OBTAIN THE USE OF THE CITY'S BUSES.

The City of Evanston, at that time, had obtained two used school buses that School District No. 1 had donated to the city, which we made available to the citizens of the city, but no one and no group would be permitted to use them unless they met the requirements mentioned in Resolution 93-19.

Councilman Nelson made a motion to adopt Resolution 93-19, seconded by Barnard. The motion passed with 5 votes in favor and 2 absent (Davis and Hutchinson).

Councilman Vranish introduced Resolution 93-20 as follows:

RESOLUTION 93-20
RESOLUTION OF THE CITY OF EVANSTON, WYO-
MING, INDICATING ITS SUPPORT OF THE EVANSTON
HOUSING AUTHORITY IN THE PURCHASE OF THE
APARTMENT COMPLEX KNOWN AS THE PINES OF
YELLOW CREEK.

The Evanston Housing Authority had approved the purchase of The Pines of Yellow Creek, and the Federal Department of Housing and Urban Development (HUD) had also approved the purchase. Gary Bolger, Director of the Evanston Housing Authority (EHA) requested that the City of Evanston give their approval for the Housing Authority to purchase The Pines, for which they needed the city's approval.

There was a lengthy discussion on this subject for a couple of meetings in which I was personally against it. I felt that the EHA had enough housing with well over 60 units for Evanston's low-income residence and elderly folks. During my first term as mayor, we formed the EHA This was during the "boom" days of rapid growth, and the purpose was to help low-income folks and senior citizens obtain reasonable housing subsidized by the U.S. Department of Housing and Urban Development (HUD) to ensure a rental rate that folks could afford. At that time the fast growth period was causing rental rates to go sky high and most folks on fixed income or low income couldn't afford the rent. Therefore we formed the Evanston Housing Authority, but it wasn't meant to get to a point where it was competing with the private sector.

After the big boom was over in 1985 we started in a "bust" period that brought rental rates down to a reasonable amount and I didn't feel we needed any more low-income housing. There was more than enough for those that really needed the EHA program. The Pines of Yellow Creek was owned by a private firm and was probably at least 80% occupied. I argued against Bolger's request because I also thought the EHA had a certain purpose and that is why I was instrumental in getting it formed. But it was not meant to be a profit organization; it was there to help the needy, and that was all.

However, at this time Councilwoman Wall was fighting me on almost everything I wanted to get done, and she seemed to have had intimidated four other city council members to go along with her: Vranish, Nelson, Davis and now Barnard. So they outnumbered me on what I wanted to do, and over the next year and a half it got even worse.

Following the introduction of Resolution 93-20, Councilwoman Wall made a motion to adopt, seconded by Barnard. The motion passed, but I felt that we had made a big mistake. Now we had a government agency in competition with the private sector. I never believed that government should compete with those in business for themselves, unless it was necessary. That is not American.

Councilman Nelson made a motion for Councilwoman Wall to be the voting delegate representing Evanston for the 1993 Wyoming Association of Municipalities (W.A.M.) Convention to be held in Sheridan in June, with the mayor as her alternate, seconded by Vranish, with all voting in favor.

Public Works General Manager Allan "Oop" Hansen reported on the 1993 Water Utility Management Institute seminar he attended in Arlington, Texas after obtaining a $2,000 scholarship to attend. He stated that it was an amazing opportunity for him to learn many things that he hadn't known about and said he felt that the seminar would help him a lot in his position in Public Works.

I again congratulated Oop for receiving the scholarship and hoped he would pass on what he had learned to those under him.

City Engineer Brian Honey reported on the Rocky Mountain Training Program he had recently attended in Durango, Colorado.

He said that it was well worthwhile and he would advise others to attend in the future.

I thanked Brian for his report and told him that I was sure what he learned will help him and others in the operations of the city.

Prior to adjourning, I announced a meeting to be held Thursday, March 25th at 6:00 p.m. to discuss the committee's cable TV findings, and I announced that the mayor and council's goal-setting session appeared to have been successful. *I only hope,* I thought to myself.

<hr/>

About this time my son, Rand, who owned Uinta Realty, Inc., made a big change which would affect me somewhat. His key salesperson, Lisa Burridge, and her husband Tim were in the process of forming a new real estate company in Evanston and leaving Uinta Realty. The franchise they were going with was Re/Max and their company would be called Re/Max Results Realty, Inc.

Rand decided to shut down Uinta Realty, Inc. and go with the new company of Re/Max, and all other agents did likewise, except for me. I moved downtown and rented an office in the Old Town Hall from Virginia Mathieson, who was leasing and managing the building. I opened a small office on the second floor, and after Rand had dropped the name of Uinta Realty altogether and had gone with the new name of Re/Max, I decided to call my company once again Uinta Realty. In the past it had always had a good reputation and was the oldest agency in the area; therefore, I couldn't see a reason to go with another name. A couple years later after I knew Rand had officially let his corporation expire I applied through the Wyoming Secretary of State's office and incorporated once again as Uinta Realty, Inc.

I was back in my own office once again. It was just like I was starting my own agency Uinta Realty, Inc. all over again, and I guess I was. I had no agents working with me. I was completely alone for the next year. I was starting from scratch again, but I did start out reasonably well. I had taken my listings with me and was the property managing agent for the Veterans Administration's foreclosures in the entire county, which helped me a lot, because not only did I get paid for that, I also got the V.A. listings when they came up for sale.

∽∾

The first regular city council meeting of the month was held on April 14th, with Boy Scout Sterling Widmer from Troop 40 in attendance to fulfill his requirements for his merit badge. He also was operating the video camera for the meeting in place of his brother, Stanton, who had been operating the camera for the past year or so.

I thanked Scout Sterling Widmer for his attendance and for offering to operate the camera. I also wished him well in his achievements in earning his merit badge.

Under public participation, Bruce Sowards made a presentation for Wyoming Communication Corporation explaining the need for more funding to update and repair the translator stations on top of Medicine Butte. Although these stations did not belong to the city, they do provide the city with communications for all the emergency agencies in the area, such as the police and fire departments. Also, they provide the city with TV for folks in the area that could not get on the cable system at this time.

I thanked Sowards for his presentation and explained that there were no funds in the current city budget; however, the city would take it into consideration and try to locate funds from other areas of the budget and let him know within the next two weeks.

Richard Honadel was in attendance to speak of the removal of Evanston's big pine trees. He said that he had noticed that more of the pines get removed each year, and that he would like the people in Evanston to be encouraged to keep their trees if possible.

I thanked Honadel for his concern and told him that some of these big old pines may have needed to come down before they fell down and ended up doing harm to something or someone. I also told him that the city was concerned and that Community Director and City Planner Paul Knopf had been keeping an eye on the tree removal that was going on in Evanston and he had talked to some of those folks about it.

The Cable TV Committee had completed their report and after the city council and I had read it and was in approval of it, Councilwoman Wall made a motion to approve and accept the committee's report and recommendations, seconded by Nelson with all voting in favor.

I thanked City Attorney Boal and his committee for their very thorough and complete report, and stated that the recommendations and suggestions in the report would not go without action taken on them. I said, *Although this report has taken many months to complete, it was well worth it, and in every way it will benefit the cable company and the citizens of the Evanston area if we implement the recommendations in the report.* I added, *I've never seen a more thorough and well thought-out report, thank you.*

Councilman Davis then made a motion to direct the city attorney to take action on the Cable TV Committee's first recommendation concerning the franchise tax, seconded by Vranish, with all voting in favor.

Under new business, Resolution 93-24 was introduced by Councilman Hutchinson as follows:

RESOLUTION 93-24
RESOLUTION AUTHORIZING THE CITY OF EVANSTON, WYOMING TO FILE AN APPLICATION FOR FUNDING UNDER THE WYOMING TRANSPORTATION ENHANCEMENT ACTIVITY PROGRAM ADMINISTERED BY THE WYOMING DEPARMENT OF TRANSPORTATION FOR THE BEAR PATHWAY PROJECT.

The Wyoming Department of Transportation had been designated by Governor Mike Sullivan as the state agency to administer programs of the Federal Intermodal Surface Transportation Efficiency Act (ISTEA) of 1991.

The resolution authorized the city to undertake all actions necessary to file an application for funding the BEAR Pathway Project under the Transportation Enhancement Activity Program for purposes of conducting an activity as defined by ISTEA.

The amount of the funding request would come from the BEAR Project Committee. Councilman Ron Barnard had recently been elected as President of the Better Environmental And River Project (BEAR), and he pointed out that the funding request would be for an 80/20 grant in the amount of $500,000 with the state paying the 80%.

Councilwoman Wall made a motion to adopt Resolution 93-24, seconded by Hutchinson. The motion passed with 7 votes in favor with a change in the wording stating that "The City of Evanston shall be committed to perpetual care of the BEAR Pathway Project."

Councilman Vranish made a motion to transfer the funds to the Evanston High School Baseball Field Project as follows: $7,000 from Landscape Park Shop #2. The motion was seconded by Davis. With a short discussion the vote was called, with all voting in favor.

Councilman Davis made a motion that a proposed resolution from the City of Evanston be prepared and presented to the W.A.M. Board concerning sales tax collected in each county and paid directly to the State of Wyoming by out-of-state vendors without regard for which county the tax was collected. The motion was seconded by Barnard, with all voting in favor.

After a short discussion concerning the lack of oil and gas production in the area, Councilman Davis made a motion authorizing the mayor to write a letter to the U.S. Bureau of Land Management (BLM) urging them to rewrite the oil and gas section of their Green River Basin Management Plan and allow more oil and gas exploration. Motion was seconded by Nelson, with all voting in favor.

Operations Manager of Public Works Oop Hansen reported that Saturday's garbage pickup would end. This had been a suggestion from Public Works which the council and I agreed upon. Eliminating Saturday's pickup would involve a little more time in picking up the garbage during the work days.

Before adjourning I announced that there would be a work session on April 21st at 5:00 p.m.

On March 22nd I and the members of the Evanston City Council held a Goals and Objective Session. During this session we all agreed that the City of Evanston needed a Mission Statement. It was the first time the city had ever had such a statement. It was voted on unanimously and read as follows:

MISSION STATEMENT
"Our purpose is to provide leadership, resources and laws needed to achieve the community's vision of a total quality of life experience. Our goal is to ensure that the residents, as well as the businesses of Evanston, always have a voice in the process."

During this March 22nd meeting we also spoke of promises, in the form of statements, that we would make to the citizens of Evanston as follows:

- To insure that all rules, regulations and services set forth by Evanston City Government are appropriate and pertinent to the quality of life of the residents of Evanston, Wyoming.
- To expect a strong sense of accountability and dedication by all city employees to the people of Evanston, and to officially recognize those employees whose service to the citizens of Evanston reflects this goal.
- To encourage the overall communication and lines of communication within the City.
- To recognize and cultivate the importance of small businesses within Evanston, as well as to encourage industry to explore the resources in our community.
- To stimulate proper management techniques so that the infrastructure of our City is functioning at the highest level of productivity.

Other items that were brought up during this March 22nd meeting were organizational structure, budget items and procedures, short-term and long-term goals and objectives, and personnel policies.

This was a lengthy session, but I felt very good about it. I only hoped that all council members also felt good about it and would take the session very seriously.

During our second regular city council meeting on April 28th I opened the meeting at 7:00 p.m. and declared that we had a quorum. Following the initial business of the meeting I opened up for public participation.

The first item of business was the request from Tim Lynch for approval of his application for a malt beverage permit for the Chili Cookoff on June 19th. After a few words from Tim, Councilman Nelson made the motion for this permit to be approved, seconded by Barnard, with all voting in favor.

Also, Judd Redden, Director of the Lincoln Uinta County Association of Governments (LUAG) reported on the Revolving Loan Fund Committee set up by LUAG, and made a request for the Town of Lyman to have one seat on the Committee.

The Revolving Loan Fund was a program set up to assist businesses in the two counties to obtain loans for improvements to their business or to start up a business or an industry. Each county and community within Lincoln and Uinta Counties would budget money based on their population for the Revolving Fund, and hopefully those funds would grow to the point where the entities could approve applications made for loans, some matching. This program had been going on for years and was a successful program which was helping the economy.

After a short discussion, a motion was made by Councilman Vranish to allow the Joint Powers agreement of LUAG to be rewritten, permitting the Town of Lyman to have one seat on the Revolving Fund Committee, seconded by Hutchinson, with all voting in favor.

John Bowns reported on his activities in arranging for new activities and events to be held at the Uinta County Fairgrounds this coming summer. He spoke of the Rodeo Series on weekends from June until the weekend prior to Labor Day weekend, when Evanston's annual Cowboy Days celebration is always planned.

Resolution 93-28 was introduced by Councilman Vranish as follows:

RESOLUTION 93-28
RESOLUTION AUTHORIZING THE CITY OF EVAN-
STON, WYOMING TO ENTER INTO AN AGREEMENT
TO PROVIDE FINANCIAL ASSISTANCE TO WYOMING
COMMUNICATION CORPORATION FOR SERVICES TO
PROVIDE FACILITIES FOR AN EMERGENCY CAPTURE
SYSTEM AND ADDITIONAL IMPROVEMENT TO THE
CITIZENS OF THE CITY OF EVANSTON.

Councilman Barnard made the motion to adopt Resolution 93-
28, seconded by Hutchinson, but before the vote there was a lengthy
discussion concerning the budget and where funds would come from.
City Treasurer Steve Widmer said that there were enough funds
available in the Reserve Account, which had not been touched yet.

Ending the discussion I called for the vote on the motion to adopt
Resolution 93-28, with 6 votes in favor and 1 vote against. I don't
recall who the dissenting vote was.

A motion was made and seconded by the council later to transfer
the funds in the budget as described by the city treasurer, with all
voting in favor.

Councilman Hutchinson made a motion to change the June 9th
city council meeting to June 15th, just prior to the scheduled fiscal year
budget hearing, because the mayor and some of the council members
would be attending the Annual W.A.M. Convention in Sheridan on
June 9th. The motion was seconded by Davis, with all voting in favor.

After new business was acted on, we had comments and announcements by the council members, staff and me.

City Engineer Brian Honey reported that bids had been let on the
street overlays and slurry projects, and that he felt good that the projects would be completed on schedule with the proper traffic guidance.

I announced that the Public Service Commission would be meeting at the Evanston City Hall on May 6th at 9:00 a.m., and that the
meeting would receive comments and give information concerning

the Evanston telephone service. There had been a request for an increase in rates by the telephone company and P.S.C. was asking for public comments on the rates and the service.

Every spring as the snow melts is a lot of unsightly garbage and debris, causing the city to look quite dirty. Therefore, I declared the 15th of April as Evanston's City Clean Up Day. City employees would be out in force to help pick up the trash. They would be asking for the cooperation of business owners and residents to join in to clean up roadways, parking lots and vacant lots.

Community Director Paul Knopf explained that this effort is an attempt to pick up around the neighborhoods and business areas. He asked those participating to place the trash in tied garbage bags and leave them near designated roadways.

City sanitation crews will work from noon to 6:00 p.m. picking up the bags left along the designated roadways. *This is a public and private cooperative effort to make and keep Evanston beautiful,* Knopf said. On May 22nd there would be the annual Spring Clean Up when residents are asked to participate. During the week of May 17th through the 22nd city crews would pick up all garbage and trash from the alleys and streets (where there are no alleys) left by the citizens.

During April, I had a number of proclamations to declare and sign such as The Week of the Young Child, proclaimed for April 18-24, sponsored by the Uinta County Child Care Coalition; Volunteer Week, also for the week of April 18-24, sponsored by the Rocky Mountain Care Social Services; I welcomed the League of Women Voters convention to Evanston by a proclamation, designating the week of April 19-25 as League of Women Voters Week; and I signed a proclamation designating the week of May 2-8 as Municipal Clerk's Week in honor of all City of Evanston clerks and office employees.

The regular Evanston City Council meeting on May 12th was a very short meeting. After roll call, I declared that we had a quorum and opened the meeting. Following approval of the minutes, payment of the outstanding bills and accepting department reports, and after public participation, we went directly into new business because there was no old business left pending to be acted upon.

The first order of new business was a motion by Councilman Nelson to approve an application for a malt beverage permit for the Police Benevolent Association for the annual Mudd Bogg to be held on July 16th and 17th. The motion was seconded by Vranish, with all voting in favor. Detective J. R. Dean was in attendance representing the Police Benevolent Association.

Councilman Hutchinson made a motion to approve an application for a malt beverage permit for the Lions Club for their annual Rib O Rama at Depot Square on May 31st. Motion was seconded by Wall with all voting in favor. Bill Alexander was in attendance representing the Lions Club.

Councilwoman Wall made a motion to approve final payment to the contractor for work done on the BEAR Project and authorize payment to be made by the BEAR Project Committee. The motion was seconded by Nelson, with all voting in favor.

The BEAR Project Committee had the funds for the diversion project, but payment had to be approved by the City of Evanston. There was an attempt and a motion made by Councilman Hutchinson to stripe a left turn lane into Incline Drive off Yellow Creek Road after the underpass of I-80, seconded by Davis, but after a lengthy discussion Councilman Hutchinson made a motion to table any action at that time until the Evanston Police Department could complete a study on the ramifications of a left turn lane at Incline Drive, seconded by Vranish, with all voting in favor.

There was no other business to come before the council. I polled the staff and council members for comments and announcements.

The Wyoming Association of Municipalities was offering a scholarship for one of their members to attend the Rocky Mountain Leadership program. I don't recall where the program was to be held, but I believe it was somewhere in Colorado. Councilman Hutchinson made a motion to nominate Councilwoman Jerry Wall as a candidate to receive the scholarship, seconded by Nelson, with all voting in favor.

Community Director and City Planner Paul Knopf presented a $4,000 check to the chairman of the BEAR Project from the

Wyoming Fish and Game Department, and reported on a recent planning conference that he had attended in Chicago, Illinois that was sponsored by the American Planning Association.

A big thank you was given to the Fish and Game Department by all and I congratulated Knopf for his attendance at the Planning Association meeting in Chicago and told him that I hoped it was beneficial not only to him, but also to the City of Evanston. He assured the council that he believed the meeting was good for him and the city.

City Treasurer Steve Widmer gave a short report on his recent attendance at a Government Finance Officers Association Convention held in Vancouver, Canada.

City Attorney Dennis Boal gave a report on his trip to a Labor Relations Seminar held in Laramie, Wyoming, concerning workers and unions and municipalities.

Both reports were very informative and thorough and I thanked Widmer and Boal for the reports. I expressed my thanks for them both taking the initiative to attend the meetings, and I hoped their attendance would also be beneficial.

A few meetings ago I had announced that I had made arrangements for City Attorney Dennis Boal and me to make a trip to Chicago in early May to meet with Mr. Ken Fischl, President and CEO of Union Tank Car Corporation and his Board of Directors.

During the city council meeting I told the council members that we were going there to let them know that the City of Evanston would have property for them to rebuild on a different location, because we definitely wanted them to remain in Evanston.

I told the council that we would not be making any definite deals with them concerning the property while there, but I wanted to let them know that the Union Pacific Resources Corporation had donated enough acreage to the city adjacent to where they are now located, and we would be taking a map and other material to U.T.C.C. to show them which land we were talking about. They would be able to see that the land was adjacent to the main line, so they could

construct rail spurs off the main. We would not be making any definite deals with them or quoting any purchase price or stating how
much property they could take. We would tell them that any deal
made would have to be made by a resolution adopted by the Evanston
City Council.

After I announced the meeting with U.T.C.C. in Chicago, the
council members all had their secret little meetings in their new
office in the back of City Hall and decided that they weren't going
to be in favor of Boal and me going alone to meet with the tank car
company.

During a city council meeting, following my announcement of
the Chicago meeting, a member of the council indicated that the city
council would like to see at least one council member go with Boal
and me. At that time Councilman Hutchinson agreed to go, so it
looked like he was going to be our watch dog to make sure we didn't
do anything out of bounds. But I think Hutchinson wanted to keep
the Tank Car Company in Evanston as much as I did. I guess they
thought we were all going to "pull a sneaky" on them and give the
land to the corporation or make some underhanded agreement without council approval. It bothered me that they didn't seem to trust
our city attorney or fellow councilman Tom Hutchinson.

Tom Hutchinson was the only one that spoke up and volunteered
to go. I got the feeling that the rest of the council was hoping nobody
would volunteer so I would have to call the trip off (though I would
have gone whether anyone else went or not, even if I had to pay
for the trip, and I'm sure Dennis Boal would have gone with me). I
wasn't going to take a chance of losing the U.T.C.C. to another community, especially in Utah where we would completely lose both the
employees and the tax base.

⚬⚬⚬

During the meeting of May 12th Councilman Hutchinson and I reported on the meeting in Chicago with the Union Tank Car Company. We indicated that the company was very receptive to the idea
of looking at the property and remaining in Evanston. We told the

council about visiting their mother plant in East Chicago, Indiana and meeting with their board. We told them that even Mr. Ken Fischl, CEO of the corporation, appeared to be in favor of staying in Evanston.

I told the council that no deal had been made and would not have been made whether Councilman Tom was there or not. "In the first place the tank car company wasn't ready for a deal, and it would probably be months before their final decision is made," I said.

During a historic committee meeting, Jerry Wall made a slight indication that I would be making a commission on the U.P. land through my real estate agency. This was heard by my wife Sandy and others. At first Sandy didn't pay much attention to it, but after thinking about it, Sandy was pretty upset with Wall's statement. She was about to ask what she meant, but someone saw that Sandy was upset and changed the subject, lucky for Wall.

Boy, what a vicious lie. I couldn't believe it. I had never even thought of such a thing, but she was out to get me even if she had to lie, and she did many times until the next election. Someone should have reminded her that it's easier to tell the truth than to lie; when you lie about something you've got to remember what you lied about. But I don't think that would have bothered someone like Wall. She just wanted revenge.

The city council members were getting sneaky and secretive towards me. Jerry Wall and others were trying their best to backstab me whenever they could. Wall already had Vranish, Nelson and Davis going along with her.

Councilman Hutchinson told me later that he didn't go to Chicago with us to keep an eye on us; he went because the majority of the members of the city council were planning to vote against the trip unless one of the city council members accompanied Boal and me. I thanked Tom for telling me this. He gave me a note from Councilman Vranish to him, Tom, proving what he said was correct. I told Tom then that I was glad he went, because those particular council members probably wouldn't have believed me or Boal when reporting back to them about the trip.

Hutchinson was the only council member that Wall wasn't able to dominate to her secretive agenda. But then, Tom had beaten her in the primaries of the 1992 election also.

As we did every year, we sent invitations to all of our State of Wyoming elected officials and our Congressional Delegation to attend our Annual Renewal Ball. Governor Mike Sullivan was the only one in a position to accept the invitation. However, we did get letters from them all stating that the date didn't fit their schedule or they had other commitments.

Governor Sullivan was also in Evanston in May to address the Wyoming Public Employees State Convention that was being held in Evanston this year of 1993. While here he purchased a rubber ducky in support of the Evanston BEAR Project from the Rubber Duck Race Committee.

Governor Mike Sullivan has been a great friend to Evanston and Uinta County, and had supported us in many ways. I believe he had visited Evanston more times than any other Governor that I know of. And believe me, it was very much appreciated.

During the second regular city council meeting of the month on May 26th, in public participation, Linda Barker, representing Uinta County 4-H, requested to use a city bus to transport 4-H children to the Wyoming State Fair in Douglas, and requested that some of the fees be waived.

After a short discussion Councilman Barnard made a motion to allow the use of the bus, under the requirements set by resolution, to waive the .50 cent per mile required fee. The motion was seconded by Nelson and passed with 6 votes in favor and 1 absent (Hutchinson).

James Abbott, representing the BEAR Project made a presentation concerning their BEAR Day, which included the Rubber Duck Race on the Bear River. He encouraged and challenged everyone to sponsor one of the ducks for $25.00 each.

I thanked Abbott for his presentation and assured him that I would be sponsoring one of his ducks. I also wished his committee to have a successful event once again this year.

The only item of unfinished business was to remove from the table a motion made by Councilman Hutchinson last meeting to stripe the Yellow Creek Road with a left turn lane turning into Incline Drive. But as there was no motion made to bring the action off the table, the whole idea died. I suppose after the police department did their research on the left turn, the council felt that striping a left turn lane at that location could cause more problems, because of the congestion of heavy traffic at certain times. The council felt that it would be much safer to leave it as it was.

Under New Business, Resolution 93-31 was introduced by Councilman Will Davis to authorize City Public Works and the City Community Development Department to hire seasonal workers and to ratify the action I had taken earlier in giving my permission to hire a seasonal worker for the Community Development Department of the city.

Apparently, Public Works and the Community Development Departments had requested to hire high school kids to work for the city during the summer months. They would be hired at a reasonable hourly rate, but would receive no city benefits. This would be a good move for the city to provide this program for kids in their teens.

A motion was made by Councilman Nelson to adopt Resolution 93-31, seconded by Barnard, with all voting in favor.

Below is a copy of the note that Councilman Clarence Vranish wrote to Councilman Tom Hutchinson concerning our trip to Chicago to meet with the Union Tank Car Company in June, 1993.

Tom, I let you go to Chicago because you wanted to keep an eye on ~~him~~ the mayor. ~~I don't.~~ I told you I wouldn't approve this trip. If you received the blessing of the majority of the council let me know. Clarence 6:21 6-17-93

BRIEFLY...

Governor's visit

Gov. Mike Sullivan addressed the Wyoming Public Employees State Convention in Evanston on Friday. Sullivan said the public needs to know that state employees are dedicated to their jobs, and that a pay compensation plan for state employees needs to be addressed.

Sullivan buys rubber ducky in support of Evanston BEAR Project

While on a whirlwind tour of southwest Wyoming Friday, Gov. Mike Sullivan paused to show his support of the Better Environment And River Project (BEAR) in Evanston.

Sullivan purchased a "rubber ducky" to run in the annual ducky race on the Bear River in downtown Evanston.

The "Rubber Ducky Race," sponsored by Key Bank of Wyoming, will be the highlight of "A Day On The BEAR" on Saturday, June 26.

"A Day On The Bear" is planned to invite residents of Evanston to come down to the parkway under construction and see how it is progressing, and what plans involve.

The Evanston Parks and Recreation Department will be holding a "Frisbee-Golf Tournament and a "Hike or Bike Scavenger Hunt" in the project. The Rotary Club will be providing free hot dogs and soda pop for those attending.

Water level in the river permitting, plans include floating through the park from the Bear River State Park on the east side of Evanston, to the middle of town where the Old Ice Ponds are being reconstructed. The float will provide a unique view of the improvements made and those planned.

Sponsorship of ducks for the race is solicited to raise needed funds to continue construction of the project. Individuals and businesses are being contacted.

Duck entries are available from Key Bank employees and various volunteer "Ducky Salesmen" throughout the community.

The winner of the "Ducky Race" receives notoriety throughout the area and a traveling trophy.

Plan to attend the race and other events planned on June 26.

Governor Mike Sullivan purchases an entrant for "Rubber Ducky Race" in support of the BEAR Project from Donna Van Riper, chairperson of the Rubber Duck Race Committee. James Abbott of the race committee is at left.

Uinta County Herald, April 25, 1993.

The new city hall was built in 1978, and after almost 15 years, the main office area was in need of new carpet. Bids were put out, with the low bid being $7,951.57. Councilman Davis made a motion to accept the low bid to re-carpet the main office area, seconded by Wall, with 5 votes in favor, 1 vote against (Barnard) and 1 absent (Hutchinson). The motion passed.

We also put out bids to re-roof City Hall, but they all came in way over the engineer's estimate. Therefore, Councilwoman Wall made a motion to reject all bids, seconded by Barnard, with all voting in favor.

City Planner Paul Knopf reported on the Third Annual Bike Race on State Highway 150 South over the High Uintas to Kamas, Utah and back to Evanston on Saturday, June 19th, and the local bike race on Sunday around town, and requested the council's permission for the in-town route. Councilwoman Wall made a motion to approve the request to close the streets as in previous years for the Annual Bike Race to be held on June 20th from 1:30 a.m. to 5:00 p.m., seconded by Nelson, with all voting in favor.

Councilman Nelson followed up with a motion to support and authorize me to continue negotiations with the Union Pacific Railroad Corporation for additional parcels of property to be used at Depot Square and for landscaping the underpass area, seconded by Barnard with 5 votes in favor, 1 abstaining (Davis) and 1 absent (Hutchinson). The motion passed. I don't know why Davis abstained, but I guess he had his reasons.

I mentioned that the annual Spring Clean-up Day was once again successful and thanked public works and the general public for their involvement, and I thanked the Beautification Committee and their volunteers for their work in downtown Evanston planting flowers, pulling weeds, cleaning store fronts and sweeping sidewalks and curbs.

There was a "thank you barbecue" held at Martin Park that evening for all volunteers that participated in Spring Clean-up Day.

Approximately 40 employees of Utah Power and Light Company (now known as Rocky Mountain Power) participated in planting about 50 trees, each 10 to 15 feet high in Hamblin Park, Ottley Park and the BEAR Project, and they also donated approximately 150 trees to the local schools to be planted by the students.

I expressed a big thank you to U.P.&L.C. for such a grand gesture to the City of Evanston, and to all their employees who participated in the tree planting project.

Prior to adjourning I called for another work session for 5:00 p.m. on June 2nd and reminded everyone of the public meeting to be held on the budget for fiscal year 1993-1994 at 7:00 p.m. on June 2nd. The meeting adjourned at 9:45 p.m.

LETTERS TO THE EDITOR

Volunteers to be commended for efforts

Dear Editor:

Beautiful, exciting, and busy. That's the only way to describe this past Memorial Day Weekend for Evanston.

A weekend to remember our loved ones and the many veterans who are no longer with us, and at the same time a weekend of fun and enjoyment.

Beautiful, not only because of the nice weather, but because of how clean the community is and how nice the cemetery was with all the flags, pinwheels and the many flowers. The people of Evanston, the young and old, should be commended for their efforts in cleaning up our City.

The Veteran's of Foreign Wars and the Eagle's Club should be commended for all their efforts in decorating the Evanston Cemetery. The flags and all the pinwheels added a feeling of pride to the entire program at the cemetery. Thanks to the Vets and the Eagles for making the Memorial Day Services so great. All this, the cleaning up, the services and the hanging of the flags throughout the community have entailed thousands of voluntary man-hours. And we all should appreciate that.

An exciting and busy weekend, because of the many events taking place. Wyoming Downs had a terrific kickoff for the season, congratulations to them.

The team roping at the Uinta County Fair Grounds, and the Evanston Lion's Clubs 4th Annual Rib-O-Rama and all the Parks drew a large amount of people, and business throughout the area appeared to be good.

Thanks again to all of you who took part in helping to make this Memorial Day Weekend such a large success. It was a great way to start off the Summer season.

Volunteers are great. They make a community worth living in. So please when you see someone volunteering their time to help our city, say thanks and give them a big pat on the back.

Thank you and God Bless you all.

Mayor Dennis J. Ottley

Uinta County Herald, June 4, 1993.

The *Uinta County Herald* of May 21st had an article headlined: UP RESOURCES BREAKS GROUND ON WAHSATCH GATHERING SYSTEM.

The article read: *Union Pacific Resources Company (UPRC) began construction yesterday on its 41-mile Wahsatch Gathering System (WGS) with a luncheon, speeches and an official groundbreaking at its permanent operations facilities located at 86 Allegiance Circle in Evanston. About 250 persons attended the activities.*

The *Herald* added an insert placed in the headline article by Publisher Mike Jensen titled, UPRC DONATES 192 ACRES TO EVANSTON.

The insert read: During the official groundbreaking ceremony of the Wahsatch Gathering System on Thursday, Union Pacific Resources Company President and Chief Executive Officer Jack L. Messman made a surprise presentation to Evanston Mayor Dennis Ottley.

Messman gave Mayor Ottley the deed for 192 acres of land adjacent to the Purple sage Golf Course.

This is the second land donation from UPRC in the past year. In the spring of 1992, UPRC donated 73 acres, also located near the golf course, to the city of Evanston. Mayor Ottley graciously accepted the deed from Messman.

"This is a surprise," Mayor Ottley responded. "This is just great. We really appreciate the Union Pacific Resources Company for this donation."

According to Ottley, he was surprised the presentation was made Thursday during the groundbreaking ceremonies.

"I didn't think it would happen so soon," he said. "We thought it might happen sometime this summer."

Ottley and other city officials have worked hard for the past five years trying to obtain the property around the golf course.

"The 265 acres of property will be used to attract new industry to Evanston area," he said. "By doing so, we'll be able to diversify the economy of Evanston."

Ottley explained that the Union Tank Car Company is planning a $17 million expansion of their facilities and the newly acquired property will play a major role in their plans.

In addition, when monies become available, the city will expand the Purple Sage Golf Course to 18 holes. The mayor said he will be putting together several committees to study and plan for the development of the newly acquired land, the insert concluded.

In the last part of May, I received a number of letters from sixth-graders at Davis Middle School, commenting on the city's recycling program. These letters were from the following students: Destiny Spruill, Tiffany Parkin, Becki Reynolds, Rebecca Bennion, and Ashley Mower.

Each letter said what a great a job the city was doing in the recycling program, and each one made suggestions on how we could better the program by adding more bins and allowing more types of materials to be recycled. One letter requested stricter laws on littering.

Each letter requested me to write back and state my concerns and express my views on their requests, and I did just that. It made me feel good that Evanston's youth was aware of the recycling program.

I also wrote a Letter to the Editor in the *Uinta County Herald* of June 4th concerning Memorial Day Weekend. My letter read:

Dear Editor:

Beautiful, exciting, and busy. That's the only way to describe this past Memorial Day Weekend for Evanston.

The letter thanked all those volunteers that were involved in decorating the cemetery, the events at the fairgrounds, and all other events that were going on during the weekend. It was all wonderful.

The 11th Annual Renewal Ball was held at the Elks Lodge on June 5th with the theme "Golden Past – Brilliant Future." Chairperson Janice Bodine reported that the Renewal Ball, once again, was a grand evening with a very successful auction and a fun night for all.

Governor Mike Sullivan and Wyoming's First Lady Jane once again visited Evanston, as he was the guest speaker at the Ball. When he arrived, Sandy and I picked him up at the Uinta/Evanston Burns Field Airport.

While riding into town the governor said to Sandy, *I hope our visits to Evanston aren't hurting the Mayor politically, because I am a Democrat and you folks are Republicans.*

Sandy replied, *The city is non-partisan, and that's what Denny likes about city politics. Besides, we don't look at a person because of their politics, we look at them because of their character and you, as Governor, have done a lot for Evanston and shown a lot of interest in us, so don't worry about you hurting us. We just appreciate you being here as often as you have.*

Then the governor told us about the ties that he had with Evanston. He spoke of the time that his grandparents had lived in Evanston; his grandfather was employed by the Union Pacific at the time. He had the address of the house his grandparents had lived in and asked if it would be much trouble to go by it if it was still standing. It was.

Governor Sullivan then handed me an address which was in the vicinity of 8th and Sage Streets. I don't recall the number, but when we got to the home he said that his grandparents had lived in the house many years ago, before he was born. He said that he had always wanted to see where they lived. After telling us a little about his grandparents, we left for the Renewal Ball.

When we got to the ball a number of folks were already there, and as we entered most of them stood up out of respect for the Governor. We proceeded to the table that was reserved for us. Then I noticed Uinta County Commissioner Paul Barnard and his wife sitting at another table. I approached them and asked Commissioner Barnard, who was Chairman of the Commissioners at that time, if he would like to join us at our table. They did, and though some folks appeared to resent it, I would have asked the chairman of the commission, no matter who it was, to sit with us.

Urban Renewal Director Jim Davis was acting as Master of Ceremonies and when he introduced me as mayor, I stood up to the microphone and introduced those city council members that were present. When I introduced Councilwoman Wall, I said, *I would like to introduce Councilwoman Jerry Wall as the only Lady on the council.*

She was already standing and about to sit down, but when I introduced her she turned her head and yelled out *I'm no lady,* and I guess that was, at that moment, the only thing she and I had agreed on 100% since she was elected and became a member of the city council once again in 1993.

But, with Governor Sullivan and his wife Jane being present, Sandy and I were not only surprised, but quite embarrassed and I believe that a lot of other folks felt the same way.

However, the event was a big success and I believe the governor and his wife enjoyed themselves. When driving him back to the airport he thanked us for a great evening and said that they both had a good time, not mentioning anything about the Wall incident. He thanked us also for allowing his pilot to be present to enjoy a nice dinner with everyone.

In early June, following the weekend of the Evanston Renewal Ball, the W.A.M. Annual Convention was held in Sheridan. Councilmembers Jerry Wall, Craig Nelson, Ron Barnard and I all attended and traveled to Sheridan.

Having a ball

Mayor Dennis Ottley gives a word of praise to all the volunteers that made the 11th Annual Rewal Ball a success. For more Renewal Ball photos see page B3.

Governor Mike Sullivan shares a humorous Story with ball attendees while Evanston Mayor Ottley looks on.

Uinta County Herald, June 8, 1993.

Wall, Nelson and Barnard left hours earlier than I did. I drove the Evanston officials' car to the Sheridan Inn, the official site of W.A.M. headquarters, registered, and then went looking for Evanston delegates.

I found Jerry Wall and Craig Nelson in the lounge of the Inn having a drink and visiting with folks. I approached them and asked where Barnard was. Jerry stated that they didn't know and didn't care, in a very sarcastic manner. She said that they ditched him because he was just a big dumb ass (those may not have been the exact words, but it was very similar).

I was quite concerned with the way they were acting and said that I better go see if I can find him. I reminded them that this was Ron's first W.A.M. meeting and he might need a little help getting around, but they didn't seem to care.

While moseying around various locations in the Sheridan Inn I finally found him talking to folks and getting acquainted. When I found him he seemed to be enjoying himself, and as I approached him I asked, *How are you doing?* He indicated that he was doing fine and then I suggested that he and I look over the W.A.M. agenda and see what meetings and seminars we would be interested in attending. We did, and after that I was no longer concerned about Barnard, because he was doing all right.

During the convention there was a committee meeting that Jerry Wall was attending and may have been conducting. During the meeting Jerry made a motion on a subject that I was strictly against. The motion had something to do with the Wyoming State officials, maybe the Farm Loan Board, but whatever it was I know it was in opposition to something that Governor Mike Sullivan was involved with.

Since I was interested in the meeting, I decided to attend. All meetings were open to members, whether they were on the committee or not. At this particular session Executive Director Carl Classen was also in attendance.

Whatever Jerry had made a motion on, Director Classen was also in favor of, but when they opened the floor for discussion I spoke strongly against it. I knew as far as Evanston was concerned, the Governor and other state officials had been more than fair with our community. I'm sorry I don't recall the issue, but I felt that both Jerry and Carl were way out of bounds and playing politics.

After I spoke and the motion was voted on, it was defeated by a large majority. I had always been well respected by most members of W.A.M., and I had never, until lately, seen the association go political. W.A.M. was always nonpartisan, as it should be, and I wanted to keep it that way.

This incident put Jerry Wall more strongly against me, but I didn't care because I was doing what I felt was best for the association and Wyoming communities.

Although I had been approached several times to run for the position of President of W.A.M., I decided a long time ago that my place was to be a good mayor.

Years ago, when Bob Burns was Mayor of Evanston and I was one of his city council members, I decided that a mayor of a city should never be president of W.A.M.

During his first term, I thought Bob Burns was an outstanding mayor and worked hard in the best interest of the City of Evanston, including increasing the economy. I learned a lot from him, and he got re-elected another term.

But, during his second term he become very much involved with W.A.M. and was elected as president of the Association during his second term. I noticed that, in time, he was starting to neglect the City of Evanston, but was doing a very good job as President of W.A.M.

When I noticed this, I told myself, *I will never be overly involved with W.A.M., including being its president.* I had a lot of respect for the Association and knew it was a worthwhile organization and it was very necessary for Evanston to remain as an active member, which I had been, both during my tenure as a city council member and as mayor, but never wanting to be president.

⚬⚬⚬

We had the dedication of the new Centennial Neighborhood Park on June 14th, starting at 6:00 p.m. with a Neighborhood Pot Luck Picnic followed by the Centennial Park Dedication Program, with door prizes and fun for all.

This was Evanston's newest city park and was made possible by funds provided by the City of Evanston. The park was named after the Centennial Subdivision that started construction in 1976, the year of the United States Bicentennial.

On the 2nd of June, the Evanston City Council held their annual public budget hearing for fiscal year of 1993-1994. It was a lengthy meeting with those in attendance requesting funds for various programs, most of which were already included in the proposed budget, so there was very little change to the proposed budget at that time.

The final action on the budget would be to adopt a resolution during the regular city council meeting on June 15th. Therefore, on June 15th I opened the meeting. Councilmembers Ronald Barnard and Craig Nelson were absent. I declared a quorum and proceeded to the initial items on the agenda. All passed by a unanimous vote, and then I went directly into public participation.

A public hearing was held concerning an application for a new restaurant liquor license by Luis Ibarra, dba El Rancho Grande Restaurant. The hearing was conducted by City Attorney Dennis Boal and would be taped and on file at Evanston City Hall. Following the hearing Councilman Hutchinson made the motion to approve the license application of Luis Ibarra, seconded by Wall, with all those present voting in favor.

Sandy, representing the Evanston High School Alumni Society, made a request for a parade to be held July 3rd starting at 9:30 a.m. at the Uinta County Library Parking Lot.

After a very short discussion Councilman Davis made a motion to authorize the Alumni Parade and the proposed route, and to notify the Evanston Police Department of the event. The motion was seconded by Wall with all those present voting in favor.

Councilman Davis made a motion to approve a malt beverage permit application for the County Fair Board for the annual Uinta County Fair on July 31st, August 3rd, 4th, 5th and 6th from 2:00 p.m. to 12:00 midnight. The motion was seconded by Hutchinson and passed unanimously.

Eugene Joyce, representing Wyoming Downs, was on hand to express his appreciation for the support in getting the racing season started with a special thanks to the mayor, Councilwoman Wall and City Planner Paul Knopf.

Mr. Joyce announced that ESPN TV News would be running a segment on Evanston and Wyoming Downs on national TV this summer.

I expressed the city's appreciation to Mr. Joyce for promoting the Downs and the City of Evanston. *God only knows that we need the publicity to help build our economy,* I said.

I expressed the city's thanks, appreciation and congratulations to Police Chief Dennis Harvey and Detective J. R. Dean and mentioned the schooling they had completed as follows:

Russell Dennis Harvey:

Attended elementary school, junior and senior high schools in Evanston, graduating in 1966.

He went into the U.S. Air Force in 1966, attended part-time college courses at Santa Maria Junior College in Santa Maria, California. His major was Criminal Justice.

He got out of the Air Force in 1970, returned to Evanston, and went to work at the Union Pacific Railroad shop.

In October 1971, he went to work for the Evanston Police Department. He was appointed as Chief of Police for the department by Mayor Dan South in 1977.

He started taking college classes in 1983 at Western Wyoming College in Rock Springs, majoring in Administration of Criminal Justice.

He also took classes at Western Wyoming College, University of Wyoming and Weber State University in Ogden, Utah.

He attained his Associate of Science Degree from Weber State University in spring of 1991. He also received his degree in Administration of Criminal Justice.

James R. Dean:

Started college in 1974 at Weber State College, majoring in Police Science.

He joined the Evanston Police Department in 1977 after being on the E.P.D. Reserves since 1976.

He took city-sponsored college courses for two years, part-time in 1983, and then received his Associate of Science Degree. He also took classes in Administration of Criminal Justice, both from Weber State University, in 1990.

He graduated from Weber State in 1993 with a B.S. Degree in Administration of Criminal Justice. Dean also took courses from Western Wyoming College through the Lifelong Learning Center in Evanston; he took teleconference courses from the University

Of Wyoming; correspondence course from Brigham Young University; and by teleconference from Utah State University, as well as driving back and forth to Ogden to attend on-campus courses from Weber State. J. R. made a ten-year commitment to finish his degree program.

Those city council members who were present also congratulated Harvey and Dean for their outstanding achievements.

As the first item under new Business, Ordinance 93-5 was sponsored by Councilman Vranish and introduced by Councilman Hutchinson. The ordinance read as follows:

ORDINANCE 93-5
AN ORDINANCE ENACTING SECTION 12-42.2.
<u>LICENSE REQUIRED</u>, OF THE EVANSTON CITY CODE
MAKING IT A CRIME FOR PERSONS TO DRIVE A
VEHICLE ON THE PUBLIC ROADS OR HIGHWAYS
WITHIN THE CITY OF EVANSTON, WYOMING
WITHOUT A VALID DRIVER'S
LICENSE.

Although the State of Wyoming already had a law making it illegal to drive a vehicle without a license, the City of Evanston was passing this ordinance to align with state law. It was made a part of "Section 12, Motor Vehicles and Traffic" of the book of Evanston Codes.

Councilman Vranish made a motion to pass Ordinance 93-5 on first reading, seconded by Davis, with all voting in favor. The ordinance was also passed by a motion and a second by the council on the second and third readings unanimously.

Opening the floor for the final budget hearing, City Treasurer Steve Widmer gave a brief explanation of the budget. With no one present in opposition to the proposed budget, I asked for someone from the city council to introduced Resolution 93-34.

The Resolution was introduced by Councilman Vranish and the title was read by City Attorney Boal as follows:

RESOLUTION 93-34
A RESOLUTION PROVIDING INCOME NECESSARY
TO FINANCE THE BUDGET AND PROVIDE FOR AND
AUTHORIZE ANNUAL APPROPRIATION OF FUNDS FOR
FISCAL YEAR 1994.

This fiscal year of 1993-1994 budget was finalized in the amount of approximately $10,250,000 dollars. It appeared that, once again, the City of Evanston ended its fiscal year of 1992-1993 with a healthy cash reserve. This was always good because with a reasonable cash reserve we could always fall back on that if we ran into a shortfall of funds.

The lodging tax program was looking healthy, with approximately $125,000 raised over the previous year, and the new Round-Up Program, recently initiated by Councilwoman Wall, had done well this past year by raising approximately $3,300 to be used for improvements of Depot Square. Also, the employees each received a 3% increase in pay.

After a few amendments were voted on during discussion, the motion to approve and adopt Resolution 93-34 was made by Councilman Davis and seconded by Hutchinson, and the motion passed unanimously.

There was no other new business, so I polled the council and staff for comments and announcements.

Community Development Director/City Planner Paul Knopf reported on the High Uinta Bike Race to be held on Saturday, June 19th. He stated that they expect 250 to 300 bikers to be involved and already had over 70 volunteers to help.

Councilman Davis stated that the dedication of Centennial Park was a big success and expressed thanks from the people involved for making Centennial Park a reality.

I, in turn, congratulated the folks of Centennial Valley for getting the park and thanked them all for putting on such a wonderful dedication of the park. It was a fun day for all and I thought everyone enjoyed themselves, and it was an opportunity to get acquainted with the neighbors.

It was announced that Councilwoman Wall was the successful candidate and would receive the W.A.M. Scholarship to attend the seminar and schooling offered by the Rocky Mountain Foundation. The city council nominated Wall in May for the scholarship.

I congratulated Ms Wall on her receiving the scholarship and stated that I hoped she came back with some beneficial information for the entire city council. The meeting adjourned at 9:12 p.m.

I don't remember what the Rocky Mountain Foundation course was, but Wall did give a report on the seminar to the council and thanked them for the nomination. I expressed my appreciation for her report and hoped that the seminar would be a benefit to her, not only to assist her in her goals as a member of the city council, but also in her membership as a board member of the Wyoming Association of Municipalities.

However, the only thing I could see that Jerry Wall had learned was to be more political, more vindictive, more arrogant and more domineering, because she had already intimidated four council members to work against me. After returning from the seminar she got those members even more opposed to the programs and projects that I was pushing for, such as the Job Corps Center and the land the Union Pacific deeded to the city, and trying to keep Union Tank Car Company from moving out of Evanston.

As far as I was concerned she not only put her own interests before the interest of the general public, but she betrayed her Oath of Office as well. She didn't seem to care about anything except the projects that she had been involved in. And she was being very sly and shrewd in working closely with Executive Director of W.A.M. Carl Classen, because she wanted to become President of the Association sometime during her term as a city council member, and she eventually did.

In a way it all kind of surprised me that she could intimidate the four city council members the way she did. Two-thirds of the city council! Quite a task, but she sure as hell knew what she was doing, and she also learned how to play dirty politics.

It didn't surprise me one bit about Councilman Craig Nelson, because she had him on a leash like he was a puppy dog right from when she was elected back on the council in 1992. He was like a "bobbing doll," always bobbing his head up and down when she wanted something. He got the nickname "Bobbing Doll Nelson" during this period. Councilman Will Davis kind of surprised me, but then he was planning to run against me in the 1994 election for mayor. When he first joined the council, he and his wife Julia went to a meeting in Washington D.C. with Sandy and me. I told Davis then that I thought he was mayor material, and I meant it. That's what I thought at the time, but I changed my mind after seeing how easily he was intimidated.

But the one that really surprised me was Councilman Clarence Vranish. Although Clarence and I had not always seen eye to eye we always seemed to respect one another. I saw Clarence as a man with a mind of his own, and whether we agreed or not, he always seemed to have the city's best interest in mind. He took the Oath of Office very seriously. However, he too became one of Jerry Wall's puppets.

And then there was Councilman Ron Barnard, relatively new to the council, but very naive and intimidated, I believe, by both Wall and Vranish. But after the way Wall and Nelson treated him at the previous W.A.M. meeting in June, I couldn't believe that he would cow-down to someone like Jerry Wall. But he too was a puppet to Wall and Vranish with them pulling the strings.

The next year and a half was going to be hell for me and I was going to have a hard time keeping the economy up, but I was bound and determined that I would keep all the programs and projects going, and continue to work on bettering the economy.

⁓

A couple of weeks after Governor Sullivan and Wyoming's First Lady Jane attended the Annual Renewal Ball, I received a letter from the Governor thanking the City of Evanston for such a wonderful evening. I had the letter printed in the *Uinta County Herald* issue of June 29th. The letter read as follows:

Open letter to Mayor Dennis Ottley:

Just a quick note to thank you and Sandy for a great day in Evanston. Jane and I enjoyed meeting and visiting with the people of your community and the Renewal Ball was wonderful and fun. We hope to repeat the experience again one day.

Again, thanks for all you, your staff and your community did to make our visit to Evanston such a pleasure.

Gov. Mike Sullivan

I also received a similar letter from Wyoming's First Lady Jane Sullivan in appreciation of the time she spent in Evanston, and the hospitality shown her during her visit and during the Renewal Ball. She said in her letter, *"The Renewal Ball was what I call a real community event. Such a win-win endeavor...people celebrating together and promoting community pride."*

Both letters were very much appreciated, and I made the city council and the Urban Renewal Agency aware of both letters before I had the governor's letter printed in the newspaper.

The second regular city council meeting of the month was held on June 23rd. Following the approval of the agenda, we went into public participation.

Evanston Cowboy Days Committee Chairman A. J. Barker and committee members Brian Welling and Darwin McLean were requested the approval of their application for a malt beverage permit for a concert to be held on the evening of July 3rd, and during the Evanston Cowboy Days Celebration on Labor Day Weekend, September 4th, 5th, and 6th, each day from 4:00 p.m. to 2:00 a.m. The motion was made by Councilwoman Wall to approve the applications, seconded by Nelson, with all voting in favor.

Next were reports from the city department heads, which were all approved and accepted by the council unanimously.

Kate Edwards spoke on an application for a catering permit to be used for Railroad Days on July 17th and 18th. A motion was made by Councilwoman Wall to approve Edwards's application, seconded by Vranish, with all voting in favor.

I re-appointed Ryley Dawson to a three-year term on the District's Parks and Recreation Board beginning on July 1st. Motion was made by Councilman Hutchinson to confirm Dawson's appointment, seconded by Nelson, with all council members voting in favor.

Diana Hennigar, representing the Uinta County Fair Board, requested a parade permit for the upcoming County Fair on July 31st. She mentioned that the parade route would be similar to the previous year's parade route. Motion was made by Councilwoman Wall to allow the parade, seconded by Barnard, with all voting in favor.

Pat Alexander, representing the Downtown Design Committee, presented the city council with a professionally printed brochure of a downtown walking tour of Evanston which included pictures and many historical events.

The members of the council and I expressed our appreciation to the all-volunteer Design Committee for the time and expertise they had given in compiling all the information that was in the booklet. I said, "The booklet is well done and the citizens of Evanston should appreciate it and get involved in the tours."

Jill Froman, a senior at Evanston High School, and Brent Boehme, High School Media Specialist, in cooperation with the Urban Renewal Agency produced an eleven-minute video promoting the Evanston area. I called for time to view the video. Thanks and appreciation were extended to Froman, Boehme and the agency for their work and efforts in producing this professionally-done video.

Evanston District Parks and Recreation Director Dennis Poppinga introduced Wyoming State Forester Dan Perko and Forester Dana Stone to the council. Mr. Perko gave a report on the tree inventory and condition and value of all the trees in Evanston within public right-of-ways, the cemetery and so on. Perko reported that the average value of each tree in Evanston is $390 with a total valuation of over $1,400,000. He stated that with a value such as that he would recommend the city pass a tree ordinance.

I wasn't sure why this study was done unless the planning department requested it, but there was no cost involved. So I thanked Perko and Stone for the information and said we will take this information and advice under consideration at a later date.

We acted on two resolutions, 93–35 and 93–36, concerning management, operation and regulation of the Evanston Parks and Recreation District; and a geological survey joint funding agreement for the operation of a stream gauging station on the Bear River in Evanston. Both passed unanimously.

Next we went into comments and announcements by the council and staff.

Public Works Operations Superintendent Allan "Oop" Hansen reported on the recent certifications received by employees Lon Richardson and David Albrecht. They both completed a course that will be beneficial to their jobs, and the council and I congratulated and thanked them both for their work and for their accomplishments. Councilwoman Wall made a motion for the City of Evanston to participate in the Wyoming Department of Transportation program to install "Buckle Up" signs throughout the community, seconded by Barnard, with all voting in favor.

Wall also reminded everyone about the Rubber Ducky Race on the Bear River June 26th and Community Day at the Uinta County Fair on August 6th.

Community Development Director Paul Knopf reported that the Green Thumb Awards Program for the most outstanding landscaping in the community would be starting soon.

Before adjourning, I extended a special word of appreciation for all the volunteers and sponsors of the many weekend activities: the Chili Cookoff, the High Uinta Classic Bike Race, the Rodeo Series, the L.D.S. Regional Conference held in Evanston, Uinta Downs Horse Races, the Renewal Ball, and many more. All these activities brought many, many people to Evanston.

I said that the 12th annual Overthrust Chili Cookoff held on Saturday, June 19th at the Uinta County Fairgrounds was once again a great success, and Tim Lynch and his committee should be awfully proud. In the first eleven years of the Chili Cookoff, the committee had raised over $163,000. This money had been donated to dozens of local programs throughout the community and was very much appreciated.

I also reminded the council of the special meeting scheduled for June 28th at 7:00 p.m. and announced that there will be work session for July 7th. We adjourned at 9:15 p.m.

I received a short letter from Evanston Police Detective Colleen Millburg, written on June 21, 1993 that read as follows:

Mayor Ottley
City Council

I recently returned from a roundtable discussion presented by the National League of Cities in Pasadena, California. The theme was centered round the family unit. I wish, at this time, to thank you for giving me the opportunity to attend.

After working with other, much larger, cities I felt that we are further ahead in the areas of community programs and community bond with families and especially the youth than others attending seemed to be. Upon completion of the two days I felt that we came away with ideas that may be implemented into our already working system. I was glad to return to Wyoming and proud to have been a part of our group.

Colleen Millburg (signed)
Detectives
Evanston Police Department

Each member of the Evanston City Council got a copy of the letter, and I thanked Officer Millburg for the letter and congratulated her for attending the roundtable session.

The first regular city council meeting of the month was held on July 14th, and after a quorum was declared we took care of the initial agenda, such as the approval of the minutes and outstanding bills.

I recognized a visiting Boy Scout, Jason Eicker of Troop #95, and I thanked him for his attendance, welcomed him with a handshake and presented him with one of Evanston's "Fresh Air, Freedom and

Fun" pins. I welcomed him to participate in the meeting anytime he desired.

Following, I reappointed Georgia Harvey and Councilman Tom Hutchinson to the Public Service Board for a three-year term. Councilman Nelson made a motion to confirm the appointments, seconded by Davis, with all 6 council members voting in favor.

Councilwoman Wall made a motion to approve a malt beverage permit application requested by the Ellis Ranch Psychos for their annual Softball Tournament at the Overthrust Ball Fields on July 17th and 18th. The motion was seconded by Barnard, with all voting in favor.

Councilman Barnard stated that he would like to be heard as a member of the BEAR Project and offered special thanks to everyone who was involved in the Rubber Ducky Race and the activities of the day: Dennis Poppinga, Robert Van Riper, James Abbot, Key Bank, Brian Honey, Allan "Oop" Hansen, Russ Robertson, all of the city departments, the Rotary Club and everyone else who made the program a big success.

The rest of the city council members and I also echoed our thanks and appreciation for a job well done.

Councilwoman Wall made a motion to approve a parade permit requested by the Evanston Cowboy Days Committee for Labor Day, seconded by Hutchinson, with all voting in favor.

In new business, Councilman Nelson sponsored Ordinance 93-6, which created a section in the city code naming hours of use for the Sulphur Creek Reservoir area and prohibiting overnight camping except by Special Permit.

Ordinance 93-6 was introduced by Councilman Hutchinson, and after City Attorney read the title Councilman Nelson made a motion to pass Ordinance 93-6 on first reading. The motion was amended by adding a few words, but the main motion as amended passed unanimously.

Ordinance 93-6 also passed unanimously on the second and third readings as amended with no changes during the next two meetings.

I hoped Evanston was still a candidate for getting the Job Corps Center in Uinta County near Evanston. The U.S. Forest Department had requested that the City of Evanston adopt a resolution showing that the city was in favor of obtaining the center.

They were still looking at Fremont County, but Wyoming would definitely get a Job Corps Center somewhere in the state. I, along with many others, was hoping it would be in Uinta County, but there was still a large group opposed, mostly led by folks living on or near Wyoming State Highway 150 South.

Resolution 93-39 came on the floor and was introduced by Councilman Hutchinson. The resolution read as follows:

RESOLUTION 93-39
RESOLUTION OF THE CITY OF EVANSTON, WYOMING, AUTHORIZING THE PREPARATION OF A PROPOSAL IN PARTNERSHIP WITH THE U.S. FOREST DEPARTMENT FOR FUNDING FOR A JOB CORPS CIVILIAN CONSERVATION CENTER TO BE LOCATED IN UINTA COUNTY, WYOMING.

Section 1: The City of Evanston, Wyoming, is authorized to take all actions necessary to prepare and to aid and assist the U.S. Forest Department in the preparation of a partnership proposal for the construction and operation of a Job Corps Civilian Conservation Center to be located in Uinta County, Wyoming.

Section 2: The Mayor is authorized to execute and the City Clerk to attest all documents which may be necessary for the preparation of said proposal.

Councilman Davis made a motion to adopt Resolution 93-39, seconded by Barnard. The main motion was amended with a few word changes and seconded. The motion as amended passed with 6 votes in favor and 1 vote against (Vranish).

Adopting this resolution gave Evanston new hopes of getting the Center, but there was still a large group of opposition, and we still had Fremont County to consider as a tough competitor. Governor

Sullivan assured the City of Evanston that the state property located on State Highway 150 was still available to the county for the Job Corps Center. Things were looking up, but I was still worried because of the intense opposition to it.

During this meeting of July 14th Councilman Vranish brought to the attention of the city council that the school crossing signs with 20-mile per speed limit located on Yellow Creek Road near Twin Ridge Avenue should be removed because they were installed without prior approval from the city council.

I said to him that the city would not remove them without the consensus of the city council. Motion was made immediately by Councilman Vranish to remove the signs mentioned and seconded with all voting in favor. Therefore, with the vote of the council, I directed Public Works to remove the signs immediately, and thanked Councilman Vranish for bringing this to our attention.

Surprisingly, we never heard anything from the School District concerning those signs, so I guess it didn't bother them to have the signs removed.

Prior to adjourning I proudly reported that the City of Evanston received a certificate for the city's Outstanding Commitment to the Stewardship of America's Public Lands and Natural and Cultural Resources from U.S. Secretary of the Interior Bruce Babbitt.

This certificate was recognized the outstanding volunteer work that the BEAR Committee had accomplished for their project on the Bear River and area.

I also received a very nice letter from U.S. Senator Alan K. Simpson offering his congratulations to the City of Evanston for receiving such a great honor from Secretary of Interior Babbitt.

Receiving the certificate made me feel great, but the letter from Senator Simpson made me feel even better. It was good to know that all the work on the BEAR Project and all the other projects that Evanston had undertaken had not been unnoticed. I made sure that each council member, the staff and commission and board members were all aware of the letter from Senator Simpson and that all had a chance to read the letter.

During the July 14th meeting I also announced two other important meetings: Wednesday, July 1st at 5:00 p.m. was a public meeting to discuss the proposed Job Corps site; and also on Wednesday there would be a meeting with representatives from WAMJPIC (the Wyoming Association of Municipalities' insurance plan) and Blue Cross/Blue Shield at City Hall from 10:00 a.m. to 12:00 noon, and 2:00 p.m. to 4:00 p.m. who would provide information about their health insurance programs.

The *Uinta County Herald* of July 16th ran an article by reporter Ann Curtis titled, CITY PONDERS VYING FOR JOB CORPS CENTER. Ms Curtis started the article as follows:

Another effort is being put forth to bring a Job Corps Training Center to Evanston. Businesses and citizens are being asked for their input on the move.

Evanston Mayor Dennis Ottley has sent out a number of letters asking politicians and business leaders to attend a meeting on Wednesday at 5 p.m. at City Hall.

Private citizens are also encouraged to attend, listen to the proposal, and express their opinions on the matter. The Job Corps Center would employ about 70 people as teachers, counselors, maintenance personnel and kitchen help.

The center would house 275 to 500 students from the ages of 16-21.

Curtis's article continued: *At Wednesday night's city council meeting, councilman Clarence Vranish was the only "no" vote on a resolution allowing the city to proceed with looking into the matter. Several council members, including Vranish, were skeptical, saying they didn't want a situation like the Majestic Ranch, near Randolph (Utah), in Evanston. Ottley encouraged them to visit the Weber Canyon Center before making up their mind.*

Ottley said the center would help bring economic stability and diversification to Evanston, the article concluded.

ALAN K. SIMPSON
WYOMING

United States Senate
Assistant Republican Leader
WASHINGTON. D.C. 20510

August 9, 1993

Honorable Dennis Ottley
Mayor, City of Evanston
1200 Main Street
Evanston, Wyoming 82930

Dear Dennis:

Congratulations! What a nice honor for
you. I was pleased to learn that the City of
Evanston was honored with a certificate for its
"Outstanding Commitment to the Stewardship of
America's Public Lands and Natural and Cultural
Resources" by President Bill Clinton and
Secretary of the Interior Bruce Babbitt. That
is tremendous!

I certainly commend you and share in your
sense of excitement and pride in receiving that
distinction. It seems most appropriate that
your efforts and dedication have been so nicely
recognized.

I've watched you over the years. You do a
fine job, Dennis. I admire you so. I know
personally of the extraordinary dedication,
energy and time you put into making Evanston a
better place in which to live. I always enjoy
my visits with you.

Ann joins in sending our best wishes and
warm personal regards to you and to Sandy.

Most sincerely,

Alan K. Simpson
United States Senator

AKS/acd

Uinta County Economic Development Coordinator Ken Klinker wrote an article for the *Uinta County Herald* issue of July 20th. It read:

Several months ago, the Uinta County Economic Development Commission was approached by a plastic injection molding company about the possibility of relocating their manufacturing facility from Wheat Ridge, Colo., to Evanston.

The facility would have employed around 150 people. Last week I found out they decided to purchase an existing 50,000 square foot building in Grand Junction, Colo., because they couldn't find one in Wyoming.

Although this decision is disappointing, I wanted to let everyone know how exciting it was to have the community come together in a united effort to do whatever we could to get them to choose Evanston.

We were extremely high on their list, having everything they needed but a building.

I would especially like to thank a number of individuals who went out of their way to get this deal done. J. D. Hall and Don Larson at Intermountain Electric took the time to evaluate the electrical systems at various buildings they were interested in.

Virginia Mathieson at VM, Inc. opened her offices on a Saturday morning at no charge to allow people to fill out questionnaires expressing interest in the positions that would be available (more than 60 people responded with one day notice). Chris Elsen at Century 21/Elsen Realty spent hours trying to find property that would fit the needs of the principals of the company.

Bob Simon at Job Service was very helpful developing the employment questionnaires. Larry Stick, principal at Evanston High School, re-scheduled several times in order to provide a tour of the high school for the company executives and their families.

His enthusiasm about the facilities and the Evanston education system made a great impression on the company. Clarence Vranish arranged an evening of entertainment and stimulating conversation at the Elks Club that I am sure they will not soon forget.

First National Bank provided free legal counsel to address numerous complex legal problems. Diane Mills at the Dunmar Inn subsidized room rates for their visits. And UP&L and the City of Evanston helped cover the cost of numerous site visits. As you can see, there was a broad base of support from the community to try to convince this company to locate here.

I'm sure there were others who helped, and I apologize for not mentioning you here.

My point is that this community is enthusiastic about growth and diversification on our economic base. Although this particular company did not decide to locate here, we proved that we have much to offer manufacturing companies and our continued efforts as a community will eventually lead to success.

Thanks again to everyone who helped with this project.

The above letter shows that there can be an enthusiastic move by the Evanston and Uinta County folks on some industry, but although Klinker's letter didn't say so, there was some opposition to the plastic injection molding company. A number of were concerned about the (awful?) odor that the plant might produce and the air pollution it may create. There were many concerns about the plant, but overall most folks wanted it.

I would have liked to have seen the same enthusiasm for the Job Corps Center as Klinker described in his letter, but the City of Evanston didn't get much consideration from either Klinker or the county's economic commission concerning the Center.

The only difference, as far as I could see, was that one was government and the other was private industry. They both would have had great benefits for the community, but both also had their downfalls.

During the July 28th regular city council meeting, during public participation, Mrs. Jesse Monroe of the Pine Gables Lodge, a bed & breakfast inn located on the corner of Harrison Drive and Center Street, complained about the loud noise and bad language coming from the city parking lot across the street from the lodge. She said it happened very often during late-night hours and was disturbing her guests considerably.

I told Mrs. Monroe that the city police would make an effort to patrol that area more often and see that the folks parked in the lot either move or quiet down and knock off the foul language. I thanked her for attending and making the city aware of the problem.

Mr. Ross Martin was expressed his support for a new testing program for plumbers in the State of Wyoming. This is a program to give successful Wyoming plumbers greater mobility between communities, and is being sponsored by W.A.M. There would be a nationally recognized test offered each month in various locations throughout the state and could possibly begin as early as September 1993.

At this time there were no state requirements for those that wished to go into the plumbing business. But there had been a move for quite some time to require some kind of certification that plumbers must acquire before going into business.

Prior to adjourning I polled the staff and council for remarks and announcements.

Parks and Recreation Director Dennis Poppinga pointed out the need of a backhoe for the cemetery, because the cemetery is maintained by the Parks Department. Poppinga was directed to get with Public Works and start advertising for bids to be presented to the city council in the next meeting or so.

City Treasurer Steve Widmer reported receiving a quarterly check for franchise fees from the power company in the amount of $13,338.33 for the first quarter of the year. All utilities within the city pay a franchise fee every quarter to the City of Evanston, which is recognized as income and placed in the general account.

Councilman Tom Hutchinson had attended a seminar on casino gambling held in San Diego, California with the permission of the City of Evanston, because we knew the state gambling issue would be coming up and possibly be a proposition to be voted on by the people in the next election in 1994.

Councilman Hutchinson expressed his appreciation to me and the city council for the opportunity to attend the seminar. He stated that it was very informative and interesting and that he would communicate the information he had learned during our work sessions, which are also open to the public.

I reminded everyone of upcoming events: Uinta County Fair in August and the City Picnic on August 26th at 5:30 p.m. at Hamblin Park. The meeting adjourned at 9:18 p.m.

On July 20th, Community Development Director and City Planner Paul Knopf put out a memorandum naming his committee for *Support Your Community Week*, which would be held the last week of October. The committee would consist of 15-20 people who would offer diversity and share work assignments, to ensure the continued success of the event, the memo concluded.

This year, as every year, I received letters from the young folks of Rich County, Utah, inviting me to their annual Junior 4-H Livestock Sale during the Rich County Fair. This year the 4-H Livestock Sale was held on Saturday, August 21st, and once again I went to Randolph to attend the livestock sale. With the help of Mr. Kay Thornock of Randolph, who helped me every year, I would purchase, on behalf of the City of Evanston, one of the 4-H members' stock. I felt it was good public relations, because the folks of Rich County did so much shopping and banking in Evanston.

The first regular city council meeting of the month was held on August 11th, with only three council members and me present. City council members Tom Hutchinson, Jerry Wall and Ron Barnard had been excused. However, with four present, I declared a quorum and opened the meeting at 7:00 p.m.

Councilman Vranish made a motion to authorize a malt beverage permit to Cowboy Joe's Liquor Barn for a Volley Ball Tournament sponsored by the Evanston Beautification Committee at Depot Square on August 14th from 8:00 a.m. to 7:00 p.m. The motion was seconded by Davis, with all those present voting in favor.

Engineering Technician Bob Liechty explained a proposed testing program for plumbers sponsored by W.A.M. that could be accepted by any town or city in the State of Wyoming that elected to participate in the program.

I thanked Bob for his presentation and assured him that most commercial plumbers would appreciate the program, because I have had local plumbers asking me why the State of Wyoming doesn't have a testing and certification requirement for plumbers.

Jake Jacobs and Bob Severe requested a street closure on Labor Day, the weekend of the Evanston Cowboy Days celebration. They requested the closure of 10th Street from Front Street to Main Street, and Main Street from 10th Street to 9th Street for a festival from 9:00 a.m. to 2:00 p.m. The motion was made by Councilman Nelson to authorize the street closures, seconded by Davis, with all those present voting in favor.

Under new business, Councilman Nelson introduced Resolution 93-45, a resolution authorizing the installation of a fiber optics Line by Union Pacific Resources Company within existing utility easements and across city public streets. The approval would be given with the understanding that UPRC bored under Wasatch Road and either bore or obtain cut permits in all other locations as required by city ordinances. The motion to adopt Resolution 93-45 was made by Councilman Davis, seconded by Vranish, with all 4 votes in favor.

In the past, the City of Evanston had always left it up to the Evanston Cowboy Days committee to select what street vendors were allowed to come to Evanston and set up booths on the street during the Labor Day weekend.

However, during this meeting Councilman Vranish brought up the subject and suggested that a letter be sent to remind the Cowboy Days committee that all street vendors must purchase a permit from City Hall before setting up. This was agreed upon by the council and me. I then directed City Clerk Welling to send out such a letter to the committee.

In adjourning this short meeting I reminded everyone of the upcoming events: the Rich County Fair, the City Picnic, Cowboy Days, the Autocross Race, the Mayor's Golf Tournament, and the town meeting in which U.S. Senator Malcolm Wallop and Congressman Craig Thomas were expected to be available for questions and answer on state and national affairs.

Senator Wallop and Representative Thomas held their town meeting in Evanston on August 16th at the City Hall building. The meeting was very informal and Evanston folks had an opportunity to ask a lot of questions pertaining to important issues such as welfare reform, Social Security, child support, taxes, and the budget.

I received a nice letter from Congressman Thomas thanking me for my attendance at the town meeting. In his letter he stated: *"Taxpayers are not the problem, as some Capitol Hill folks suggest. Overspending is the problem."* I had to agree with him 100%.

The second regular city council meeting of the month was on August 25th with all members of the council present. I declared a quorum and opened the meeting at 7:00 p.m.

During public participation, Councilman Ron Barnard, Chairman of the BEAR Project Committee presented future plans for the Bear River area and reported that the committee was beginning to receive the signage for the BEAR Project. He displayed one of the signs the committee had recently received.

Councilman Barnard also expressed the city's and the committee's appreciation to the Wyoming Game and Fish Department for providing the signs, and he gave a special thanks to Community Development Director and City Planner Paul Knopf for working closely with the Game and Fish Department on the wetland project.

He also reported that the Rubber Ducky Race on the Bear River was a big success and had raised $7,055 that would be used for improvements to the BEAR Project, and he thanked all those involved in making the duck race successful.

Lisa Wesselius requested that the city provide a fence around the new Centennial Valley Park so when her horses got loose from her property they wouldn't get into the park area, as they had. However, the council did not accept the idea, and I let Mrs. Wesselius know that we had never fenced any of the city's neighborhood parks, and that we were not going to start now.

The council also questioned the cost of fencing, and ended up telling Mrs. Wesselius that folks that own horses have to be responsible for them and do their own fencing, especially if the horses are in the city limits. The subject was dropped.

After reviewing and acting on several bids on vehicles, we addressed new business. The first item being introduced by Councilman Nelson was Resolution 93-44, authorizing the city to enter into an agreement with the Gibbon & Reed Company for overlay on streets in the city that were badly in need. The motion was made by Councilman Hutchinson to adopt Resolution 93-44, seconded by Nelson. Motion passed unanimously.

Councilman Hutchinson followed up by introducing Resolution 93-46 to authorize the City of Evanston to enter into an agreement with X-It Construction for construction of sidewalks in areas within the city known as the Red Mountain Road and Yellow Creek Road.

The council voted that the sidewalks would be five feet wide and would be constructed immediately. Motion was made by Councilman Nelson to adopt Resolution 93-46, seconded by Wall, with all voting in favor.

The Red Mountain residents were finally going to get the sidewalk that they had been asking for the last two years, to go from Highway 89 to the Red Mountain Subdivision. Yellow Creek Road would also have additional sidewalks.

After acting on a few more resolutions I, as mayor, sponsored Ordinance 93-7 and was introduced by Councilman Nelson.

ORDINANCE 93-7
AN ORDINANCE AMENDING SECTION 15-11.1. DISTURBING THE PEACE, OF THE EVANSTON CITY CODE, TO ELIMINATE THE REQUIREMENT THAT A WRITTEN WARNING BE GIVEN BEFORE A PERSON CAN BE CITED FOR DISTURBING THE PEACE.

Sec. 15-11.1. Disturbing the Peace.
It shall be unlawful for any person to cause, or to continue to cause or make a disturbance of any excessive or unusually loud noise so as to disturb the peace, quiet and comfort of any reasonable person

of normal sensitivity residing in the same vicinity, neighborhood, trailer or mobile home park, apartment house or complex within the limits of the City of Evanston.

The City of Evanston had been receiving numerous calls and complaints concerning loud stereos and other noises, especially during late hours. Although the city already had an ordinance pertaining to loud noises, it required a 24-hour written notice from the city to stop the loud noise. Ordinance 93-7 would remove that requirement because when people got the 24-hour notice, those making the noise would just continue making it until the 24 hours were up.

Ordinance 93-7 would require them to immediately stop the noise upon the first warning or they could possibly pay a fine or serve time in jail if they disturbed the peace after they were warned.

Motion was made by Councilman Vranish to pass Ordinance 93-7 on first reading, seconded by Wall, with all voting in favor. The ordinance was passed on the second and third and final readings during future meetings.

Councilman Nelson made a motion that Councilman Ron Barnard be Evanston's voting delegate at the upcoming National League of Cities Convention to be held in December, and Councilwoman Jerry Wall would be the alternate, seconded by Vranish, with all voting in favor.

I reminded everyone that there would be a work session on September 1st at 5:00 p.m., and also about the upcoming City Picnic, the Mayor's Golf Tournament, and other events just before adjourning.

Every year in late August, just before the school year started, Uinta County School District No. 1 would have a New Teacher Orientation get-together for new educators and other new school officials. This year the Orientation was held at the Western Lamplighter Motel (now known as the Days Inn) on August 24th. A number of local folks, including the mayor, were always invited to attend. It was an opportunity for new school personnel to get acquainted with the local leaders and other citizens.

This year, as other years, I was once again invited to attend and asked to say a few words to welcome the new people to our community, and tell them a little about Evanston's history and special places to visit, also to mention some of our annual events. My talk was never very long, but I always felt privileged to be included and to have the opportunity to speak and welcome new people to our community.

The 4th Annual Mayor's Golf Tournament was held on Friday, August 27th. The public was invited to the "4-Person Scramble." There were cash awards for men and women. It was an eighteen-hole tournament and brunch was served following the ninth hole. We had a full slate of participants and everyone enjoyed themselves.

On August 31st I received a letter from Linda Barker, Uinta County 4-H Coordinator, thanking the City of Evanston for waiving the fees for their use of the city bus to take the Uinta County 4-H participants to the Wyoming State Fair in Douglas. She stated that they were able to transport over twenty 4-H youth to the State Fair and back safely and reasonably.

I thought it was a good move to let the 4-H coordinator use the city bus without any additional cost for such an important event, and I really appreciated the letter and made sure each city council member received a copy of it.

During the regular meeting of September 8th, a very short meeting, I spoke of the recent death of James (Jim) W. Vanderbeek and all he had done for Evanston. Jim had passed away on August 22, 1993 at the age of 67. He spent 42 years with Amoco before retiring. He had been a very good friend to Evanston during the Overthrust oil and gas boom.

During the boom days of Evanston Jim was Senior Vice President for Amoco Production Company. His office was located in Denver, Colorado. His position was to oversee the Overthrust area, including Northern Utah and Western Wyoming. During my first term as mayor, Jim and I became close, you might even say good friends, but most of our association pertained to business.

My Assistant Steve Snyder and I made many visits to Denver to talk to Jim about some of Evanston's problems. One of the last visits was when I asked him if it was possible for Amoco to change their mind about locating the proposed East Anschultz Gas Plant in Wyoming rather than Utah.

An announcement had been made by Amoco that the plant would be located in Summit County, Utah. This got my attention because most of the road going to the plant would be in Uinta County and most of the workers would be from Evanston. I asked myself, *Just why can't the plant be built in Uinta County rather than Summit County? Why couldn't the plant be moved a few hundred yards into Wyoming?* After our visit with Jim he told us that he would look into the possibility.

A few days later he notified me that the plant would be built in Uinta County. As a favor to Evanston and Uinta County he acknowledged my request, and the Anschultz plant was officially located in Wyoming just across the Utah/Wyoming state line. This was a great move for the County and Evanston because of the tremendous increase in property tax revenues, and because most employees would be living in the Evanston area.

Yes, Jim Vandereek was a great friend to Evanston and Uinta County and never hesitated to do what he and Amoco could for the area, whether it was planning, research, funding or just assisting us through the boom period. He was also a U.S. Navy Veteran of World War II.

Jim was one of the principal founders of the Overthrust Industrial Association (O.I.A.) and a big supporter of the Evanston Recreation Center, among many other new structures that Evanston gained because of the boom.

When I received a copy of Jim's obituary from the *Casper Star Tribune* it made me sad that he had passed away at the early age of 67, but I was very happy to know that I had the opportunity to have been associated with him. The City of Evanston sent flowers to his family and condolences and voiced appreciation for what he had done for Evanston.

On September 12th, the new Evanston Alliance Church was having their Day of Dedication. They invited Sandy and me to the ceremony, and asked me to give a short talk.

The Alliance Church had purchased the building that was originally Billy's Bar, Lounge and Dance Hall. After the oil and gas boom was over, Billy's went into foreclosure. The Church purchased the property from the bank.

When I arrived at the church I received a grand welcome from a tremendous group of local folks. In my speech I first apologized that Sandy could not attend because of other commitments. I said, *Though I am not of your faith and don't attend church often, as our Great President Abraham Lincoln once said, "When I do good, I feel good; and when I do bad, I feel bad; and that's my religion." One of the great blessings of America is freedom of religion, the right to worship and seek God in your own way. Without that, America would not be America.*

I also said, *There was a man who once said that if he ever had the opportunity to build a church he would put this sign on every door: "You are not too bad to come in. You are not too good to stay out." I know that this will be true also with your Church,* I said.

The dedication of the Alliance Church was a big success and I was honored to have had the opportunity to be invited and to say a few words.

This year, as every year, I received letters of appreciation from the young 4-H members who had entered their livestock in both the Uinta County Fair and the Rich County, Utah Fair. The letters thanked me for the City of Evanston's participation in the stock sales of both fairs, and for purchasing one of the livestock entrees.

On September 20, 1993 I wrote a letter to the Honorable C. Stuart Brown, who had been a member of the Wyoming Supreme Court, but had recently retired. My letter was an invitation for him to attend the Saturday Night Honor Banquet during Support Your Community Week as the keynote speaker.

Judge Brown was well known to Evanston because of his time as District Judge in Western Wyoming before his appointment to the Supreme Court.

Several days later I received noticed from the Judge that he would be honored to accept my invitation. I was very grateful for his answer and early reply.

The second regular city council meeting was held on September 22nd. Following roll call, with all council members present, I called the meeting to order, and after acting on the early business we had the public participation segment.

I read a letter from Mary Hyde stating that she wished to resign from the Evanston/Uinta Joint Powers Board for Human Services. Councilman Nelson made a motion to accept Ms Hyde's letter, seconded by Davis, with all voting in favor.

The council and I expressed our appreciation to Ms Hyde for her voluntary time and assistance while serving on the Board, and wished her the best in the future.

Robert Lowham, residing on Lombard Street, just across the street from the Best Western Dunmar Motel, presented a hand-written plat to the city council with a diagrammed list of vehicle accidents that had happened at his residence since 1970. Over the years, a number of vehicles driving that curve or leaving the Dunmar Motel have slid off Harrison Drive into the vacant lot on the curve, sometimes continuing on to Mr. Lowham's property. Therefore, he requested the city to install some kind of barrier on the corner to stop vehicles from leaving the street.

The council was very sympathetic to Mr. Lowham's problem, and Councilman Vranish made a motion to either install a guardrail or some other kind of barrier to protect the Lowham property and prevent any serious accidents. Years ago there had been at least one death from a roll-over at that location that I was aware of. The motion was seconded by Wall, and the vote was unanimous.

I directed City Engineer Brian Honey to take care of this. I mentioned that Harrison Drive was still under the Wyoming Highway Department's jurisdiction and directed Honey to approach them first, because they might already have the material for a guardrail.

In the end, the Highway Department ended up installing a guardrail at the requested location. They did this right after Honey made them aware of the problem.

John Bowns gave his report on the 1993 summer activities at the fair and rodeo grounds. In his report he stated that he might continue on a twelve-month basis in order to have the time to properly promote events. The council and I agreed with him and thanked him for the activities that he had promoted during the summer of 1993.

I told John that he was doing a great job in helping to promote Evanston and improving the economy, and to keep it up. It was appreciated.

City Engineer Honey presented a proposed change order on the street overlay project to install a fabric material under the overlay to give more stability to the road surface on City View from Sioux Drive to Del Rio Drive.

Councilman Nelson made a motion to authorize this proposed change order and fabric installation concept suggested by Honey, seconded by Barnard, with all voting in favor.

Councilman Hutchinson reported on the Wyoming Conference on Telecommunications to be held on October 8th, and that he would be one of the panelists on Wants and Needs of Wyoming for Telecommunication Services. I congratulated Tom on his appointment to the panel on such an important service to the State of Wyoming.

Evanston wasn't one of the Wyoming cities initially selected to have the technology they call the compressed video network, but when I was approached by the folks at the Lifelong Learning Center to call Governor Mike Sullivan and request that Evanston be put on the list, we were immediately added. Governor Sullivan never hesitated at all—in fact, he apologized for not having Evanston on the list to start with. Thanks to those at Life Long Learning for bringing it to my attention!

I asked Councilman Barnard to explain just what compressed video services were and how the technology could benefit Evanston. He explained that it gave Evanston access to speak to people or different parties live from anywhere in the state of Wyoming that had the system available. The intercom system would be very beneficial to Evanston and the Center to have the ability to speak directly to someone elsewhere by video. The Center would also be able to hold classes and small seminars at the Center benefiting everyone who had need or interest.

Prior to adjournment I reminded everyone of the public meeting on October 6th to receive input for a Tree Ordinance.

During September I had met with Mr. John L. Harmer of Bountiful, Utah. He stated that he planned to re-open what they now called the Oxbow Refinery, which had been shut down a few years ago. The Oxbow Refinery had been constructed in the mid–1980s by Lair Petroleum, Inc. of Denver, Colorado. After it had been opened for operation it did business under a few other names, but when they shut it down it was known as Oxbow Refinery.

On Tuesday, September 21st, the *Uinta County Herald* came out with the following article:

Evanston Mayor Dennis Ottley announced Monday that the Oxbow Refinery, which has been closed for three years, could re-open as early as Jan. 1, 1994.

Ottley said that John L. Harmer of Eyring Energy Inc., of Bountiful, Utah, had stated that they had plans to expand the refinery so that it would produce 12,000 barrels of diesel fuel and unleaded gasoline per day. The Oxbow Refinery is located on Divide Road [formerly the old U.S. Highway 30 South], eight miles east of Evanston on 40 acres of property.

"This is something that would really help diversify our economy. They would be using local crude and condensate," Ottley said. Twenty-six employees will be hired when the refinery opens and 12 to 14 months later, 44 employees would be in the ranks, according to Ottley.

Two conditions that Harmer wants met are that the refinery's sewer and water be hooked in with the City of Evanston, the *Herald* article concluded.

When Harmer requested that they be hooked into the city's water and sewer systems, he didn't mention the City of Evanston would also be paying for it, but later he did. He requested that the city pay the cost of running city utilities to the refinery. He stated that since they were opening up the refinery and helping the economy by putting people to work, as well as increasing the county's tax base, that it would only be right that the City of Evanston pay for the construction of the water and sewer hookups.

LETTERS TO THE EDITOR

Fossil Butte superintendent foresees Job Corps Center projects

Editor's note: The following letters were addressed to Mayor Dennis Ottley.

Dear Mayor Ottley: We have heard the city of Evanston, in partnership with the USFS, has proposed a Job Corp. Center (JCC) for the Evanston area. Good luck with your proposal. We, along with the BLM and USF&WS, had some momen-

tary thoughts about an Interior JCC partnership proposal for the Kemmerer area. But, we quickly recognized that the potential is perhaps much better near Evanston. If you do succeed in getting a center with a construction curriculum and associated projects, there is much potential for federal work projects in the Kemmerer

area. That was perhaps the most compelling incentive for doing a proposal in our area. The BLM Kemmerer Resource Area, Seedskadee National Wildlife Refuge, and the newly authorized Cokeville Meadow Refuge, the Kemmerer Ranger District of the Bridger-Teton National Forest and Fossil Butte National Monument all

have an abundance of infrastructure construction needs.

Those needs might be of interest when JCC impact on nearby federal properties is evaluated. Enclosed is a letter of endorsement for inclusion with your proposal.

David McGinnis
Superintendent
Fossil Butte National Monument

Sen. Simpson lends support to Job Corps Center proposal

Dear Dennis:

How goes things with you? Thank you for contacting me to urge my support for the Uinta County Economic Development Commission's proposal for a Job Corps Center in Evanston.

I agree with you that there is a great deal of merit to this

proposal and I want to share with you that I have written to Secretary of Labor Robert B. Reich to express my enthusiastic support for this project. As one of just a few states in the nation that does not currently have a Job Corps Center, Wyoming would benefit tremendously from such a fa-

cility. It is also important that you and so many others in the community are supporting this proposal.

We are fortunate to have a very dedicated and capable group of people pursuing this at the local level. Please know that I will continue to closely monitor the progress of this

project.

Thank you again for your thoughtful letter, Dennis. Take care and be well. Stay in touch. I'll always appreciate hearing from you. Ann joins in sending our kindest personal regards to you and to Sandy.

Alan Simpson
United States Senator

Proposed Evanston Job Corps Center has support of Rep. Thomas

Good morning Dennis:

Thanks for letting me know about your request for a Job Corps Civilian Conservation Center in Evanston.

I am happy to give my support to this proposal and

hope the letter that was sent to you will be helpful in gaining approval for your application. A number of organizations in Evanston have also asked for my support.

It's good to know that many

folks in Evanston are clearly in favor of this proposal. I agree that the establishment of this center will provide jobs, income, and be very beneficial for the entire community and our state.

Again, thanks for sharing your thoughts. If there is anything else I can do for you, my friend, please feel free to contact my Rock Springs office.

Best regards,
Craig Thomas
Member of Congress

Uinta County Herald, September 14, 1993.

LETTERS TO THE EDITOR

Reader defends Job Corps Center and its residents

Dear Editor:

I am writing in response to a letter to the editor in your recent issue regarding the Job Corps Center possibly locating in Evanston.

It concerned me greatly at the presumption that poor, under-privilidged persons are all categorized in the letter as "troubled youth."

I have toured the Job Corp facilities in many areas and have given educational talks and workshops at some of them. I have found the population of the centers to very closely mirror the general population in the manners, behavior and goals of its residents. Some may have committed crimes. Some may be troubled. But then... the same might be said about some neighbors that live by us now.

I applaud any service that will assist people to improve their living and educational conditions. I believe we should help single mothers and their children to help themselves and remove themselves from the welfare system. I am more than happy to accept the very small risk that may arise from a minority of the Job Corps residents in order to give the others a chance for a better life.

During the depression, the Civilian Conservation Corps was the answer for many of our successful citizens to get help in the form of lodging, food and jobs at a time when the whole country was suffering. Perhaps the Job Corps will produce outstanding leaders in all fields of endeavor that will contribute to society in the future.

In addition, we ask our political leaders to improve our economy – then we fight them when they have a way of engendering 80 jobs as well as all the income to our local businesses. I, too, ask the residents of Evanston to review the proposal and to do everything possible to help not only ourselves economically, but people who need our help and encouragement.

Denice Wheeler of Evanston.

Uinta County Herald, October 10, 1993.

The city council said that they did not have the money, and that they have never done that for any other industry. Someone asked them; "Just what kind of guarantee are you going to give us that you will stay open for many years down the road?" Because the refinery was bought and sold so many times during the few years it was opened before, folks questioned whether or not it would be successful in the future.

The council refused their request concerning the water and sewer, but that wasn't what killed their efforts to open the refinery up. According to Mr. Harmer, it was a case of lack of money and production. Hopes of re-opening the refinery were not looking too good at this time.

However, later in 1994, I was approach by another group that did finally get the refinery open. They approached me for assistance in getting the refinery operating again, but that is a story for the next chapter.

The question of whether or not Uinta County was going to get the Job Corps Center was a continuing issue. Although I felt that the majority of the folks in the county were in favor of having it in Uinta County, the opposition was increasing and getting louder. This worried me.

The Letters to the Editor column of the *Uinta County Herald* was becoming a large part of the local newspaper; some were in favor of the Job Corps Center and some were in opposition. Some of these letters were sent to me directly, and then I would send them on to be published in the Letters column of the *Herald*.

Some of the letters that I received were from very important people. I received letters of support of the project from U.S. Senator Alan Simpson, U.S. Representative Craig Thomas and surprisingly, even from Superintendent David McGinnis of the Fossil Butte National Monument in Lincoln County.

Also, there were a number of locals writing letters to the paper stating that they were in favor of the Center being located in Uinta County. There was an awful lot of support, but there were still folks in Uinta County in opposition and they were loudly making their point. This worried me.

During the first regular city council meeting of the month held on October 13th, and after the initial business was acted on, I appointed myself to serve on the Human Services Joint Powers Board to fill the vacancy left by Mary Hyde. Motion was made by Councilman Vranish to confirm the appointment, seconded by Barnard, with 5 votes in favor and 1 vote absent (Nelson). The motion passed.

I appointed Frank Sheets, Jr. to serve on the Personnel Board. Motion was made by Councilman Hutchinson to confirm the appointment, seconded by Davis, with 5 votes in favor and 1 absent (Nelson). By ordinance I was not permitted to vote on my own appointments.

Councilman Vranish followed up with a motion to approve a catering permit for serving liquor, applied for by Kate's, for the Octoberfest to be held on October 25th between 5:00 p.m. and 9:00 p.m. in the Beeman-Cashin Building at Depot Square, seconded by Wall, with all voting in favor. The Octoberfest was part of the week's Support Your Community Week program, which was scheduled to run from October 23rd through October 29th.

During the public participation segment of the October meeting, Dallas Reynolds addressed the city council with concerns about the lack of crosswalks on Yellow Creek Road south beyond the traffic light on Cheyenne Drive and Yellow Creek.

After some discussion Councilwoman Wall made a motion for Public Works to have the three intersections on Yellow Creek Road striped with pedestrian lanes on Barrett Avenue, Twin Ridge Avenue and Herschler Avenue, and to install pedestrian signs and speed signs where necessary. Motion was seconded by Barnard, with all voting in favor.

The City of Evanston was looking at licensing and insurance requirements for the taxicab business. City Attorney Dennis Boal suggested that the existing city code concerning the taxicab business be amended and updated to address the present concerns. He stated that he would have an ordinance to amend the city code ready to act on for this meeting of October 13th.

Under new business I sponsored Ordinance 93-8, introduced by Councilman Davis to amend portions of Section 25 of the Evanston City Code, regarding the regulation of taxicabs. This ordinance defined the duties and regulations for operating a taxicab business, including the required city license and liability insurance.

Motion was made by Councilman Vranish to pass Ordinance 93-8 on first reading, seconded by Hutchinson. The motion passed by 6 votes in favor and 1 absent (Nelson). The Ordinance also passed unanimously on the second and third and final readings.

It had been previously announced that the City of Evanston received federal funding in the amount of $500,000 from the Wyoming Transportation Commission for the pathways at the BEAR Project as part of a transportation enhancement activity project.

Councilman Barnard, Chairman of the BEAR Committee was so delighted at receiving the funds that he couldn't stop thanking all those involved and the Transportation Commission for all their support and interest in the BEAR Project.

In closing the meeting of October 13th I announced that there would be a work session on October 20th at 5:00 p.m. with a special city council meeting to follow at 6:00 p.m. I also reminded everyone that Support Your Community Week was coming up October 23rd through October 29th and nominations for honoring senior citizens should be coming in soon.

The meeting adjourned at 9:17 p.m.

On October 8th I wrote an article to be printed in the next issue of the *Uinta County Herald*. They printed the article as a guest column. My article was titled, "A MESSAGE TO THE PEOPLE OF EVANSTON."

In this article I thanked the citizens of Evanston for their cooperation and patience during the city's recent street maintenance projects. I explained that the city budget had been increased $100,000 over last year giving the city a budget of $390,000 for overlays, slurry seals, crack sealing and striping.

Due to the fact that many folks had asked what the difference was between an overlay and a slurry-seal, in the article I tried to explain the difference. I wrote that a *slurry- seal* is only ⅜ inches thick and is used to repair small surface defects and seal the surface to preserve the existing asphalt. An *overlay* is a layer of new asphalt placed to a thickness of 1½ inches, and is used to repair major surface defects and construct a new driving surface. I mentioned that, at that time, the cost for slurry seal was 70 cents per square yard, while the cost for overlay was $3.00 per square yard.

I apologized to the folks for the inconvenience of a rough year of street maintenance. I explained that having nice streets was important to the city officials and the contractors because it gave us better traffic control and made our streets safer for the public. The contractors, because of the street closures and unexpected delays to motorists, had commented emphatically how polite the Evanston motorists were during the construction.

I reminded folks that the primary key to Evanston's street maintenance program was the city's street department crew. They worked year in and year out to seal cracks, repair potholes and maintain our streets, and they kept the streets passable by removing the snow during the winter months.

I have always been committed to providing funding for well-maintained streets, and I am very proud of all city personnel and the work they do to maintain all services.

I concluded my article with: *Thank you all again for your patience and understanding.*

⥲

We had a special meeting on October 20th to act on two resolutions only. In opening the meeting I declared a quorum with three city council members present (Vranish, Nelson and Barnard) and me. Davis, Wall and Hutchinson were excused.

The first order of business was Resolution 93-53 introduced by Councilman Barnard authorizing the City of Evanston to apply for a grant from the federal Police Hiring Supplement Program to receive funding for additional personnel that the Evanston Police Department was in need of. The police budget did not have enough funds to hire additional officers. This resolution would only be acted on if there was a need for additional personnel in the department. Motion was made by Councilman Nelson to adopt Resolution 93-53, seconded by Vranish, with all 4 votes in favor.

Resolution 93-54 was introduced by Councilman Vranish as follows:

RESOLUTION 93-54
RESOLUTION OF THE GOVERNING BODY OF THE CITY OF EVANSTON, WYOMING URGING FULL FUNDING FOR AMTRAK AND REQUESTING CONTINUANCE OF DAILY AMTRAK SERVICE ACROSS SOUTHERN WYOMING.

Section 1: The City of Evanston, Wyoming urges the United States Congress to authorize full funding of Amtrak's $381 million operating grant.

Section 2: The City of Evanston, Wyoming requests that Amtrak take whatever steps are necessary to insure continued daily service through Evanston and across southern Wyoming.

Motion was made by Councilman Nelson to adopt Resolution 93–54, seconded by Barnard, with the 4 votes in favor.

All communities across southern Wyoming, cities, towns, and counties, adopted a similar resolution to encourage Congress to continue funding Amtrak passenger service across southern Wyoming. Efforts were also made by Wyoming's three Congressmen, Governor Mike Sullivan, and other elected state officials. I'm sure there were many folks from Wyoming and other states that were also involved in trying to continue the Amtrak system across Wyoming.

However, on October 25th Evanston received an immediate release, as they called it, from the National Railroad Passenger Corporation (Amtrak) that there would no longer be passenger rail service across southern Wyoming as of November 4th. This was not good news and the folks of southern Wyoming were very disappointed.

KATHY KARPAN
Secretary of State
Cheyenne, Wyoming 82002-0020

OCT 1993

October 21, 1993

The Honorable Dennis J. Ottley
Mayor of the City of Evanston
1200 Main Street
Evanston, WY 82930

Dear Mayor Ottley:

Thank you for your October 5 letter asking that the Farm Loan Board lower the Joint Powers Act interest rate to 6%.

I'm happy to report that the Board, at its October 7 meeting, approved proposed rules to lower the rate to 7.25%. The matter now goes out for public comment and will come back to the Board for final approval. While the rate is not as low as the Wyoming Association of Municipalities recommended, I do think it is a good compromise and will be of real benefit to our local governments.

I hope all is well and thanks for keeping me apprised of your Job Corps project.

I haven't been to Evanston since commencement — we'll have to cook something up.

Sincerely yours,

Kathy Karpan
Secretary of State

KK/atn

Margy White
Deputy

Recycled Paper

The Capitol
(307)777-7378

On October 5th I wrote a letter to Wyoming's Secretary of State Kathy Karpan requesting that the Wyoming State Farm Loan Board lower their interest rate to six percent (6%). W.A.M. had acted on this during their last directors' meeting, and requested that all members write to Secretary of State Karpan requesting the lower rate of interest. The letters needed to be sent out immediately because the Wyoming State Farm Loan Board's next meeting was scheduled for October 7th.

On October 25th I received a very nice letter from Secretary of State Kathy Karpan thanking me for my letter and letting me know that during the Farm Loan Board's meeting of October 7th they had agreed to lower the rate to 7.25%.

She also stated that the matter would now go out for public comment and would come back to the Board for final approval. She also said that although the rate not as low as W.A.M. recommended, she thought that the 7.25% rate was a good compromise.

The Wyoming State Farm Loan Board, made up of five elected officials, had always been good to Evanston, and they appeared to unequivocally be in favor of Evanston getting the Job Corps Center.

We now had the annual Support Your Community Week to look forward to, a week-long celebration that gave folks of all ages an opportunity to show their pride in living in this community of Evanston, Wyoming.

An article in the *Uinta County Herald* of October 19th by reporter George Hammond-Kunke read as follows:

Festivities for the Seventh Annual Support Your Community Week begins Saturday with the seven-day event running through Friday.

New to the celebration this year is a Locals Art Show on Sunday, Oct. 24 at the First National Bank from noon until 4 p.m.

"The Locals Art Show is something new to Support Your Community Week. If it is successful, we'll continue with it," Evanston Chamber of

Commerce Director Diane Hodges said. "The Hot Air Balloon Demonstration is also new."

The Hot Air Balloon Demonstration was sponsored by Aspen Elementary School to promote their Books Across the World program, and would be held on Monday, October 25th. Some 450 students were on hand to see the balloon rise about 30 feet into the air.

Herald reporter Hammond-Kunke's article continued:

"The whole week is about volunteerism. Support Your Community Week is more attended each year. We don't have any problem with attendance when it involves people of Evanston. The whole community is invited to everything," Hodges said.

Mayor Dennis Ottley started Support Your Community Week in 1987 to try and get people motivated to do something about what was a national economic problem. "In 1987 the economy was down and we were hoping that it would help boost things a little. Even though things were down on a national scale, we felt that we could still do something," Ottley said.

"The week is a chance for people and families to come out and have a lot of fun," Ottley said. *"This is a week of goodwill."*

The week started out with the Kids Day on Saturday, October 23rd at Depot Square, though adults could also be involved if they desired. The day's schedule included a Paper Plane Contest, Pumpkin Carving Contest, and Cow Chip Tossing.

Other events throughout the week included the new Locals Art Show and a Tour of Evanston, both very successful.

The Oktoberfest, with the Bavarians once again performing, was held at the Beeman-Cashin Building at Depot Square on October 25th. During the Oktoberfest, the Evanston Voluntary Firefighters were invited to attend for the city to honor them and present them with a token of appreciation for their terrific service over the many years.

The Mayor's Prayer Breakfast was held at Lotty's Family Restaurant on Tuesday, October 26th. The Honorable Greg Phillips, State Senator of Wyoming, District No. 15, which included Evanston, was the morning's keynote speaker. Also on that day, the essay contest on "Why I Love Evanston" was held for school children only, and a pizza_luncheon was served at noon, at which time the essay winners were named.

The Senior Recognition Day Lunch at noon on Thursday was held at the Weston Plaza (Days Inn). Local folks were asked to bring their favorite senior citizen(s) to lunch. The featured speaker was Max Maxfield, Director of the Wyoming Department of Commerce.

Following the luncheon there was a Dedication of the Wall near the flagpole at Depot Square to celebrate the 125th year (the Quasquicentennial) of when the Community of Evanston was established. A special plaque and the Wall had been built, and the unveiling was today. A good crowd attended with speakers Jim Davis, Paul Knopf, and Mark Harris. Cake and ice cream were served and everyone sang "Happy Birthday" to the Community of Evanston. The day was topped off with the Chamber of Commerce Mixer held that evening at Dave Madia's Evanston Motor Company.

October 25, 1993

Mayor Dennis Ottley
City of Evanston
Evanston, WY 82930

Dear Mayor Ottley,

On behalf of Pack 54, we would like to extend our "Thanks" to you for the State
Flag you donated. Den 5 would like to send you their "Thank you's" also. Den 5 had
the privilege of conducting the Flag Ceremony at the monthly Pack meeting held on
October 25th. This would be the first of many Flag Ceremonies that the State Flag
would be presented in the Color Guard. Our Pack meetings are the last Monday of
each month so this is why our "Thank You" has been a little late in coming. Den 5
wanted to get a signature from each of the Dens and the Webelo groups to show you
our appreciation. Thank you again for your generous gift.

Sincerely,

Kathy Rigoli
Den 5
Kathy Rigoli, Den Leader

On Friday night October 29th the annual Support Your Community Week Honor Banquet was held at the Legal Tender. The dinner honored those senior citizens who had been nominated.

During the banquet Evanston Chamber of Commerce President Patsy Madia and I made the presentations to those senior citizens nominated for their outstanding love for Evanston and for their many years of voluntary service to make the community a better place to live. Honored were Eugene and Beth Anderson, Andrew (Andy) Horne, Gilbert Bills, and former Mayor Robert (Bob) Burns.

Our featured speaker for the evening, introduced by Master of Ceremonies Tony Vehar, was the Honorable C. Stuart Brown, retired Supreme Court Justice. Justice Brown was well received, partly because so many folks in the area were already acquainted with him from when he held the position of District Judge and had his office in Evanston.

On October 25th a letter was written to me, in which I received a few days later, from Kathy Rigoli, Leader of Den 5 of Cub Scout Pack 54. The letter thanked me for donating a Wyoming State Flag to Den 5 to be used in their ceremonies.

In her letter Mrs. Rigoli stated that *"Den 5 had the privilege of conducting the Flag Ceremony at the monthly Pack meeting on October 25th. This would be the first of many Flag Ceremonies that the State Flag would be presented in the Color Guard...Den 5 wanted to get a signature from each of the Dens and the Webelo groups to show you our appreciation.*

I appreciated the letter, on which approximately 20 names were signed, and was more than happy to donate the flag to them. The Scout programs have always been among my favorite youth programs. They have done a tremendous amount of good for America's youth.

The second regular city council meeting was held on October 27th. Following the roll call and after declaring a quorum, the Evanston High School Cheerleaders opened up the meeting with a few cheers to enliven everyone's spirits for this council meeting held during Support Your Community Week.

All city council members were present, except Councilwoman Jerry Wall, who was excused because of other commitments, but as every year, during this special week's council meeting, there was an extra-large attendance on hand.

During public participation the student essay winners were recognized, with the winning students reading their essays on "Why I Love Evanston."

After each essay was read, the student received a big round of applause, and after all essays had been read we gave them another resounding round of applause. At this time I called for a ten-minute recess, giving everyone an opportunity to congratulate each student and time to leave if so desired.

After the recess, the meeting was called back to order and the council addressed old business, with a few items to act on which were shortly completed.

In new business, Councilman Nelson introduced Resolution 93-55. This was a resolution authorizing the city to execute a water agreement with the Wyoming State Highway Department to sell them water from the Bear River for a construction project they were planning, for improvements on a portion of Wyoming State Highway 150 South.

The city of Evanston is the appropriator of record for certain water rights for the Bear River, and the city had the rights to sell water as it deemed necessary. The agreement, an attachment to Resolution 93-55, allowed the State of Wyoming to purchase approximately 20,000 gallons of water per day from the Bear River during the construction of a portion of State Highway 150.

Motion was made by Councilman Nelson for the adoption of Resolution 93-55, seconded by Barnard, with all 6 votes voting in favor.

After the completion of some additional new business I polled the council and staff for comments and announcements, and called for a work session for November 3rd at 5:00 p.m.

Community Development Director/City Planner Paul Knopf announced that a field trip to the Weber Basin Job Corps Center in Ogden, Utah would be available on Saturday, December 4th. Two buses would leave the Evanston City Hall at 10:00 a.m. and return at approximately 5:00 p.m. The first 80 people to sign up for the trip will get to go. "It'll be done on a first-come, first-serve basis," Knopf said. He added that the tour would give the public a better understanding of what Job Corps is all about.

He also stated that reservations for the bus tour should be made with Sharon Constantine at City Hall before December 2nd at 5:00 p.m. This announcement concerning the Job Corps trip to Ogden was also announced in the *Uinta County Herald* of November 19th.

After a few comments from the council members concerning Support Your Community Week, I thanked all who had taken part in the week's events and for their efforts in making the event another big success. I said, *It seems to be getting more people interested and involved with new ideas every year, making the event more successful than ever.*

I especially mentioned the dedication of the new Wall and plaque in celebrating Evanston's 125 year (Quasquicentennial) anniversary. I thought that was a nice event to add to the Week's celebration.

I also mention that it was 125 years ago next month in December when the first train went through Evanston.

In the past Congress had passed federal unfunded mandatory legislation, such as housing regulations, handicap regulations, safe drinking water and so on. When these unfunded mandates were passed by Congress it often put a financial burden on cities and towns that were affected.

This question was recently brought up at one of the Board meetings of W.A.M. at which time they put out notice that they were opposed to federal unfunded mandates and requested that each W.A.M. member write to each of Wyoming's Senators and Representative requesting that changes be made to federal unfunded mandates when they financially affect cities and towns.

As soon as I got the message from W.A.M., I wrote letters to Wyoming's two senators, the Honorable Alan Simpson and Honorable Malcolm Wallop, as well as to Wyoming's lone representative, the Honorable Craig Thomas, and explained to them W.A.M.'s position on unfunded federal mandates.

I got letters of reply from each of them. They all basically stated the same thing: Senators Simpson and Wallop both stated that the senate had two bills in committee which would prohibit federal mandates from being enforced against a state or local government unless they were fully funded by the federal government, and that the appropriate federal agency must publish a schedule of compliance costs. Both bills were being considered by the Senate Governmental Affairs Committee.

Representative Thomas stated that he had joined with other members of Congress in co-sponsoring a bill stating that no state or local government would be required to comply with a federal mandate unless funds were provided by the federal government, as well as a bill that would seek to roll back or simplify existing unfunded mandates.

All three stated that they would be staying on top of these bills to see them through, and they all thanked me for bringing the issue to their attention, although they had already been aware of the problem and had already started acting on the bills.

During the November 10th regular city council meeting, Councilwoman Wall made a motion to approve the Torch Light Parade on November 16th, seconded by Nelson, and Councilman Nelson made a motion to approve the Teddy Bear Parade to be held on December 4th, seconded by Hutchinson. Both motions passed for approval by a vote of 5 in favor and 2 absent (Barnard and Davis).

During public participation, Mr. Ken Robison made a lengthy presentation concerning casino type gambling and the Gaming Initiative that would be on the ballot in the 1994 general election in November.

The State Legislature passed a bill to let the Gaming Initiative be on the next ballot and let the people decide, which as far as I was concerned, was the right way to go.

Robison also spoke on some interesting projections on potential income that the state and local entities would gain if the Gaming Initiative was successful.

I thanked Ken for his very interesting presentation and told him we would just have to wait and see how it turns out.

Under New Business I sponsored Ordinance 93-9, introduced by Councilman Nelson, stating that the City of Evanston would support the 1% additional optional sales tax, which by law must be voted on, I believe, every four years. The ordinance spelled out that the City of Evanston was in favor of keeping Uinta County's four 4% sales tax: 3% state and 1% optional.

Councilman Nelson made a motion to pass the ordinance on first reading, seconded by Wall. But after some discussion Councilwoman Wall made a motion to table any action on Ordinance 93-9 until the

March 23, 1994 regular city council meeting, seconded by Vranish. Motion to table was passed by 4 votes in favor, 1 vote against (me) and 2 absent (Barnard and Davis). However, Ordinance 93-9 was never acted on again; it became a dead ordinance.

I later talked to City Attorney Dennis Boal about it and told him I wanted this ordinance passed as soon as possible, and he suggested that we rewrite the ordinance, give it a new title and take the 4% out because it got folks confused. They didn't think the 3% state tax was part of the 4% mentioned. Therefore, Boal said he would try to have a new ordinance prepared for sponsorship in early 1994, and would mention the 1% optional sales tax only.

Although I was the only one voting in favor of the original Ordinance 93-9, after receiving a copy of the new proposed ordinance and having a chance to read it, I agreed that it was good that we waited and had City Attorney rewrite the ordinance. So I was kind of glad that City Councilwoman Wall made the motion to table Ordinance 93-9. However, by law, we were required to get an ordinance passed on all three readings and presented to the Uinta County Clerk's office within at least ninety days prior to the general election; therefore, I didn't want to wait until the last meeting in March to first act on it.

The majority of the cities and towns within Uinta County had to pass ordinances and present them to the county before the Uinta County Commissioners could adopt a resolution, required by law, stating that the county was also in favor of it before the Optional Sales Tax Initiative could be put on the ballot.

I guess I was just a bit overly anxious to get the ordinance passed on all three readings and over to the County Clerk's office. I felt that getting it in sooner would give Uinta County more time, and it would show the other incorporated communities in the county where we stood, and just might be a signal to them to get moving on their ordinances if they were also in favor.

During this November 10th meeting Mr. John Bell was in attendance and expressed opposition to the Job Corps Center being in the Evanston area. I told Mr. Bell that he had the right to feel the way he did and nobody was going to take that right away from him.

I also told him that I didn't know for sure how the city council was going to vote, but months ago they voted in favor. However, after saying that, according to the minutes, City Council members Clarence Vranish, Jerry Wall and Tom Hutchinson each expressed their concerns, and apparently one or two of them must have said that they were no longer in favor of the Center.

It kind of upset me because it showed that some of the council members were starting to ride the fence. Everyone had a right to change their mind but I couldn't see anyone, especially city officials, if they were really concerned about the economy, changing their minds just because a few people got to them.

There was no doubt in my mind that the Job Corps Center would have been a big benefit to the entire county, just as the Wyoming State hospital and the Mountain Regional Services have been.

The *Uinta County Herald* printed what I said in the paper. My quote was: *It's a shame to start riding the fence and being wishy-washy at this point."*

In the *Herald's* issue of November 30th, Councilman Clarence Vranish published a Letter to the Editor stating that he felt that I owed the Evanston City Council an apology for what I said in the *Herald* article. I agree that I may have owed Vranish an apology because he was the only council member that voted against Resolution 93-39 during the July 14th meeting. However, he did write a letter to Utah Senator Orrin Hatch in 1988 requesting the senator's support in getting the Job Corps Center in the Evanston area when the issue first came up. So I really didn't feel that I owed any of them an apology, because they all had voted previously, one time or another, in favor of the Center. I don't believe I gave the *Herald* any particular names but all I can say is, "If the shoe fits wear it." I never offered an apology.

If anything, they owed me plenty of apologies. They told lies about me a number of times, publicly and in print, but not to my face.

Prior to adjourning the November 10th meeting Councilman Vranish made a motion to cancel the second meeting of the month on November 24th, because that was the week of Thanksgiving, seconded by Wall, with all those present voting in favor.

I once again reminded everyone of the trip to Ogden, Utah to tour the Weber County Job Corps Center on December 4th.

One of the recent actions of the Evanston City Council was to increase water and sewer rates. This was an issue that a number of the folks didn't like to see, especially just before the holidays. However, the city had no choice due to price increases and the cost of upkeep in providing the City of Evanston with good potable water that is safe for consumption, and keeping the sewer system and plant up to standard.

A memo was sent out to the public explaining the purpose of the rate increase. In part the memo read:

After 7 years of maintaining the same water rates, it became necessary, this fiscal year, to increase both the water and wastewater rates by 25 cents for every 1,000 gallons of water used. This increase will begin to offset the annual losses in the water and waste water funds, which has averaged $250,000 in each fund.

Because water, sewer and sanitation are enterprise funds; by law they must be self-supporting and only money collected from these funds can be used to support themselves. Increased inflation rates and because State Law requires us to depreciate all of the new facilities, it has become necessary to finally raise the rates.

Speaking of the $250,000 annual deficit of the water and sewer funds, the public had to be made to realize that in order to overcome any deficit, an Enterprise Fund must come out of the General Fund. This was something we needed to get straightened out.

⁓⁓

Every holiday season during the month of November, an Evanston committee selects a "Miss Merry Christmas" and a "Little Miss Merry Christmas." This year, my niece's daughter Mandi Tueller was selected as Miss Merry Christmas. Mandi, a teenager at the time, was the daughter of Bruce and Larna Julie Tueller, and the granddaughter of my sister, Terry (Ottley) Hutchings and her husband, Elby (Johnny) Hutchings (both deceased).

My sister Terry had died in December of 1990, just three years before Mandi had been crowned Miss Merry Christmas, but I know she would have been very proud of her beautiful granddaughter. My entire family was very proud of her. Mandi is a beautiful girl and well deserving of the honor.

Miss Merry Christmas and Little Miss Merry Christmas

MANDI TUELLER
Miss Merry Christmas

ASHLEY O'DRISCOLL
Little Miss Merry
Christmas

Uinta County Herald, November 23, 1993.

Also, congratulations to Ashley O'Driscoll who was selected Little Miss Merry Christmas, I'm sure her family was very proud as well; she was an adorable little girl.

<center>~~~</center>

As mayor I wrote an article to the citizens of Evanston and published it in the *Uinta County Herald* of December 3rd. The Herald titled the article, MAYOR OTTLEY GIVES HOLIDAY GREETINGS TO CITY RESIDENTS. In part it read the following:

> *Happy holidays...*
>
> *As we bask in the afterglow of Thanksgiving and look forward toward Christmas and the New Year, I think it is timely to reflect on many reasons we can be both thankful and proud as a community.*
>
> *First of all, Evanston is blessed with a civic spirit, unmatched anywhere. This spirit is so well represented at this time of year, through the unselfish efforts of those assisting the needy with food and toys. In Evanston, however, it is not just the holiday season that brings out goodwill.*
>
> *Throughout the year, our citizens help others in need, whether travelers or friends; we contribute volunteer hours for community events; and we strive to promote our own quality of life. We are truly a community of friends and neighbors working together for the common good...*
>
> *This concept of togetherness is our strength. It is also what makes this time of year special.*
>
> As such, let us take time, not just during the holiday season, but throughout the year to appreciate each other, and to reaffirm our commitment to our community.
>
> *The future depends upon our resolve, our vision, our enduring love of Evanston.*
>
> *Wishing everyone a joyous holiday season.*
> *Mayor Dennis J. Ottley*

I thanked the *Herald* for publishing the article and expressed my appreciation to them for keeping the citizens abreast of what has happened throughout the year of 1993.

During the December 8th meeting of the Evanston City Council, I declared a quorum and called order. Councilmembers Jerry Wall and Craig Nelson were excused.

After the initial business was taken care of, during public participation, Councilman Hutchinson made a motion to approve the application from the Veranda Bar for a catering permit for the Uinta County Employees' Christmas Party for December 17th at the Uinta County Complex from 4:00 p.m. until 2:00 a.m., seconded by Davis, with all present voting in favor.

The 1993 financial report and all monthly reports from the various city departments were read and accepted by motion with very little discussion. The city department heads always gave good, thorough monthly reports and kept the city council members and me well informed of what was happening.

During this meeting I expressed my appreciation to all of them for their efficiency and for their outstanding performances in their positions throughout the year.

I made two appointments to the Beautification Committee: Barbara Couture and Diane Taggart. Councilman Vranish made the motion to confirm the two appointments, seconded by Davis, with 4 votes in favor, 2 absent and 1 abstaining. I had to abstain from voting because it was my appointment.

Councilman Hutchinson made a motion to authorize City Engineer Brian Honey to proceed with an Environmental Protection Administration (E.P.A.) grant for a water quality study, seconded by Davis, with all present voting in favor. This E.P.A. grant would have to be acted upon by resolution as soon as Honey got the information and application to move forward. The resolution would be prepared by City Attorney Boal.

A lengthy discussion took place concerning the ordinance which would authorize the continuance of the optional local 1% sales tax. City Attorney Boal informed the Council that he was in the process of preparing a different ordinance, with a different and under a different title number. The council agreed that Boal was doing the right thing.

Councilman Barnard expressed his appreciation for being able to attend the National League of Cities Convention held in Orlando, Florida, and reported that he felt that Evanston was way ahead of most cities, both in facilities and public participation through volunteerism.

∽✤∽

The December 4th bus trip that was scheduled to take folks to Ogden, Utah to tour the Weber County Job Corps Center was called off because Evanston learned on December 3rd that we lost our bid for the Job Corps Center. It was a big disappointment to me and many others, but it was not a surprise. I was doubtful that we would get the bid because so many local officials became opposed to the Center.

The *Uinta County Herald* of December 7th headlined: EVANSTON HANDED PINK SLIP IN BID FOR JOB CORPS CENTER. The article by reporter George Hammond-Kunke read:

The U.S. Department of Labor turned down Evanston's bid for a Job Corp Center Friday.

Evanston Mayor Dennis Ottley said he "was disappointed but not surprised" by the rejection. "If we were going to get cut, I'm glad that it happened now and not in February. I'm disappointed because this would have been a good boost for Evanston's economy. It would have been an asset for Evanston to have a Job Corps Center," Ottley said.

"We thought that the cost would be a factor in their decision," Ottley said. "There's some vacant military camps that they could use. Also, they base the need for a Job Corps on population. That's a big factor," Ottley said.

"I don't think the opposition had a valid reason for being against [a Job Corps Center]," he said.

The article continued: *Evanston's proposal was for a state-of-the-art construction, housing 300 students. It would have been a co-ed facility. Ottley was backed by the United States Forest Service in the attempt to bring a Job Corps Center to Evanston. Ottley said earlier that the city, county and Forest*

Service put together a Job Corps Center proposal in 1988-89, but it was also denied...There are no Job Corps Centers in the Cowboy State.

"*We're still trying to encourage industry to come to Evanston,* Ottley said. Hammond-Kunke's article concluded.

However, many years later the Cowboy State did finally get a Job Corps Center located in Fremont County. The center is known as the Wind River Job Corps Center near Riverton, Wyoming. Good for Riverton!

⬥⬥⬥

Most citizens would like to see their community prosper and maybe progress a little, but they are often like the foolish guy who was out duck hunting, and fired at one, hit it, and watched it fall. He commented, "It was stupid of me to waste a shot on that duck. Hell, the fall would have killed it anyway." Many citizens are just as foolish in their thinking. They figure: *Why should I waste my time and efforts to help promote my community, the city will progress anyway.*

I have always believed that if you want your community to enjoy prosperity and progress you, as a citizen, need to get involved and help keep up the economy. A city is like a field of corn: if you don't actively cultivate it, it will eventually dry up.

Anyway, back to the story: we no longer needed to worry about getting a Job Corps Center, but we still needed to work hard to keep the Union Tank Car Company in Evanston, and that was going to be my biggest goal next year, 1994, as well as a big push for the folks in Uinta County to vote *yes* on the 1% optional sales tax during the general election in November. Failing to pass this optional tax would cause a financial problem for the entire county's economy.

RECORDS

Hats off to Police Benevolent Association and community

Kudos to the Evanston Police Benevolent Association and all the many contributors who made Saturday's first ever Shop With A Cop program such a success.

According to the latest figures, police officers received more than $3,200 in donations from various groups and individuals to support the event. Thanks to these efforts, this Christmas holiday season was made a little brighter for some 75 Evanston youth who might otherwise have gone without gifts.

And while presents and gifts do not represent the true meaning of Christmas, love, caring and good will to others does, and this is exactly what Saturday's event was all about.

Once again, Evanston's true colors come shining through.

Donation

Evanston city employees collected $665 dollars for the "Shop With A Cop" Christmas program. "Shop With A Cop" was sponsored by the Evanston Police Benevolent Association to help kids have a better Christmas. From left to right are Evanston Police Department Detectives Mike Putnam and J.R. Dean and city employee Frank Workman.

Uinta County Herald, December 14, 1993.

As in other years the Evanston Police Benevolent Association completed their Shop With a Cop Christmas program to help local kids have a better Christmas, some to have a Christmas at all. Another program, among many, that the Police Department either sponsors or helps sponsor to convince Evanston's youth to become responsible citizens and live an ethical and decent life.

The second regular city council meeting of the month and the last meeting of 1993 was held on December 22nd. During public participation we had several not-so-serious problems and complaints from those citizens in attendance. There was nothing that was considered an emergency. Therefore I referred all complaints to the various departments to look in to.

Resolution 93-58 had been tabled at the last meeting on December 8th by a unanimous vote, but during this meeting Councilman Hutchinson made a motion to rescind the action taken previously and bring the resolution back on the floor for a vote, seconded by Wall with all 7 votes in favor.

This resolution was initially introduced by Councilman Hutchinson at the previous meeting, authorizing the City of Evanston to enter into a cooperative agreement with the Western Wyoming Rural Conservation and Development Council (RC&D Council), affiliated with the United States Department of Agriculture, Soil Conservation Service, for funding assistance in obtaining a compactor/baler for the Evanston Recycling Project. The motion to adopt Resolution 93-58 was made by Councilman Davis, seconded by Hutchinson. The final vote on the main motion was unanimous, and the recycling staff received their compactor/baler, which was a big help to the program.

Prior to closing the December 22nd meeting we all wished everyone a Merry Christmas and a Happy New Year for 1994, and I expressed appreciation to all who had participated in the recent activities such as the "Nutcracker" stage play, the City Christmas Dinner, and the Shop With a Cop program. I also reported on the possibility of the Oxbow Refinery reopening and the Union Tank Car Company expansion.

The meeting adjourned at 10:05 p.m.

I don't know why the issue of Councilman Vranish involving himself in a police investigation of a recent theft didn't come up in the meeting of December 22nd, especially after the *Uinta County Herald* of December 21st headlined: COUNCILMAN INVOLVES SELF IN POLICE INVESTIGATION OF THEFT, written by *Herald* reporter George Hammond-Kunke. I can't imagine why Councilman Vranish took it on himself to get involved with police work, and for the life of me, I couldn't figure out why he and the police department would intentionally keep it from the city council and me. As mayor, I was the Police Commissioner.

The article in the *Herald* had a subtitle: *County Attorney: Surveillance job was amateurish.* The article read in part:

An Evanston City Councilman under the auspices of the police department used police equipment to conduct surveillance at a friend's business in an attempt to catch a thief, but botched the job, according to the Uinta County Attorney.

Clarence Vranish conducted the clandestine surveillance work at Sunridge Service Sentre, where more than $10,000 in money and goods was reported stolen from July through mid-October, 1993.

The surveillance work was authorized by Evanston Police Department Chief Dennis Harvey, but Vranish's role in the operation was kept from Mayor Dennis Ottley and other city officials.

"It's a Pandora's Box that we don't need to open. I don't know where you got that information. I don't know if someone is trying to embarrass me or the police department. I haven't done anything wrong," Vranish said Friday. "My part was installing the video tape. Yeah, it was police equipment. I'm not a police officer but I am interested," Vranish said.

Police Chief Dennis Harvey wouldn't say much about the incident Friday: "There was an investigation going on about the theft of some stuff. I don't know much about it."

Asked if it was police department policy to lend out equipment to private citizens, Harvey refused to comment.

A suspect was developed from a tape from a hidden camera, but no charges were filed because Uinta County Attorney Jim Anderson determined the tape recording was inconclusive. Poor camera placement and audio problems contributed to inconclusiveness of the tape, he said...

"Part of my decision to not press charges was the poor quality of the video," Anderson said.

"This was amateurish at best," he said. "The long and short of it is they [the police department] shouldn't have loaned that stuff out."

Mayor Dennis Ottley said he was very upset over the incident.

"I guarantee that something like this will never happen again," Ottley said. Vranish's involvement in the incident was 'sneaky and underhanded'," Ottley said.

"I didn't even find out about it until two months later. It came down to me through the grapevine," Ottley said.

"It's not right for a private citizen to do something like that. The policy for any city department is not to loan out property to a private citizen. I don't care if it was me or anybody else," Ottley said.

"For one thing, it puts too much liability at risk. It puts city personnel in a bad position. I did feel that it was a matter that could have been straightened out in-house," Ottley said.

Vranish, however, defended his role in the matter, saying, "I would probably do it again. I was always raised that there's a right and wrong. When you're a councilperson, you're intimately associated with the city," Vranish said.

"It's not a big deal and I don't want it blown out of proportion. I'm not upset. I try to be straightforward and upright. There was a local business with an extreme problem with theft. I'm friends with the store owner," Vranish said. Vranish went on to say that someone was trying to "defame my character."

Vranish said the reason police did not investigate the matter themselves was because an Evanston police officer worked part-time at the business.

"He (the police officer) was never a suspect in the matter," Vranish said.

Yet by not having the police do the surveillance work it made it look like the police officer "was a suspect," Mayor Ottley noted.

"The officer was completely exonerated. I wanted to protect the policeman who was employed there," Vranish said. "He was never a suspect. No one ever thought he was doing it."

"The police (department) don't have an internal affairs department. I didn't tell them where I was going to put the equipment," Vranish said.

Evanston City Attorney Dennis Boal also would not discuss the incident. "As far as I'm concerned, it's still an internal matter. I won't comment on it. It involves personnel and staff," Boal said. "It's improper and wrong (to comment) and I won't comment on it...It should be worked out in-house. If it's a personnel matter, it should be kept confidential. That's the state statute in process. That way nobody's unfairly damaged with rumor and innuendo," Boal said.

Although the incident was not illegal, some say it was inappropriate.

"It's not good form, but it's probably not illegal," said Mike Cornia of the Evanston Public Defender's Office...

"I don't think there's any law or statute that prohibits it. I just don't think it's a very good idea," Anderson said.

Anderson (County Attorney) added that the Evanston Police Department failed to consult with him before the investigation started.

Evanston Police Detective Lieutenant J. R. Dean, who was also involved in the investigation, said: "I was against it from the beginning," and although it was approved (by Harvey), the chief was leery of doing it too."

Asked if it was police policy to involve private citizens in investigations, Dean said, "I would say no. I know it won't be any more for sure. We learned a lesson out of it – a dumb lesson. In Clarence's infamous way, he wanted to help out."

Ottley said the matter "would probably be brought up at the next City Council meeting [Wednesday, 7 p.m. at Evanston City Hall]," the Herald article concluded.

<hr />

The incident was even published in the Sunday December 26th issue of *the Casper Star-Tribune*. But the incident was not brought up at the meeting, according to the minutes. I don't why, but it was finally brought up during the first meeting of 1994 on January 12th.

I was quite upset and disappointed with Councilman Vranish, but I was more upset with Chief Harvey and let him know that things like that don't happen while I'm mayor. I told both of them that what upset me more than anything was the sneaky and secretive manner it was executed, without council's and my knowledge. I do feel that both meant well, but I don't think that either realized what they were doing, or what the consequences would be whether they were successful or not. But both assured it wouldn't happen again.

However, Vranish said publicly in the *Uinta County Herald*, "*I was always raised that there's a right and wrong. When you're a councilperson, you're intimately associated with the city.*"

But then he also said in the same article, "*I would probably do it again.*" That statement did bother me. Just because he is member of the city council, it does not give him any special privileges to do something like that without the knowledge of the mayor and council.

I recently read a quote by Chuck Yeager: "*You don't concentrate on risks. You concentrate on results. No risk is too great to prevent the necessary job from getting done.*" I think this quote kind of fit Vranish, because I don't think he was concentrating on either risk or results.

Well, 1993 had come to an end and although we had some problems and lost the Job Corp Center and Amtrak, I believe it was still a successful year. The ongoing programs were all a success, thanks to the council, the staff and the boards, commissions and committees of volunteers.

However, I do expect a tough year in 1994, election year, and I wonder how all the city officials will perform, including me, because the city council members seem to have their own agenda that they don't want to share with me. We will just have to wait and see.

CHAPTER 28

1994....A year that I consider to be a tough one; not only because it is election year for me if I decide to run for re-election, but also because I'm not looking forward to working with council members that don't care about the economy or upholding their Office of Oath, and I don't need to name names.

It was January 12th, the first regular city council meeting of the year, and following the approval of the agenda, the minutes of the previous meeting and payment of all outstanding bills, I proceeded to present the State of the City Address (which was printed in the minutes at length) as follows:

"1993 is now a year of history. It was not an easy year, it was a productive year. Although it was productive, we were not without problems, problems not so much publicly, but problems within our own organization. We have had disagreements, but at the same time we have had harmony. Regardless of the problems we have had this past year, I want you all: city council members, staff and employees, members of the boards, commissions and committees, and all those volunteers who have taken part in making this past year successful, to know that you all have done a terrific job.

We have done a lot. Just to name a few of our accomplishments: the completion of Bear River Drive, Red Mountain and Yellow Creek Sidewalks, Water Tank Repairs, the continuous effort to improve our streets, water, sewer and drainage. We have been successful in obtaining a very large grant for the BEAR Project, and, through the assistance of Public Works and the Planning Department, we have completed the design and construction of the ice pond piping and level control structures to make it possible to run water into the ponds...."

I praised the Parks and Recreation District for the completion of the Centennial Valley Park, the ice skating rink at the ponds, the baseball fields and other areas of recreation. I commented on the success of purchasing properties for the Red Mountain and Overthrust Community Park areas. Hopefully, if budget allows, we will be able to have these parks also constructed soon.

I mentioned the Recycling Program and the progress made. We had a lot of community support for the program. The city had received a number of letters from university students, high school students, and governmental officials commenting on the recycling program. It has saved the city tipping fees, and it has kept hundreds of thousands of pounds of garbage from going to the landfill. It has been a tremendous saving for the city and the landfill.

I commended the Evanston Police Department for their outstanding work in keeping crime at a minimum, and animal control for doing such a terrific job. I mentioned how busy the City Court had been with their case loads getting bigger because of the terrific job the police department had done.

I also mentioned how well personnel at City Hall were doing, keeping up with the budget changes and other administrative duties. I told of the new "Expenditure Control Budget" system that was implemented this past year.

I spoke of all the programs and ongoing projects that were accomplished in 1993. I mentioned that 1993 was the 125th year since the Community of Evanston was founded, and all the historic programs that were continuously being worked on.

My address continued:

"The strength and leadership must start at the top. Every community needs the leadership to move forward. You, members of the Council, are those leaders. This is where the <u>strength</u> must start.

<u>Vision</u>, a word we hear often, a word that we should give a lot of thought to, a word that our City Planner uses time and time again. One of the big benefits of living in Evanston is our reliable infrastructure, the underlying basic framework of our community..."

"We also must continue to build toward the high quality of life that we are accustomed to. In doing this, as leaders, we must look at our own values: values such as <u>integrity</u>, a firm adherence to a code of moral values; complete

honesty is a must to run a strong organization; *courage*, a value that gives us the strength to do what's right regardless of the consequences. We must have the courage to be successful in our endeavors. *Enthusiasm*: nothing great was ever achieved without enthusiasm. This is a must with all of us, the value of *well-being* and *contentment*. There is no *well-being* and *contentment* in an organization unless we try to understand one another and be willing to give forgiveness; *confidence*: the confidence to think big and get big results; *aspiration*, the expectation of success. When you live with *aspiration* in your heart and mind you live with success. And last, but certainly not least, is *love*, a selfless concern for all others: love for your community, its people and others. For without love, your dedication means nothing. Remember, it has been said that the opposite of love is not hate, it is apathy. *Apathy* is something that no community can tolerate and still expect itself to be successful and strong. But for our community's sake give these few values a lot of thought and try to adhere to them.

Integrity, courage, enthusiasm, well-being, confidence, aspiration and love, values that should mean so much to all of us.

In closing I want to say thank you again to all of you for making 1993 another successful year.

Now let's look to the future, let's continue to have the vision, the strength and the elasticity to go forward. Let's focus on making things better, not bigger.

Thank you and God bless you all."

Following my annual State of the City Address, the city council members expressed themselves, thanking the staff for their cooperation, and giving special thanks to each other and the public for placing their confidence in them as representatives. They expressed the need for cooperation in promoting Evanston and tolerating each other's ideas and feelings. 1993 was a good year and each councilmember stated they were optimistic for a good 1994 year. Councilman Vranish presented the following statement:

"1993 was a good year. We shared in many accomplishments. We have water in the ice ponds and ice ponds are truly that — there is ice! The ice rink on 6th Street still has high levels of usage and I have also viewed large numbers skating on the ponds. To me, it demonstrates a large increase in the total number of our citizens enjoying Evanston's recreation opportunities.

The greatest single accomplishment for which this council should be proud is their introduction of the expenditure control budget system. Historically, federal, state and local governmental agencies went on a frantic buying binge just prior to the end of the fiscal year. Simply put, it meant that [you] spend it all now or lose it. This new budget states 'what you don't spend in your current budget is yours to keep and spend later.' You can save these dollars to purchase something you need later.

The response has been overwhelming! It encourages thrift and has saved the city considerable funds.

The citizens of Evanston can also be proud of civic pride. The city and county have been heavily involved in economic development. Several times this past year, businessmen have come to Evanston in consideration of locating here. Universally, they go into the business district and supermarkets to ask the local citizenry their opinion of Evanston. They always obtain a truthful and unbiased opinion because those asked don't know who the party is that's asking the question. From the reports I've received, citizen pride has increased substantially in Evanston. That is an accomplishment that speaks well for our community.

Thank you for the past year. God bless all of you."

The above statement by Councilman Vranish was taken from the minutes of January 12, 1994. He had requested that City Clerk Don Welling print his statement in full, as he would the mayor's State of the City Address, which is fine and proper if requested.

I made the following appointments of Department Heads:

Chief of Police..Dennis Harvey
Community Development Director/City Planner.............Paul Knopf
City Clerk & Assistant City Treasurer.........................Don U. Welling
City Treasurer & Assistant City Clerk.............................Steve Widmer
City Engineer/Director of Public Works.........................Brian Honey
City Court Judge..John Phillips
Assistant City Court Judge...Greg Phillips
Assistant City Court Judge...Bruce Barnard
City Attorney..Dennis Boal
Assistant City Attorney...Rick Lavery

Councilman Nelson made a motion to confirm the above appointments, seconded by Davis with 5 votes in favor, 1 absent (Ron Barnard) and 1 abstaining (me). The motion passed.

I then appointed all remaining members of the Evanston Police Department, which included a total of 26 patrol officers, detectives, animal control officers, a parking attendant and all secretarial staff.

Motion was made by Councilman Hutchinson to confirm the police department appointees, seconded by Nelson, with the motion passing with the same vote as above.

I went on to make all the appointments to the city boards and commissions, except the appointments to the Evanston Tourism Board, which was requested to hold back until a later regular city council meeting.

Councilman Nelson made the motion to confirm all of my appointments, seconded by Davis, with all voting in favor. I named the new Police Commission to be Councilmen Tom Hutchinson, Ron Barnard and me as the Police Commissioner. Also, I named the following as City Council Liaisons to the various boards and commissions:

Planning and Zoning..Dennis Ottley (me)
Housing Authority...Ron Barnard
Historical Preservation.......................................Jerry Wall
Urban Renewal..Jerry Wall
Recycling...Will Davis

During public participation, Councilwoman Wall made a motion to permit two parades to be held during the Annual Chinese New Year's Celebration: the Torch Light Parade on February 11th and the Parade of Dragons on February 12th. Motion was seconded by Hutchinson and passed unanimously.

The only item under Unfinished Business was Ordinance 93-10 for second reading. The ordinance proposed a zone change in the Evanston Industrial Center from a Highway Business Developing

Zone to an Industrial Established Zone as requested by the First National Bank.

Ordinance 93-10 was passed unanimously on both first and second readings, and would be passed on third and final reading, also by a unanimous vote, during the meeting on January 26th.

Under new business, Ordinance 94-1, the first ordinance of the year, was sponsored by Councilwoman Wall and introduced by Councilman Vranish for the City of Evanston to regulate basic cable television rates, equipment and customer service standards. It also set regulations and duties of franchisees for the right to use public streets and alleys for cable television service lines.

This ordinance was based on the findings of the long-standing Cable Television Commission, and was passed unanimously on all three readings.

Thanks were given to City Attorney Dennis Boal and the Cable Television Commission for their time and effort for preparing Evanston with an ordinance that would help provide good cable television service to the citizens of Evanston.

Following other action taken in new business, City Engineer Brian Honey expressed his appreciation and thanks to the mayor and city council for their dedication and service to the community, and Councilman Davis recognized Councilwoman Wall for her appointment to the National League of Cities (N.L.C.) Human Development Committee, and congratulations were also given by other city officials.

At this time Councilman Tom Hutchinson made the following remarks, taken from the minutes, concerning the recent incident involving the use of city property, a police surveillance camera, by a city council member:

"During the past few weeks, Councilman Vranish determined, on his own, to take an action that has created some discussion in the news media and also among many of our constituents. In response to this, I sent Mr. Vranish and the Council and Mayor's office a memo requesting a time to discuss this matter. As I have had no response to this request other than a discussion with Mayor Ottley, I am tonight requesting again that we meet to discuss not

just this matter, but perhaps to again discuss ethical behavior and the basic duties of members of a city councilperson. I perceive that our basic duties are to set policy and budget. Individuals are appointed by the Mayor to carry out the policy and administer the budget. Maybe it would be an appropriate time to refresh us on these responsibilities. I do not wish to infight nor waive judgement here; however, when one of us acts on our own in the name of the City, we are placing each of the other council members in a position of accountability, also.

Would the Council be willing to do this and if so, when should we meet? I believe this is very important and that this matter should not be glossed over or ignored. This may clear the air for the Council as well as for the interested citizens we represent. Further, we should perhaps feel responsible to give a report to the community regarding the outcome of this meeting. Or maybe they should participate in the meeting. Above all, we should want to serve this community to the best of our abilities.

Could we please have some discussion on this matter?"

Immediately following Councilman Hutchinson's statement, I asked for further discussion, but according to the minutes there was no discussion at that time.

Councilwoman Wall changed the subject by discussing the activities of the Historic Preservation Committee and made a motion to create a budget account and transfer one thousand dollars ($1,000) from the Council budget to the Historic Preservation Committee, seconded by Davis, with 6 votes in favor and 1 absent (Barnard).

Councilman Vranish followed by asking for a study on the possibility of a left turn light on Front Street going to 6th Street to lessen congestion.

This would be a decision of the Wyoming Department of Transportation (D.O.T.) and was turned over to City Engineer Brian Honey to contact the Highway Department and make them aware of the concern. The D.O.T. did end up in correcting the situation.

I then suggested a work session be held January 19th at 5:00 p.m. to discuss Oxbow Refinery, the budget, high school bus congestion, and the TV ordinance. I also announced that on January 18th at 10:00 a.m., an employee's committee meeting would be held. The committee had requested that city council members and I be present if possible.

Prior to adjourning, Councilman Vranish made a motion to go into executive session to discuss a personnel matter, seconded by Wall, with motion passing unanimously.

I don't recall what this executive session was called for, unless it was over the video camera incident.

Executive sessions are called for whenever a personnel problem comes up, and generally the city attorney is present and sometimes the city clerk; however, no minutes or action are taken during the session. Any action to be taken must be brought back on the floor during the public meeting. There was no action taken on this particular executive session.

I then called the meeting back to order, but with no further business, I called for adjournment at 10:30 p.m.

The *Uinta County Herald* issue of January 18th printed my entire State of the City Address. It was printed on the front page, and I thanked the *Herald* for the article, and I thanked them once again for keeping the public informed of what was going on in city government.

Also in this same issue of the Herald was an article titled, COUNCILWOMAN WALL GETS WARD II INVOLVED.

The article went on to read the following:

Evanston City Councilwoman Jerry Wall has started publishing a newsletter, "City Notes," for her constituents in Ward II.

"Several of the residents in Ward II are interested in getting some neighborhood associations started. Our idea is to provide a vehicle for citizen input to City Hall and to empower you as a resident of Evanston," Wall said.

"Also, an association based in your own neighborhood would provide a forum in which to discuss issues and solutions pertaining to your idea. Get to know your neighbors," Wall said. All organizational meetings will be at 7 p.m. at City Hall. Meeting dates, places and contact persons are as follows:

Tuesday – Uinta Meadows, Tina Pruitt
Jan. 24 – Aspen Groves, Gale Curtis
Jan. 25 – Crestview, Cindy Barnard
Jan. 31 – Brookhollow, Becky Eskelson

There was no doubt in my mind why she started something like this. I just wondered what she would do if I just happened to show up at one of their meetings at City Hall. It would be something.

Well, I said when she returned from her trip in Washington D.C. last year, I could see that she had learned to play partisan politics like the "Big Boys" in D.C.

But then, this was election year, and she was out to get me, but I didn't mind her starting the program mentioned in the *Herald* if she was doing it for the benefit of her constituents and not for her vindictive self-interests.

I knew what she was up to, and at that point, I just didn't care. All I was interested in was continuing to work on the ongoing projects and new programs that might come up for the benefit of the people of Evanston with integrity and dedication. I was hoping that the rest of the council would do the same.

The second regular city council meeting of the month was held on January 26th with all city council members present. After roll call and declaring a quorum, a public hearing was held concerning budget revisions for the remainder of the fiscal year. City Attorney Dennis Boal was directed to be the hearing officer, and that the hearing would be recorded and the tape would be on file at City Hall.

There were no protests or changes made during the hearing and Resolution 94-4, pertaining to the budget revisions would be introduced and adopted by motion at a later time during this meeting under New Business.

The next order of business was the annual request from the Liquor Dealers Association requesting the four days of extended hours of operation allowed by state law for 1994. The request was made by Liquor Dealers Mack Lott and Miles Alexander. The days requested were approved by motion and seconded, with all voting in favor.

Next I read a letter from Councilwoman Jerry Wall requesting to resign from the Evanston Tourism Board. Councilman Davis made the motion to accept her letter of resignation, seconded by Hutchinson, with all voting in favor.

Wall's letter of resignation was a surprise to me, because the day before this meeting I had received a memorandum dated January 25th from Jerry Wall, offering some recommendations for the Evanston Tourism Board. She stated in her memo that the board often does not function well and she thought that there should be some things done to help the situation. Those recommendations were as follows:

As this is a City Board that is responsible for expenditures of a special tax, there should be at least one, preferably two, City Council members on board.

Board members should not engage in personal attacks during meetings. This is not only in poor taste, but is unacceptable in ANY public meeting. The tirade against Councilman Davis was abominable. The presiding officer should certainly not have participated and should have put a stop to it. When I tried to move the agenda along, I was glared at and the attack continued. I finally walked out, knowing that the attack would probably then focus on me. This was confirmed by reading the minutes of the meeting on Monday.

As the Evanston Tourism Board is a public board spending tax revenue, the members should know that their votes should be recorded and public.

As this is an official board of the City of Evanston, I recommend that a staff person be made available to act as a recording secretary. This is common practice on other City boards such as Renewal, Human Service Center Joint Powers, Historic Preservation Commission, Planning & Zoning, etc. This eliminates a slanting of the minutes to a member's point of view and bias. Also, it is an unpleasant, time-consuming task for most volunteers.

For the life of me I couldn't figure out why she had sent this memo to me and nobody else. She at least could have sent a copy to the Tourism Board. As far as I know, I was the only one who got the memorandum, and I still have it.

However, referring to her first recommendation, that's why we had appointed her to the board in which she wished to be on at the time.

As for her second recommendation, I suppose she was referring to a memorandum concerning billboards that Councilman Davis sent to the members of the Tourism Board on December 15, 1993. The Davis memo suggested that he was not in favor of the method of use for the billboards that they were leasing from YESCO, Inc. He suggested that there should be more information on the boards, or new boards if need be, describing the various annual events going on in Evanston, which I too thought was a good idea.

Councilman Davis's memo was only an opinion and nothing derogatory was mentioned in it. He did state at the end of the memo *"I look forward to discussing this further with the board members."*

I have no idea what was said in the meeting to make Jerry Wall upset enough to leave, but it was the wrong thing to do. She should have just told them that she would invite Davis to the next meeting and have him explain to them what his thoughts were.

She stated that she was afraid the board's next move would be about her. If that was the case, she should have stayed in the meeting to protect herself, but she left, and the way she left was what probably caused them to talk about her afterwards.

Wall knew that minutes of all board and commission meetings were public knowledge and made available to anyone that requested to look at them. Her suggestion of hiring a recording secretary or someone to take care of records would have to be up to the Board because funds to pay for someone like that would have to come out of the Board's funds.

Anyway, Councilwoman Wall had resigned and new appointments would be made to fill the Board at the next meeting.

❧

During the city council meeting of January 26th, Councilwoman Wall and Recycling Director Barry Constantine made an announcement that Evanston had been selected as the community to host the Wyoming State Recycling Conference in mid–September of 1994.

This was great to hear and I expressed my appreciation to both of them for their efforts in getting Evanston chosen for the Conference. I said, "Events like these always help the local economy, and we are always ready to welcome them to Evanston."

Councilman Barnard then made a motion for the Evanston City Council to go on record in support of the Recycling Conference, seconded by Vranish, with all voting in favor.

Evanston Urban Renewal Agency Director Jim Davis announced that this year's Annual Renewal Ball for 1994 was set for Saturday, June 4th, and Evanston District Recreation and Parks Director Dennis Poppinga announced that cross-country skiing would be available at the Bear River State Park and some locations in the Uinta Mountains.

City Engineer Brian Honey, who had just recently attended a Transportation Service Advisory Group (Wyoming's counterpart of the Federal Department of Transportation), sponsored through the Intermodal Surface Transportation Efficiency Act of 1991 (ISTEA), and reported on state funding for urban streets. He stated that these funds were used to construct the Washington Street extension and the improvements recently made to 6th Street. He also mentioned a new funding program that would be available for improvements to Holland Drive and Holland Drive Bridge.

I thanked Honey for attending the meeting and for his report and said that his information would be useful to Evanston in the future for street improvements.

Councilman Nelson, wasting no time, made a motion to authorize City Engineer Honey to write a letter of intent for street and bridge improvements on Holland Drive, seconded by Barnard, with all voting in favor.

I then, prior to adjournment, called for a work session for February 2nd at 5:00 p.m. The meeting adjourned at 9:50 p.m.

The *Uinta County Herald* of January 28th had an article written by reporter George Hammond-Kunke titled, GREAT MUSIC WEST ASKS COUNCIL FOR $10,000.

The article went on to read, *Great Music West asked the Evanston City Council to consider giving them $10,000 for their summer music festival this summer in Evanston.*

Great Music West Executive Committee Board Member Norman B. Stephen, asked the council for the money on behalf of Janice Bodine, who was unable to attend Wednesday night's city council meeting. Bodine is the vice president of the Evanston area Chapter.

The festival will run for five weeks, opening June 19 and running through July 23. Great Music West promises to bring to Evanston some of the world's top musicians.

The *Herald* article continued, *Last year, the city of Evanston donated $5,000, according to Stephen, to the Bear Lake Music Festival for one concert in Evanston. Councilman Clarence Vranish publicly balked over the donation. Councilmen Ronald Barnard and Tom Hutchinson spoke favorably of the festival.*

"That contribution was necessary and (money) well spent. This is a wonderful thing. What attracts them is the grassroots aspect of this whole thing. This is about people who love music. That's what this is about, people who love music," Barnard said.

"I'd do it as an economic development and I see it as money well spent," Hutchinson said.

Mayor Dennis Ottley said the council would take the request for the $10,000 donation under advisement.

Although the article continued with other action taken during the meeting, it said nothing more concerning the article's title. I explained that there are certain restrictions the city has to look at whenever they make donations, but I indicated that this could be considered a service to our community and not a donation. I also made the statement that we would have to take a look at our budget, because this would be paid, if approved by the council, before the end of the fiscal year.

❦

As part of the lawsuit filed against the City of Evanston by former police officer Russell Dean over his dismissal from the Evanston Police

Department, Mr. Dean and his attorneys also named the following: Evanston Police of Chief Dennis Harvey, Evanston Police Sgt. Jake Williams, Evanston Police Lt. Mitch Allmaras, Evanston City Councilman Clarence Vranish, and me, Mayor Dennis Ottley.

This lawsuit had been settled almost a year ago. We finally got a letter dated January 31, 1994 from Russ Dean's attorney dismissing all claims against all of the above. Although I had almost forgotten about the incident, it was great news and a relief.

The first regular city council meeting in February was held on Wednesday the 9th, with Councilman Clarence Vranish, President of the City Council acting as Mayor pro tem, as I was out of town. I had an appointment in Casper concerning City of Evanston business. Councilman Hutchinson was also absent and excused.

Following roll call, Mayor pro tem Vranish declared that there was a quorum with Councilmembers Vranish, Jerry Wall, Craig Nelson, Ronald Barnard and Will Davis all present.

After the initial business was taken care of, a public hearing was the first item of business during public participation, concerning an application from William G. and Leila L. LaCoe to transfer the liquor license of Cowboy Joe's Liquor Barn to the IGA Grocery Store located at 524 Front Street (later Jubilee Food and Drugs). The hearing was conducted by City Attorney Boal.

During the hearing, Mr. LaCoe and Chris Bauman spoke in favor of the transfer, but there were other Evanston liquor dealers present, Bonnie Alexander, Kilburn Porter and J. D. Kindler, who spoke in opposition to it. After a lengthy discussion City Attorney Boal closed the hearing, and Councilman Davis made a motion to approve the transfer of the liquor license to the IGA Grocery, seconded by Nelson. The vote was 3 in favor (Davis, Vranish and Barnard), 2 against (Wall and Nelson) and 2 absent (Hutchinson and me). Motion passed.

After Unfinished Business and New Business were acted on, Mayor pro tem Vranish recognized the Beautification Committee and commended them for decorating the downtown area in preparation for the Chinese New Year celebration scheduled for February 11th and 12th.

Mayor pro tem Vranish also reported on the recent legislative meeting that was held with all mayors in the county, including me, and a number of city and town council members and staff present. A special invitation was sent to all of the state legislators representing parts of Uinta County, such as Senators Greg Phillips of Evanston and Mark O. Harris of Green River; and Representatives Gordon Park and Wayne Morrow, both from Evanston, and Elwin McGrew of Rock Springs.

Vranish reported that he felt that the meeting, which was held at the Legal Tender Restaurant, was well worthwhile and that more than a dozen issues were discussed, such as the Farm Loan Board, Workers Compensation, Public Works Construction Standards, the Gaming Initiative, the Sales Tax Exemption Study, Peace Officers Jurisdiction, and several other issues.

Most of these issues discussed during the legislative meeting in Evanston would be in the form of legislative bills to be acted on during the upcoming 1994 legislative session in Cheyenne, to begin on February 21, 1994.

After calling for a work session for February 16th at 5:30 p.m. at City Hall, Vranish adjourned the meeting at 8:02 p.m.

The annual Chinese New Year celebration was held on February 11th and 12th, kicked off on Friday with the Torchlight Parade at 6:30 p.m., followed by a Calcutta auction for the Rickshaw Races at Kate's on Main Street.

Saturday was a full day of events, with the Parade of Dragons at noon followed by the Rickshaw Races, table tennis and racquetball tournaments on both days, the annual ball drop and several other traditional Chinese activities.

Councilwoman Wall reported that the celebration was once again a big success, and Councilman Vranish reported on the increased activity of the Ham Radio Operators during the Chinese New Year celebration, as there were more calls than the previous years from all over.

I thanked all those involved in making the celebration a big success once again. I said, *The Chinese New Year celebration seems to be getting bigger each year, thanks to all that are involved. According to Councilman Vranish and his Ham Radio Operators, it seems to be getting a lot of national attention, if not worldwide. That's great!*

The City of Evanston was now waiting for nominations for Evanston's Citizen of the Year, which needed to be submitted no later than February 15th. After receiving the nominations, the Evanston City Council members and mayor would vote on the nominations by secret ballot and announce the winner at the Agri-Business Banquet to be held on February 24 at 7:00 p.m. at the American Legion Hall in Fort Bridger.

We received six nominations for Evanston's Citizen of the Year: Norm Stephens, Randy Ottley, Bruce Sowards, Brenda Roberts, and Russ and Alisa Noel, all very active citizens of Evanston, and all well deserving of the honor.

Because of my son Randy being nominated for Citizen of the Year, I withdrew from voting. I felt that if Randy was the one to receive the honors, people might think I was pulling some strings.

However, the winner ended up being Norm Stephens, owner, president and manager of Frac-Tanks, Inc., a company he started in Evanston in 1979. As Mayor of Evanston I had the honor of presenting the award to Norm. I was very proud, because I knew that he had been involved in a number of committees, chairman of some, and that he and his wife always offered their assistance anytime it was needed. It was an award well deserved.

The second meeting of the month was held on February 23rd with a full quorum. I called the meeting to order, and after the approval of the previous minutes and so on, I continued with my unfinished annual appointments by starting with the Intermodal Surface Transportation Efficiency Act 1991 (ISTEA).

I appointed the following to a one-year term:

City Councilmembers Clarence Vranish and Tom Hutchinson, City Engineer Brian Honey, City Planner Paul Knopf, Public Works Director Allan "Oop" Hansen, Uinta County Supervisor Marion

Malnar, Wyoming State Highway Engineer Marlin Wright, Jerry Nelson, and myself.

Motion was made by Councilwoman Wall to confirm the ISTEA appointments, seconded by Barnard, with all 6 voting in favor. The motion passed. I then made the following appointments to the Evanston Tourism Promotion Board: Councilman Will Davis until January 1997 and myself until January 1995. Due to the problems that City Councilwoman Wall seemed to have had while serving on the board and with her resigning, I felt that it would be a good idea for me to be on the board for the rest of her term to help Davis out if there were problems. Davis was filling a vacancy which called for a three-year term.

Motion was made by Councilman Hutchinson to confirm the two appointments, seconded by Nelson, with all voting in favor. Motion passed.

I then appointed City Treasurer Steve Widmer to the Lincoln-Uinta Association of Governments (LUAG) Revolving Fund, a subcommittee for a three-year term. Motion was made by Councilman Vranish to confirm the appointment, seconded by Davis, with all voting in favor. The motion passed.

Following the appointments, Parks and Recreation Director Dennis Poppinga requested a waiver for 25 cents of the mileage fee for the city bus. This was for a trip to take some Evanston young folks to the Governor's Council on Fitness to be held in Laramie on Saturday, February 26th.

However, upping the waiver fee, Councilman Barnard made a motion to grant the Parks and Recreation District a waiver of 50 cents of the mileage fee concerning the city bus, seconded by Nelson with 7 votes in favor of passing the motion.

Under New Business, Ordinance 94-5 sponsored by Councilman Davis and me and introduced by Councilman Davis was brought on the floor. This was a new ordinance to replace Ordinance 93-9, which was tabled during the November 10, 1993 regular city council meeting, but was never brought back off the table.

Ordinance 94-5, replacing the tabled Ordinance 93-9 read as follows:

ORDINANCE 94-5
AN ORDINANCE OF THE GOVERNING BODY OF
THE CITY OF EVANSTON, WYOMING, AUTHORIZING
THE CONTINUATION OF AN EXCISE TAX OF 1% AS AU-
THORIZED BY WYOMING STATUTE 39-6-412(b) (I), UPON
THE RETAIL SALE OF TANGIBLE PERSONAL PROPER-
TY, ADMISSIONS AND SERVICES MADE WITHIN UINTA
COUNTY, WYOMING.

Ordinance 94-5 was passed on first reading by a motion made by
Councilman Hutchinson, seconded by Nelson with 6 votes in favor
and 1 against (Vranish). The ordinance was also passed on second
and third readings during the March meetings with everyone voting
in favor except Vranish. I don't recall why Clarence was against the
motion, but he had some objections.

Next order of business followed with Councilman Hutchinson introducing Resolution 94-5 [not to be confused with Ordinance 94-5).
It was a resolution to amend the Personnel Manual of the City to permit certain city employees to reside outside the corporate city limits.

Although the personnel manual states that the City of Evanston
encourages all employees to reside within the city limits, this addition
to the resolution does state that employees requesting to live outside must receive written authorization from the governing body and
must live within the boundaries of the Bear River Drainage.

Councilman Davis made a motion to adopt Resolution 94-5, seconded by Barnard, but after a lengthy discussion Councilman Barnard made a motion to table the resolution until a later meeting,
seconded by Nelson, with all voting in favor.

⁓

During the March 23rd meeting Councilman Davis made a motion
to remove Resolution 94-5 from the table for additional discussion
and to act on the motion from the February 23rd city council meeting. The motion was seconded by Barnard with 4 votes in favor, 2
against (Wall and Vranish) and 1 absent (Nelson).

After a short discussion on Resolution 94-5, I called for the main motion that was made in February to be voted on. Motion failed by 5 voting against, 1 in favor (Barnard) and 1 absent (Nelson). The issue became a dead issue.

⤝⤞

Also during the February 23rd meeting, prior to adjournment, Councilman Hutchinson made a motion for the council to hold an executive session for discussion on the purchase of property, seconded by Nelson with all voting in favor.

The discussion during the executive session was whether or not the City of Evanston should make an offer to purchase the recycling building, which at this time we were only leasing.

After calling the meeting back to order, Councilman Barnard made a motion to direct the city attorney to negotiate with the bank, who was holding title to the property through foreclosure, on a price for the purchase of the recycling building. The motion was seconded and passed unanimously.

The meeting adjourned at 9:47 p.m.

The *Uinta County Herald* published a Letter to the Editor that I had written concerning the new Compressed Video network that the Lifelong Learning Center (now known as Uinta BOCES #1 Education Center) now had available. My letter was published in the *Herald's* March 1st issue:

Dear Editor:

On Feb. 25, I had the opportunity and privilege to attend the Evanston Open House at the Lifelong Learning Center to witness the new technology of Compressed Video. Through this network system, I was able to speak to Wyoming's Governor Mike Sullivan and at the same time see him on the video screen. It was just like sitting in the same room talking to each other while I was in Evanston and the Governor was in Cheyenne. It was amazing...

As stated by Gov. Sullivan in a letter to me dated July 6, 1993, "The community of Evanston – through its lifelong learning program, the state agencies located here and the local school district – will need to commit to a usage level that will cover the network's operational cost to go into Evanston."

Through this commitment, and the support and confidence of the governor, Evanston has been able to be included in the network. And, as mayor, I want to thank Gov. Sullivan for all this. The governor has always been a good friend to the City of Evanston and we should all appreciate him.

I also want to thank Bob Fry, and his staff at the Lifelong Learning Center, for their efforts and assistance in making it a reality for Evanston to become a part of the Compressed Video network, and bringing it to my attention. This system will be a tremendous benefit to our educational needs, our economy and will have a positive impact to Evanston's workforce.

Dennis J. Ottley, Mayor

At that time, the Compressed Video system was very new, but since then there has been technology that has either improved it or has overcome it. In 1994, Evanston was not included in the system until Bob Fry came to me and asked me to call the Governor and request that Evanston be included along with other cities in Wyoming: Cheyenne, Laramie, Powell, Sheridan, Riverton, Torrington, Rock Springs, Casper and Gillette. When I called the Governor and asked to be included, he immediately added Evanston to the list.

Also in the February 22nd issue of the *Uinta County Herald*, reporter George Hammond-Kunke wrote an article titled, COUNCILMAN WILL DAVIS TO SEEK MAYOR'S OFFICE. The article indicated that Davis was running to change the leadership style. He stated, *"We need to improve on communication between the mayor's office and that of the (Evanston) City Council; and between the mayor and staff."*

I couldn't believe that because it was the city council members who were having their little secret meetings in the back office, sometimes not even including Councilman Tom Hutchinson. They never would come into my office and talk to me about city issues.

Oh, sometimes Councilman Vranish came in to talk to me about some city issue, Councilman Hutchinson came in quite often letting me know what was brewing with the rest of the council. Councilwoman Wall and her four puppets weren't doing anything to help the economy of the city. They were only interested in trying to make me look bad.

As far as the staff went, I had a very good relationship with all of them and communicated with them every day, sometimes several times a day. However, those five council members wouldn't know about that because they never came to my office to find out anything.

In Hammond-Kunke's article, Davis also stated, *"I consider myself a friend of the current mayor, Dennis Ottley. I am seeking this position because I feel my leadership style is more in line with the needs of the community."*

All I can say to that is, *"With friends like that, who in the hell needs enemies?"*

He also was quoted as saying, *"I would be far more aggressive in the recruitment of industry for Evanston. We need to expand on our current growth and recruit new business. Right now we have almost zero recruitment. We should be marketing property instead of sitting around and waiting for it to happen. Now is the time to be more aggressive. There's property around that could be used for a lot of things."*

Apparently, Davis must have been asleep during all of my State of the City addresses, because I spoke on that exact issue every time, but apparently he didn't get the message. He also had not been aware that he and four other council members were ignoring their Oaths of Office.

While I was working hard to get land from Union Pacific Land Resources so that we wouldn't lose the Union Tank Car Company, and to get the Job Corps Center in the Evanston Area, the five city council members, including Davis, were trying to do everything they could to undermine the projects. I couldn't figure out how Mr. Davis thought he was going to do any better, because he sure hadn't done much as a council member.

What's ironic about this whole thing is that four years ago, when I was running for my third term as mayor against Jerry Wall and Tom Hutchinson, council members Davis, Vranish, and Nelson were all in favor of raising the mayor's salary from $12,000 to $30,000 so I would run again. What changed them? They became puppets to Ms Wall.

The first regular city council meeting for the month of March was held on March 9th with a full council. Therefore, after roll call and declaring a quorum I opened up the meeting. After all the initial business was taken care of I opened the public participation segment of the meeting.

Apparently Mountain Regional Services (M.R.S.) was looking to add another group home in a neighborhood near 17th Street and West Sage Street. Some folks residing in that neighborhood were present at the meeting to express their opposition to the home.

Dane Hutchings introduced some of the neighbors who would be close to the property. Hutchings explained that they would speak in opposition to having group homes with residents from M.R.S. residing in their neighborhood.

Some employees from M.R.S. were also present, and several voiced their opinions and concerns. Employees from M.R.S. tried to explain that they would not be able to keep a group home out of their neighborhood because it was federal law and part of the Federal Fair Housing Act (FHA) requirements, but that didn't matter to those in opposition: "Not in my backyard" was their feeling.

However, after an hour and twenty minutes of discussion I suggested that any further discussion on the subject could best be taken care of by direct contact with the director of M.R.S., and then I called for a ten-minute recess.

After the recess I called the meeting back to order for Old Business. Ordinance 94-4 came up for second reading. This ordinance proposed a zone change of Lots 2 and 3 of the Butte Church Subdivision, from Medium Density Residential-Developing Zone to Rural-Residential Zone, as requested by Hal Collier and Monty Stiglitz, represented by the Church on Straight and Narrow Street, who owned the property. Both lots were over 2 acres and the owners wanted to change the zone to match the adjacent property to the northeast.

Councilman Nelson made the motion to pass Ordinance 94-4 on second reading, seconded by Hutchinson, with 5 votes in favor and 2 votes against (Wall and Vranish). The motion passed. This ordinance came up for third reading during the March 23rd meeting and passed with a vote of 5 in favor, 1 against (Vranish) and 1 absent (Nelson). For some reason or other Councilwoman Wall changed her mind and voted in favor of the ordinance.

Following new business I polled the staff and city council for comments and announcements.

Councilman Nelson made a motion for the council to go into an executive session to discuss a personnel matter and property purchase, seconded by Hutchinson with all voting in favor.

After the executive session, I called the meeting back to order and Councilman Vranish made a motion for health insurance to continue for employees who are on the City Disability Program and for the city to continue to contribute its normal share to the premium, seconded by Nelson, with all voting in favor.

Councilman Davis made a motion to direct the city attorney to continue negotiating on a price for purchasing the recycling building at 61 Allegiance Circle within the parameters designated during the executive session, seconded by Barnard with all voting in favor.

Prior to adjournment, I called for a work session to be held on March 30th at 5:00 p.m. and reminded everyone that on April 12th there would be a meeting to discuss and review the Evanston 2000 Comprehensive Plan.

The meeting adjourned at 10:40 p.m.

I wrote another article which was published in the *Uinta County Herald* of March 4th. The *Herald* put it in the paper as a Guest Column and titled the article, VOLUNTEERISM AND THE ECONOMY.

My article began, *The City of Evanston is a community of giving. A community with folks that give countless hours of volunteer services every year.*

Evanston is known throughout the State of Wyoming and the Rocky Mountain area for its extraordinary voluntary services, and the citizens of Evanston and surrounding areas should realize this...

The article spoke of all the dozens of programs that were made successful through folks volunteering their services and seeing each program to its completion, as well as how much their services help the economy. My article continued:

I want to point out the importance of those services, the economic importance:

First, the enormous amount of people in the area that give their services to the public is an indication of their love and caring of the community, and the positive attitude and sentiment that is shown by the people...And this helps the economy.

Second, all of the volunteer services that are provided by those special and outstanding citizens create many different and unique activities such as sports, drama, social, etc., plus creating family recreation and historic interests for the public to enjoy...These activities also help build the economy...

These programs bring people out where they have the opportunity to patronize our local businesses and with that the commercial district has the opportunity to provide more jobs.

And third, an active community such as Evanston, with their volunteer services and their outstanding facilities, helps to entice industry, business and others to the area. People are attracted by the friendliness, the high quality of life, vision and class of our community.

Let's keep those values and maintain a good life for our families as well as ourselves. This is all Economical Development...We'll never be able to replace people like you.

This was the conclusion of my Guest Column article, and as I read it again it brings back so many memories of all the folks that were involved with all these projects and what terrific citizens they were. A lot of them are no longer with us, but I will never forget them.

After the March 9th city council meeting with the long debate about the group homes, the issue really got hot and heavy. Letters to Editor started flowing in to the *Herald* in opposition to the group homes.

The *Uinta County Herald* of March 11th published an article by reporter George Hammond-Kunke titled, RESIDENTS SAY 'NOT IN MY BACKYARD' TO GROUP HOMES.

This was a very lengthy article that started out:

More than 100 residents attended two meetings to voice their opinions about the existence and potential influx of group homes in Evanston. The meetings were at the planning and zoning meeting Monday and the city council meeting on Wednesday, both at Evanston City Hall.

Dane Hutchings indicated that he already had a group home located one and one half blocks from his home at W. Sage. He was quoted as saying, *"We're very concerned about the safety of the children. We need to take into consideration the area that is being purchased."*

He also mentioned the possibility of his property decreasing in value because of the close vicinity of the group homes, but City Attorney Dennis Boal pointed out to him that group homes could be no closer to each other than 750 feet. The *Herald* quoted me telling Hutchings that *"we [the city council] have our hands tied by federal government regulations."*

The article went on, but there was nothing local officials could do about it because of federal regulations. And checking the police reports, I could see there had been no serious criminal acts caused by these homes in the past.

Those folks in opposition to the group homes had a very valid concern, but I also had to agree that those disabled and handicapped people had some rights.

The *Herald's* March 11th issue also had another article written by Hammond-Kunke about my announcement of running for a fourth term as Mayor of Evanston.

He quoted me as saying, *"With my knowledge in city government, I feel that I have a lot to offer to the people of Evanston. The city is more solvent now than it has ever been. The budget is in good shape. There is very little indebtedness. We have carry-over money and a cash reserve to keep us going if we had a disaster."*

The mayor said the city is running smoothly, but that he has some projects he wants to complete before leaving office...

"I still have a vision. All of these projects come from the planning and goals that were set in my first term. I still have that vision to upgrade the community. I still have the ambition and vision to be a good mayor and to build a good community."

The *Herald* continued with, *Ottley has been involved with Evanston's economic development for more than 30 years,* and quoting me saying, *"Economic development goes far beyond industry. There's a broader criteria than just industry. There's tourism and local volunteerism to build the economy. We need the promotion of different ideas for the town and making the community a place for retirees and other people to come here and live.*

There are individuals who are very competitive. You build your economy from within. Tourism is a big thing that we build on. It provides a lot of revenue for the city and the county..."

The *Herald* article concluded: *Ottley has also been working hard to try and get Ox Bow Refinery back in Evanston. Ox Bow left Evanston nearly two years ago.*

"The main thing for the people of Evanston is to not give up. We've got to keep that confidence and that positive attitude going," the article quoted me.

When I said *"the city was running smoothly,"* I meant it. Although the five council members were doing everything they could to make it tough for me, I still had the staff doing a terrific job helping me. My secretary, Sharon Constantine, and all my appointed staff and all other city employees were doing everything they could to help me keep the City of Evanston moving in the right direction. I owed them a lot and Councilman Tom Hutchinson was also trying to do what he could to help me.

I have received many letters and cards from folks that had moved from Evanston, because of a job transfer or the completion of their job, or for some other reason. They always commented how bad they felt about leaving Evanston, a community they learned to love.

Their comments were always about what a wonderful community Evanston was, and how much they enjoyed living here. They often mentioned the friendliness of the folks and how active the citizens were, and they always seemed to comment on the cleanliness of the entire community. They would even sometimes comment on how clean the activities were and that most activities provided fun for citizens of all ages.

I also had many citizens approach me at City Hall or on the street telling me the same things about Evanston, and I would always thank them for their comments. To me, these comments and complimentary remarks made me feel like everything we had done was well worthwhile, and that the town was running smoothly and in the right direction.

⤳

The March 10th issue of the *Casper Star-Tribune* came out with a short article on their "Border to Border" page titled: WYO TOURISM GROUP PART OF NATIONAL RALLY.

The article read: *Jim Davis of Evanston, representing Tracks Across Wyoming, will be in Washington for a National Coalition for Heritage Areas rally March 13-15, Davis said.*

Davis said he has been asked to speak to the group "because we're one of the first grassroots organizations in the West" involved in "heritage tourism."

Tracks Across Wyoming – in existence for just over a year – is attempting to create a tourism corridor across southern Wyoming following the path of the Union Pacific Railroad.

Davis said he would be accompanied by David Kathka, director of the state Division of Parks and Cultural Resources, and David Clark, city attorney for Rawlins.

The Tracks Across Wyoming (TAW) group started last year under the direction of Evanston's Urban Renewal Agency Director Jim Davis to involve all communities across southern Wyoming following the U.P.R.R. Tracks. The group has included members from most of the communities within the five counties across the southern railroad corridor.

The committee is a large group of historic inspired folks, and Davis had arranged many trips for the group to visit historic sites along the Wyoming corridor. The TAW project was another successful program that produced a lot of Wyoming history. Evanston was very appreciative of Davis for his efforts in taking the lead in such a worthwhile program and keeping the City of Evanston in the limelight.

In opening up the second meeting of the month on March 23rd I recognized two scout troops under the direction of Cub Scout Master Peri Vastardis and Webelos Leader Stephen Fowler of Cub Scout Pack 45. Mr. Vastardis introduced the following Cub Scouts who were in attendance to fulfill a requirement for their Citizenship Award and the Arrow of Light Award: Jason Kraft, Ryan Holloman, Christopher Shives, Matt Gray, Joseph Vincent, Joshua Fowler, Stephen Fowler, Brad McInnis, Alex Vastardis and James Dunker.

I also recognized Boy Scout Master Dean Bowen of Scout Troop 75 and he in turn introduced Scout Leader Richard Hatch and Boy Scouts Brandon Barker, Kris Hatch, Brad Taylor, Justin Barker, Jason Denson, Todd Smith, Cody Webb, Tim Davis and Steve Kelly. They too were present for their Citizenship Merit Badges.

After their introduction and a few comments from their leaders, I requested that they each approach the bench where I presented each scout and leader with an Evanston "Fresh Air, Freedom and Fun" promotional pin, and thanked them for attending the meeting. I also told them that they were welcome to stay, and if they had anything to say in regards to the agenda to please feel free to be recognized and step forward.

During this meeting a public hearing was held concerning an application to transfer a liquor license held by Uinta Investment Corporation, dba Pink Elephant, to the B.A.D. Company located at 1021 Front Street.

City Attorney Dennis Boal acted as the hearing officer, and after a few comments from Ann Wallace, who was the only one present speaking in favor of the transfer, Mr. Boal closed the hearing. There was no one present in opposition.

Councilwoman Wall made the motion to allow the transfer to the new holder of the license to B.A.D. Company, Inc., dba Pink Elephant, seconded by Barnard with 6 votes in favor and 1 absent (Nelson). The motion passed.

Under New Business, Councilman Vranish introduced Resolution 94-10 ratifying the purchase of the real property and building located at 61 Allegiance Drive, which was currently being used as the city's Recycling Center.

This resolution ratified and approved the purchase of the property pursuant to the terms set forth in the Closing Statement. I don't recall how much the city paid for the building, but it was held by the bank under foreclosure, so if I remember right it was within the parameters of what was discussed during the executive session held during a February meeting.

Motion was made by Councilwoman Wall to adopt Resolution 94-10, seconded by Hutchinson with 6 votes in favor and 1 absent (Nelson).

After other new ordinances and resolutions, were acted on and unanimously passed, I polled the staff and council for comments and announcements just prior to adjournment.

Councilman Barnard made a motion to authorize the mayor to write a letter to Union Pacific Resources regarding a land transfer to the City of Evanston, seconded by Hutchinson, with all present voting in favor.

If I remember right, I believe the U.P.R.R. property they were talking about had something to do with property adjacent to the BEAR Project.

I announced that there would be a work session scheduled for March 30 at 5:00 p.m., and I reminded the council that there would be a public meeting at City Hall at 6:00 p.m. to discuss the use and zoning of the 265 acres of property that Union Pacific Resources deeded to the City of Evanston.

Meeting adjourned at 10:43 p.m.

⟜⟞⟋

Recently the Evanston City Council members and I discussed the possibility of the council have a meeting each year away from City Hall to discuss city problems, budget and future plans. We called the meeting a "Retreat" and the idea was to rent a motel room in Evanston for a day with lunch brought to us by the motel restaurant. It would be a private meeting for discussion purposes only; there would be no business acted up on. To help the local economy we all agreed that we should keep the "Retreats" local in Evanston, but would only be limited to the mayor and council members.

We decided to go to a different motel each year as long as it had a restaurant where we could get lunch, but the day of the meeting had to be on a day where all members of the council and I could make a day of it, even if it had to be on a weekend.

This year of 1994 we made arrangements to meet at the Weston Plaza. Each member got a packet of materials. Included in the packet was an agenda put together by me, a copy of the adopted city's mission statement, a copy of the city's organizational structure, and other materials that might be helpful to them.

At the start of the meeting I first asked them to open up their packets and look at the material that was in them, I then asked them if they had any problems with the agenda. Some appeared unhappy with it, but accepted it with a couple of items added.

We first discussed the mission statement and went through it to get it right and to everyone's satisfaction. I then went into planning (long- and short-range) and the operation and duties of the city council and mayor.

I mentioned the team approach, how we all should be working as a team. I discussed the thought of being present at the meetings. It seemed like almost every meeting there would be one or two (sometimes more) members of the council absent.

I asked, "What do you feel are our internal strengths and weaknesses?" I got several replies from the council, and I felt like they were all trying to be honest and upfront with their comments.

I reminded them of the Oath of Office they took when sworn in. Of course they all appeared to agree with me that they should uphold the oath, but I reminded them that our duties were to the citizens to keep the economy up and to do whatever we could to make the community safe and clean. That we must keep the infrastructure in good working order and the streets in good shape, including removing the snow as soon as possible and keeping the streets clean.

I mentioned that you need total integrity while performing your role as a city council member. I told them that if they had any questions of me or complaints, my office was always open to them for discussion. Whether it be a problem they were having with me or a project, or even if it was a city problem in general.

We talked about the duties and authority of the mayor, and the duties of each council member. Everyone appeared to agree on what was discussed.

I asked them to please be open and honest with each other including with me. I reminded them that the mayor was also a member of the city council and that I also took part in any legislation that the city might act on.

I presented the City's Organizational Chart to them. We discussed the chart and everyone appeared to agree on it with very few changes. I went through my personal goals for the city, which was to keep close communication with each of them, to build close relations with each of them, to build a good working team among us, keep them all informed as to where I stood on different issues, to be 100% honest with each of them, and to treat them all as my equal.

I told them that I had heard through the grapevine that some of them were dissatisfied with some of my appointments for liaisons to the different departments and boards. I told them that I had always tried to let them know beforehand when and who I was going to appoint, and if they were not satisfied, they should let me know at that time. I was only trying to be fair. I told them in order to meet our goals and to make the city function as it should, I needed them to work with me.

We talked at length about the budget and priorities. Of course everyone had different priorities, but I told them if we communicated as we should, priorities and goals could be worked out to everyone's satisfaction.

We met all day long and I don't think that anyone's goals or priorities didn't get discussed. I didn't think there were any departments or major positions that weren't mentioned. At the time, I thought the meeting was a success because everyone seemed to be well satisfied.

At least, I was hoping the meeting would make a difference in the way the council members performed.

❦

On April 12th I received a disappointing letter from the Uinta County Conservation District stating that the Uinta County Rural Development Committee would no longer be sponsoring the yearly Agriculture-Business Banquet. The letter stated: *Due to the redirection and workload of the sponsoring agencies the time required to do a successful job has been greatly affected.*

The letter went on to read: *Members of our group will be more than happy to assist any group or organization who would like to continue with the banquet.*

I personally felt bad receiving a letter like that, because I think the entire Agri-Business Program brought a lot of folks throughout the county together. It was not only a time for each community and the county to name their various outstanding citizens, but also a time when the agricultural industry could get acquainted with the commercial industry, and have the opportunity, county-wide, to discuss each other's problems and concerns. I was just hoping that this would not be the end of the banquet. I was hoping that another group would pick it up.

During the first regular city council meeting of the month on April 13th, the Chili Cookoff Committee applied for a malt beverage permit for the 13th Annual Overthrust Chili Cookoff event scheduled for June 18th from 10:00 a.m. until 6:00 p.m. at the Uinta County Fairgrounds. Joe McGinnis was present to represent the Chili Cookoff Committee and to remind me that I was invited to be a judge once again, which I again accepted.

After a short presentation by Joe on how well the Cookoff had done in previous years, Councilman Nelson made a motion to approve the malt beverage permit application for the Cookoff Committee, seconded by Wall, with 6 votes in favor and one absent (Vranish). The motion passed.

In the next order of business Lisa Burridge, Chairperson of the March of Dimes Committee requested a parade route for the Walk

America parade on April 23rd at 11:00 a.m. She described the route and stated that the local event was being sponsored by Key Bank (now known as Bank of the West), and the official sponsor of the national event was Lipton Tea Company.

"Things are going really well, we've already had 15 teams sign up to participate," the *Uinta County Herald* of April 15th quoted Lisa.

Councilwoman Wall made a motion to approve the parade and the route, seconded by Hutchinson, with all present voting in favor.

During public participation Barry Constantine, Recycling Coordinator, gave a short update on the upcoming Recycling Conference to be held in Evanston in September, and he reported that a compactor-bailer had been purchased. *The compactor can make $640 per load in cardboard,* he said.

I commented how well the recycling program was coming along and thanked Barry for his efforts in making the program a success.

Under New Business, Councilman Hutchinson made a motion to appoint Councilwoman Wall as Evanston's voting delegate at the upcoming Wyoming Association of Municipalities (W.A.M.) Convention to be held in Rock Springs on June 8th through the 10th, and Councilman Nelson as alternate voting delegate, seconded by Davis, with all voting in favor and 1 absent (Vranish). Motion passed.

Prior to adjourning I polled the council and staff for any comments and announcements.

The City Council and I complimented Urban Renewal Director Jim Davis for the way the Beeman-Cashin Building and Depot Square had been kept so clean and in a fine state of repair. Jim made a short report on what was being done to improve the area and about some additions to the Joss House.

Operations Superintendent Allan "Oop" Hansen read a letter from the Uinta County Engineer stating landfill fees would be waived for the City of Evanston's Annual Spring Cleanup Drive scheduled for May 16, 17 and 18. He stated that he would write a letter to the county thanking them for their generous offer. I told Oop that I too would be writing a letter to the county commissioners thanking them for waiving the fees.

In adjourning the meeting I reminded the city council and staff that there would be a work session at 5:00 p.m. on April 20th.

Once again I was invited to attend and say a few words at the annual Drug Abuse Resistance Education (D.A.R.E.) Graduation Exercises held at the Davis Middle School on Friday, April 22nd.

Principal Fred Ball opened the ceremonies with the presentation of the Flag and the Pledge of Allegiance, performed by a number of sixth grade students. He also gave the welcome and introduced Police Officer Alan Stahl, Evanston's officer overseeing the D.A.R.E. Program in conjunction with the school.

There were several videos shown and awards given. There were approximately 165 sixth grade students in attendance to receive their 1993-1994 Graduation Certificates. I felt very proud that I was invited to attend such a worthwhile program, and in my comments I congratulated all the students and told them that their parents and everyone should be very proud of each one of them for their efforts in completing the D.A.R.E. program. I said, "What you have learned through the D.A.R.E. Program will be with you the rest of your lives. As you grow older and the temptations arise, remember the things you have learned...remember to say NO."

After the ceremony everyone was invited to the cafeteria to enjoy refreshments and have the opportunity to mingle and get acquainted. It was a great program and a fun time.

On April 29th, the *Uinta County Herald* published a news article written by reporter George Hammond-Kunke titled, COUNCIL VOTES TO FINANCE GREAT MUSIC FESTIVAL.

The article began: *The Evanston City Council passed a motion to give $10,000 to Great Music West for their summer festival at Wednesday night's meeting at the Evanston City Hall Chambers.* The meeting was held on April 27th, but the article continued: *Two council members, Clarence Vranish and Jerry Wall opposed the $10,000 funding. Vranish did not feel it was an appropriate use of taxpayers' money. Wall said she felt it was too much.*

Councilman Will Davis, Craig Nelson, Tom Hutchinson and Ronald Barnard voted for the motion, as did Mayor Dennis Ottley.

The April 27th city council meeting was the second meeting of the month, and other business included the recognition of more Boy Scouts and their leaders. While welcoming them to the meeting I had Wade Williams, the Team Leader of Varsity Team #23 introduce his scouts: Dusty Jensen, Ira Hinckley, Jason Privett and Nick Baird; and I had Nephi Jensen, Scoutmaster for Troop #23 introduce the scouts of his troop: Trent Baird, Jake Schroeder, Ryan Bodine and Nathan Hinckley.

D10   UINTA COUNTY HERALD   Friday, June 17, 1994

Mayor welcomes Great Music West participants

It is a pleasure to extend a most cordial welcome to Great Music West participants.

We are most pleased and honored that these talented musicians will be in our community offering outstanding concert entertainment to the citizens of Evanston and all those who wish to attend.

We would also like to thank the volunteers who worked so diligently to bring the renown musicians to our community and a special thank you to Janice Bodine for spearheading this tremendous project.

City of Evanston
Dennis J. Ottley, Mayor

Members of the Evanston City Council welcome members of the Great Music West Festival to Evanston.

Great Music West major financial sponsors

City of Evanston, Evanston Tourism Promotion Board, Wyoming Division on Tourism, Idaho Travel Council, Frac Tanks, Wheeler Enterprises, Barbra Patterson Foundation, Cache Valley Tourism Council, George and Delores Bore Eccles Foundation, Uinta County School District No. 1, Union Pacific Resources, Bridger Valley Chamber of Commerce, Lifelong Learning Center, City of Lyman, City of Mountain View, CallAir, Simplot, Town of Afton, Lincoln County School District No. 2, Star Valley State Bank, Zions Bank, Utah Arts Council, Idaho Commission on the Arts, US West Foundation, Cache–Rich Tourist Council, Town of Laketown, Friends of Bear Lake, Town of Randolph, Town of Garden City, Pacific Power Foundation, West One Bank, Phone—Poulenc, Monsanto, Kings, New West, Town of Soda Springs, WDCI, Wyoming Council of the Arts, Town of Thayne, Town of Alpine, Town of Cokeville, First National Bank of Evanston, Wildwest Travel, Cazin & Houtz, Maverik Country Store, First Security Banks, Superior Rental, Evanston Motor Company, Blyth and Fargo Company, Dalton and Company, Chevron Oil, Verne Call, Chevron, U.S.A. and Gene and Beth Anderson. Major financial contributions and support for the Great Music West Festival came from the Wyoming Arts Council. To all these sponsors, we extend our appreciation and gratitude.

Major Service Sponsors:

KSL Television, Salt Lake City, Utah; Uinta County Herald, Evanston, Young Sign Company, KMER Radio, Kemmerer; Smith's Food King, IGA Market, Westar Printing, Evanston; and PrintStars, Afton.

Scholarship donations: Mr. and Mrs. Joseph Barker, Mr. and Mrs. Donald Barnard, Mr. and Mrs. John Coles, Mr. and Mrs. John Faddis, Iram Kirlin, Fay and Thomas Mealey, Mr. and Mrs. Hight Proffit, Mr. and Mrs. John Crandall, Josephine Walton, Dr. Gregory M. Yasuda, Mr. and Mrs. Ken Robison and Evanston Civic Orchestra.

After thanking the scouts and their leaders, I had them each approach the mayor's bench where I presented each with a "Fresh Air, Freedom and Fun" Evanston promotional pin.

During public participation, Pete Straub and Jim Neiner, representing the Wahsatch Gathering System, reported on the system that gathers and pipes sour gas from the Yellow Creek Field to the Whitney Canyon Processing Plant. They indicated that no incidents or mishaps had occurred and that all safety measures were taken care of.

I thanked them both for taking the time to come to the council meeting and assuring the public that Wahsatch Gathering System was working out fine and the System's main concern was safety.

Ordinance 94-12, sponsored by Councilman Nelson and introduced by Councilman Barnard, was brought up. The title of the ordinance was:

ORDINANCE 94-12
AN ORDINANCE APPROVING AND AUTHORIZING
A ZONE CHANGE FOR REAL PROPERTY LOCATED
NORTH OF CHAPARRAL ESTATES SUBDIVISION AND
PROPERTY LOCATED NORTH OF OVERTHRUST MEAD-
OWS SUBDIVISION, IN THE SE1/4 Of SECTION 30, T15N,
R120W, IN THE CITY OF EVANSTON, WYOMING, FROM
A MEDIUM DENSITY RESIDENTIAL-ESTABLISHED AND
LOW DENSITY RESIDENTIAL-DEVELOPMENT ZONE
TO A RURAL-RESIDENTIAL ZONE, AS REQUESTED BY
POWDOS PARTNERSHIP.

This ordinance was presented by Cloey Wall representing Uinta Engineering and Surveying, Inc. Wall was one of the partners in the POWDOS Partnership, and husband to Councilwoman Jerry Wall. Therefore, Jerry Wall dismissed herself from the Chambers and declared a conflict of interest.

Ordinance 94-12 ended up being a very controversial issue because the Rural- Residential Zone permitted housing of horses and other animals used for riding or packing, causing concern for a number of the residents living in Medium and Low Density Residential zoned subdivisions Chaparral Estates and Overthrust Meadows. Mr. Neil Lesmeister and Mrs. Lisa Parkin both spoke in opposition to Ordinance 94-12. They were residents of the two subdivisions immediately south of the new area requesting to be zoned Rural-Residential.

According to the April 29th article published in the *Uinta County Herald* by Hammond-Kunke, Mr. Lesmeister said in the meeting, *"The people in our subdivision are opposed to having horses in our neighborhood. We don't feel that POWDOS has the best interest in mind for our neighborhood, and we do have in mind what is the best interest for our neighborhood."* Lesmeister said 12 people in his subdivision were against the ordinance.

The Hammond-Kunke article continued: *Lisa Parkin offered, "Our subdivision has not been taken care of properly by this company [POWDOS],"* adding there were *"vacant basements that were dangerous to children. Rezoning will be a detriment to our subdivision.*

"Wall [Cloey] put fences around those basements...My goodness, if I put that type of fence around my yard, Planning and Zoning would not have approved of it. It's metal poles with wires stretched around it. There are no fences to speak of," Parkin said.

After ending discussion I called for a vote on the first reading of Ordinance 94-12. The vote was 4 yes votes (Barnard, Davis, Hutchinson and Nelson), 2 no votes (Vranish and me) and 1 abstaining (Wall).

On the second reading of Ordinance 94-12, during the May 11th meeting, the vote changed to 4 yes votes (Davis, Hutchinson, Nelson and me), 1 no vote (Vranish), 1 absent (Barnard) and 1 abstaining (Wall).

It was obvious that I had changed my vote, but after talking to Cloey Wall and several of the folks that resided in the two effected subdivision, I decided that the area north of the residential areas wouldn't have much of an effect on them because the prevailing winds were mostly from the south and southwest.

But on the third reading of the ordinance during the May 25th meeting Councilman Nelson made a motion to pass Ordinance on third and final reading, seconded by Hutchinson.

There were more folks present at the meeting in opposition to the ordinance than previously, causing a lengthy discussion, until Council Nelson made a motion to table Ordinance 94-12 until September 14th, seconded by Davis with 5 votes in favor, 1 vote against (me) and 1 abstaining (Wall).

I voted against tabling the ordinance because I didn't feel that it would make any difference, and when the September meeting came up and Ordinance 94-12 was brought off the table for a vote on the third and final reading, the vote turned out with 5 yes, 1 no (Vranish) and 1 abstaining (Wall). The motion passed, making Ordinance 94-12 law. Tabling Ordinance 94-12 made no sense in my opinion, because the vote ended up being the same.

Under new business during the April 27th city council meeting, Resolution 94-15 was introduced by Councilman Hutchinson giving the City of Evanston authority to submit an application to the Wyoming Farm Loan Board, Mineral Royalty Grant program, for funds to construct capital improvements on 265 acres of real property donated by Union Pacific Resources. The grant application requested funds in an amount not to exceed fifty percent of the total estimated cost of the improvements.

Motion was made by Councilman Nelson for the adoption of Resolution 94-15, seconded by Hutchinson, with all 7 votes in favor.

This vote kind of surprised me because of the way five of the city council members had been trying to make it so hard for me to get the land so we would be able to keep Union Tank Car Company in Evanston. They fought me all the way.

However, although we might have been a little premature in adopting Resolution 94-15, passing the resolution early gave the city time to work on it, showing U.T.C.C. that we were very serious about keeping them in Evanston. They had not committed to staying in Evanston at that time, but we felt that they were talking favorably and we wanted to be ready.

In other business, Councilman Vranish made a motion to change the regular city council meeting dates for the month of June. The

June 8th meeting would be changed to June 15th and the June 22nd meeting would be on June 21st, and they would be advertised as such. Motion was seconded by Nelson with all voting in favor.

The Annual W.A.M. Convention was being held from June 7th to June 11th, and the City of Evanston's public budget hearing was set by law to be held on the third Tuesday of June, which would be June 21st. This meeting change would accommodate both events.

Prior to adjournment I announced that there would be a work session on May 4th at 5:30 p.m., and a special city council meeting would be held on May 4th. The meeting adjourned at 10:20 p.m.

The special meeting of May 4th with a full council, I called the meeting to order at 7:05 p.m. and explained that the meeting was for the purpose of acting on two agenda items only. The first item of business was Resolution 94-19, introduced by Councilman Davis authorizing the City of Evanston to execute an agreement with Uinta Engineering & Surveying, Inc. (U.E.S.I.), for all design, plan and permit preparation services necessary to complete the Reclamation of the Gravel Area located in the Evanston Union Center.

This resolution gave the city the authority to complete all preparations necessary to reclaim the gravel pit located just west of the Old Roundhouse that is now a part of the 265 acres of property donated by U.P.R.C. It is located within the boundaries of the planned Union Center Subdivision and possibly part of the property that the Union Tank Car Company might need to relocate.

Motion was made by Councilman Hutchinson for the adoption of Resolution 94-19, seconded by Nelson, with 6 voting in favor and 1 abstaining (Wall). She felt that as her husband Cloey was one of the principals of U.E.S.I. that she had a conflict. The motion passed. We were trying to get things put together so that, when U.T.C.C. was ready, the property would be available.

The second item of business that was on the special meeting agenda was the proposal of W.A.M/J.P.I.C, the insurance committee of the Wyoming Association of Municipalities, who had offered special optical benefits with the city paying the same proportionate share as they did for other health coverage.

Councilman Vranish made a motion to adopt the optical benefits proposed by W.A.M. for city employees, seconded by Nelson, with all voting in favor.

With no other business I adjourned the meeting at 7:14 p.m. This had to be the shortest city council meeting I had ever conducted, at only 9 minutes.

The *Uinta County Herald* of May 6th stated in an article by reporter George Hammond-Kunke:

"The reason we needed a special meeting is because we needed to get started on it [the Union Center Subdivision] so we could get the figures for the other grant," Evanston Mayor Dennis Ottley said.

"We've gotten a pretty solid commitment from Union Tank Car Company of Chicago," Ottley said. "Now it's a matter of coming up with a negotiable agreement and we're very close to that.

"We've decided to call it the Evanston Union Center because it involves so many entities with the state and city," Ottley said. "This project could mean a big increase in the tax base as far as city, county and state taxes go. It will also have a sizable payroll, plus it could have an effect on a lot of other business," Ottley said. "It all helps a little here and there."

The *Herald* article continued: *Ottley has high hopes that the grant will arrive on or before June 2. The grant is from the Farm Loan Board.*

"This has been a long time coming. I've worked on it very hard over the years and we're looking forward to seeing the expansion. It's going to be a long term industry in Evanston. It will be a benefit and a real asset for many, many years to come," Ottley said.

Evanston is expecting to receive a grant in the amount of $486,000 for the Phase 1, Part 1 portion of the project, the article concluded.

⤜∽∾⤏

At one our meetings a few months ago, Ms Loni Tyler and part of her second grade class at Clark Elementary School were present to ask me about the Monarch Butterfly, and how the annual spring spraying of mosquitoes might affect them. I told her that I would look into her concern and get back to her.

It took me a while to gather the information that she requested, but after meeting with Les Burrough, Uinta County Extension
Agent, and Mr. Scott Shaw of the University of Wyoming, I wrote
Ms Tyler a letter with a large amount of information concerning the
butterfly. I had received this information from the extension office
and the university and they said there was no danger to the butterfly
from the spray.

On May 5th, I received a letter inviting me to attend Amoco Production Company's ribbon cutting ceremony to help celebrate the
opening of Amoco's new LNG (liquefied natural gas) facility located
at Amoco's Painter Gas Complex. The ceremony would be held at
11:40 a.m. on Tuesday, May 17th. Lunch was served following the
ribbon cutting.

The letter ended with the following statement: *Amoco hopes to be
a leading supplier of LNG in what we see as a growing market. Our LNG
facility is also a way we can add value locally to the natural gas we produce in
Uinta County.*

I was very pleased with the letter, and I did accept the invitation.
I attended the ceremony and had a chance to talk to a lot of the head
folks of Amoco. The information I got made me feel good about the
economy, because the opening of the LNG plant was another move
that would upgrade our economy and county tax base. It was a nice
ceremony and lunch, and I enjoyed it very much.

Apparently the six members of the Evanston City Council were
planning on a meeting excluding me concerning the fiscal year budget for 1994-1995 sometime in May. Why? I had no idea. However,
Councilman Vranish entered my office on Friday, May 6th at approximately 4:55 p.m. asking me if it was okay if the council had a
budget meeting without me in attendance. After a short discussion
with Vranish, against my better judgment, I told him that I didn't
give a damn what the council did, but honestly I did care, it did

bother me. I had never seen that happen in the 24 years I served on the council and as mayor.

I told Vranish that I appreciated him letting me know about it, but I still didn't feel good about it, although I told him to go ahead. I don't know whether Vranish was assigned to come and talk to me about it or whether he just felt that it was the thing to do. But I wouldn't have known about the meeting if he hadn't come and told me. I did have a lot of respect for him for making me aware of the secret council meeting.

But after talking to Vranish and telling him that I didn't care, I met with our budget officer and treasurer Steve Widmer. During the discussion with Widmer he explained what he thought was the reason for their meeting without me: they thought they could get a few things past me if I wasn't in attendance all the time. This was only his opinion; however, it made sense.

This really upset me and I called in my secretary, Sharon Constantine to put out a memorandum to each member of the city council. That memo, dated May 9th, read as follows:

Last Friday, May 6th, 1994, approximately 4:55 p.m. council member Clarence Vranish approached me at City Hall to request my approval for Steve Widmer, City Treasurer, to meet with the City Council, with the exception of the Mayor, concerning the FY 1995 city budget. I told him that I had no objections. However, after conversing with Steve and after giving this a lot of thought I have decided against this.

I have no idea what is behind the council's intention, but I have decided that it would be unfair to me, as Mayor, and Steve, and would be bad government. I would never allow any of the city staff to be put in a position such as this. It's hard for me to believe that all 6 members of the council would allow such action. As I said at the last work session we all need to discuss the proposed budget together.

I must, once again, remind the council members that the Mayor is also a part of the governing body. Therefore, the Mayor should be included in any meeting that the board may have regarding city business.

It seems to me that if there is anything to say, it should be said where all can hear. I will be at City Hall tonight in the Mayor's office between 6 p.m.

and 8 p.m. If any of the members of the council would like to talk to me at that time or any other time I will be available.

That memo was signed by me and delivered to each city council member. I don't recall whether or not any of the council members came in to meet with me, but they still had their little unofficial sessions with each other and discussed the budget secretly.

During the first city council meeting of the month on May 11th Terry McCarthy from the High Country Athletic Club presented plans for a half marathon (13 miles) to be held August 6th. She stated that the race would start at the Uinta County Courthouse, then go along Front Street and south on Highway 150 to Bear River Crossing, and return to the Courthouse.

After a short discussion Councilman Vranish made a motion to allow the High Country activity, seconded by Wall, with 6 votes in favor and 1 absent (Barnard).

Kathy Ball, representing the Uinta County Fair Committee, made a presentation and requested that their application for a malt beverage permit for the Rodeo Arena be approved. She stated that this would be during the County Fair scheduled for July 30th, August 2nd and 4th from 6:00 p.m. to 10:00 p.m.

Councilman Vranish made a motion to approve the application for a malt beverage permit requested by the Fair Board Committee, seconded by Wall.

A lengthy discussion followed the motion, because there was a lot of opposition to selling beer anytime during the fair. Aaron Martin, an educator with the 4-H program, spoke out against selling alcoholic beverages at the fair.

"I feel very opposed to the selling of alcoholic beverage at the fair," Martin said. "I saw a lot of kids drinking in the sheds at the fair last year," he added.

Ed Beaty, who is on the fair Board, said when a youth is seen drinking, "we dump the beers ourselves."

In ending discussion I called for the vote of the motion with 6 voting in favor and 1 absent (Barnard). Motion passed.

Under New Business, Resolution 94-16 was introduced by Councilman Nelson authorizing the City of Evanston to apply for a Community Development Block Grant (CDBG) from the State of Wyoming Economic Development and Stabilization Board (ED&SB) in the amount of $25,000 to develop a Master Use Plan for the 265 acres of land donated to the City of Evanston by Union Pacific Resources Company.

Councilman Hutchinson made the motion to adopt Resolution 94-16, seconded by Davis, with 6 votes in favor and 1 absent (Barnard). Motion passed.

Following, Councilman Hutchinson introduced Resolution 94-20 authorizing the City of Evanston to apply for a CDBG, infrastructure grant, from the State of Wyoming ED&SB in the amount of $150,000 to be used for Infrastructure Development on approximately 80 acres of the property to accommodate the expansion of the Union Tank Car Company's repair operation.

After a short discussion and an amendment to the resolution in the correction of a word, Councilman Davis made the motion to adopt Resolution 94-20, seconded by Nelson with all those present voting in favor. Motion passed.

Following New Business, I polled the council and staff for announcements and comments.

Urban Renewal Agency Director Jim Davis reported on three grants received for the BEAR Project, totaling $64,000. $24,000 was received from the State Land and Conservation Fund, $20,000 from Wyoming Game and Fish for fish pond rehabilitation, and $20,000 from Wyoming Game and Fish for a Handicapped-Accessible Fishing Pier.

Councilwoman Wall reported on a recent Saturday cleanup and painting project in the Yellow Creek Road area.

I announced that there would be a work session on May 18th at 5:00 p.m. and adjourned the meeting at 9:17 p.m.

On May 19 I received a letter from the Wyoming Elks Association, who had recently held their Annual Spring Convention in Evanston. The letter stated the following:

Dear Mayor Ottley;

On behalf of the Wyoming Elks Association, I would like to thank you, your officials and your citizens for the hospitality shown to the members of the Wyoming Elks Association during our recent Spring Convention, hosted by Evanston Lodge No. 2588...

Evanston is a fine city, and you may well be proud that Evanston Lodge is a strong link in the great Fraternal chain of Elkdom. Thank you again for the many courtesies extended by the City of Evanston.

Fraternally yours,
Steve Kant, Chairman (signed)

At this time local Elk Member Ken Williams was President of Evanston Lodge No. 2588 and I had commended him for bringing the Spring Convention to Evanston.

⤳〰〰

The city council and mayor's work session was held on May 18th. It was a very informal meeting for discussion of the 1994-1995 fiscal year budget. There were a number of requests from those in attendance that year, but we had to be very careful in setting priorities and staying within our means to come up with a balanced budget.

One item that Councilwoman Wall brought up again was the landscaping along Yellow Creek Road, an item that we all had wanted and she had made a campaign promise on. But it apparently had been low priority during the last couple of budget years. My problem was that I wanted to bury the overhead power lines before we did any landscaping, especially trees on the west side of Yellow Creek Road, because as those trees grew they would, in the future, cause problems and the city would be pruning them so they wouldn't interfere with the power lines, in addition to being unsightly. So I mentioned checking with Utah Power and Light (now Rocky Mountain Power) about the cost of burying the overhead wires from the I-80 underpass to where the power lines cross south on Yellow Creek Road.

The previous year I had said to the council that if we had the funds we could landscape the east side of Yellow Creek Road where there are no overhead power lines, but the council declared that they would rather wait until the city could do both sides.

Since Councilman Craig Nelson was an employee of U. P. & L., he was asked to find out how much they would charge the city to bury the overhead lines. He came back with a figure of $50,000, which we thought was high, but I told the council that I didn't want to see the west side of the Yellow Creek Road landscaped until we could bury the unsightly overhead power lines, and at the time they all seemed to agree with me.

Therefore, we prioritized the project and were able to find the $50,000 to bury the lines and appropriate funds in the 1994-1995 budget to do the landscaping on both sides of Yellow Creek Road, to be completed the next season of 1995.

However, when the 1995 season came upon us, Councilwoman Wall, who had made big promises to her constituents, managed to go ahead with the landscaping on both sides of Yellow Creek Road without burying the power lines first, which we had budgeted for. To this day those trees on the west side of the road are growing into the wires, but by then I was no longer mayor and Wall, with no vision, went ahead and completed her promised landscaping. Why Mayor Davis didn't have her wait until the high lines were buried, I'll never know, but then Davis was one of her puppets.

❦

The second city council meeting of the month landed on May 25th, and after the initial business had been acted upon, Sandy, representing the Evanston High School Alumni Society, requested a parade permit. She explained that the parade would be on July 2nd starting at 9:00 a.m. She also said that the parade would start at the Uinta County Library Parking Lot and then go down Main Street to Harrison Drive (11th Street), over to Front Street, and end up at Depot Square.

After a short discussion Councilwoman Wall made a motion to approve the parade permit and route, seconded by Barnard, with all voting in favor.

After taking care of unfinished business and new business I polled the council and staff for comments and announcements.

Community Development Director Paul Knopf brought the council up to date on the upcoming High Uinta Downtown Bike Race. He said that on Sunday, the day after the High Uinta Bike Race from Kamas, Utah to Evanston was completed, the Downtown Race would begin, using the same route as previous years, and he asked permission to block off certain streets.

Councilman Davis made a motion to allow road closures in the residential areas on June 17th as needed from 11:30 a.m. to 5:30 p.m. for the Downtown Race, the same streets that had been used the past 5 years, seconded by Nelson, with all voting in favor.

I reminded everyone that there would be a special city council meeting on June 1st at 5:00 p.m. to act on a few resolutions. I then adjourned the meeting at 9:35 p.m.

When I opened the June 1st special city council meeting I declared a quorum with four city council members present. Councilmembers Hutchinson and Barnard had been excused for personal reasons.

I explained to those present that the purpose of this meeting was to adopt five resolutions so that certain projects could get started and finished before the season was over. The first resolution was Resolution 94-21, introduced by Councilman Nelson, authorizing the City of Evanston to execute an agreement with Darby Enterprises for the completion of all work as set forth in the specifications of the landscaping and irrigation system project at the Animal Control Shelter.

Councilman Davis made a motion to adopt Resolution 94-21, seconded by Nelson. The motion passed with 4 votes in favor (Davis, Nelson, Vranish and me), 1 vote against (Wall), and 2 absent (Hutchinson and Barnard).

The next item was Resolution 94-22, introduced by Councilwoman Wall, authorizing the City of Evanston to execute an agreement with X-IT Construction for the completion of all work as set forth in the specifications of the Depot Square Parking Lot Project.

Councilman Nelson made a motion to adopt Resolution 94-22, seconded by Davis. But Councilman Vranish made a motion to amend the Contract, Article 3, 3.2, that after the word "owner" we insert "$500.00," to specify the late charges per day if the contractor didn't meet the deadline. Motion to amend was seconded by Nelson with all those present voting in favor. The main motion by Nelson, as amended, also passed with all present voting in favor.

The next item of business was Resolution 94-23, introduced by Councilwoman Wall, authorizing the City of Evanston to execute an agreement with Flare Construction, Inc. for the completion of all work as set forth in the specifications of the Water Drain Line and the West Sage Street Sewer Improvements Project. Resolution 94-23 was adopted by motion with all voting in favor.

After unanimously agreeing to amend the present agreement with the City of Evanston-Uinta County Human Resource Center Joint Powers Board, authorizing the Board to issue refunding revenue bonds to refinance its debt to the Wyoming Farm Loan Board by Resolution 94-25, also introduced by Councilwoman Wall, Resolution 94-26 was introduced by Councilman Vranish to express the City of Evanston's continued support of the City of Evanston-Uinta County Human Resource Center and its Management Board, if at all possible, given future budgetary constraints.

Resolution 94-26 was amended by motion to change a few words but passed unanimously, and the main motion, as amended, was also adopted by same vote.

The special meeting adjourned at 5:45 p.m.

The first regular city council meeting for the month was held on June 15th, and when the motion to pay the outstanding bills was made by Councilman Nelson and seconded by Barnard, Councilman Vranish made a motion to amend the main motion to pay all outstanding bills with the exception of a bill to the *Uinta County Herald* for a full page advertisement (though the city had done this a number of times before and nobody objected) for the amount of $775.00.

Motion to amend was seconded by Davis. Motion to amend failed with 3 votes in favor (Vranish, Wall and Davis) and 4 votes against (Barnard, Nelson, Hutchinson and me).

However, the main motion to pay all bills, including the $775.00 *Uinta County Herald* bill, passed with all voting in favor unanimously. What surprised me was, why did Vranish make a motion to not pay the $775.00 bill with Wall and Davis agreeing with him, yet they all voted in favor of the main motion to pay all bills? It didn't make much sense to me, but then it didn't surprise me either.

Other business that came up during the June 15th meeting included the following:

I reappointed Kevin Smith to a three-year term on the Parks and Recreation District Board with Councilman Nelson making the motion to confirm the appointment, seconded by Wall with all council members voting in favor.

Councilman Nelson made a motion to approve an application for a malt beverage permit submitted by the Evanston Police Benevolent Association for a Truck/Trailer Pull Contest to be held at the Rodeo Grounds on July 15th and 16th. Motion was seconded by Hutchinson with 6 votes in favor and 1 absent (Vranish was excused early because he had an Airport Board meeting to attend).

Councilman Davis made a motion to approve a malt beverage permit, also submitted by the Police Benevolent Association, for an activity called Bull Wars, also to be held at the Rodeo Grounds on July 29th. The motion was seconded by Nelson with 6 votes in favor.

Janet Jackson, representing the Evanston Cowboy Days Committee, requested a parade permit for Labor Day, Monday, September 5th. Councilwoman Wall made a motion to allow the parade, seconded by Hutchinson, with all present voting in favor.

After some other business, I called for a ten minute recess. Councilman Vranish had returned from his Airport Board meeting.

After the recess was over I called the meeting back to order and continued with more new business that was on the agenda and dealt with, followed by me polling the staff and council members for comments and announcements.

Police Chief Dennis Harvey announced that the City of Evanston was turned down by the Wyoming Justice Department for funding for two additional police officers. This was a disappointment and I commented as such.

Councilman Davis gave a report on the recent Wyoming Association of Municipalities (W.A.M.) Convention in Rock Springs and announced that Councilwoman Jerry Wall had received a special leadership award and plaque at the convention. A word of congratulations to Councilwoman Wall was made by everyone, including me. I mentioned that she was well deserving of the award because of her hard work and time she had put in as a board member of W.A.M.

And she was. I just didn't appreciate the way Wall and Director Carl Classen were trying to make W.A.M. a political organization when it was meant to be non-partisan. I didn't like the way they had bad-mouthed the Wyoming State officials, especially Governor Mike Sullivan and Secretary of State Kathy Karpan (both Democrats). They both had given Evanston a tremendous amount of help and I appreciated both of them.

Councilwoman Wall then made a motion for the council to hold a work session at 6:00 p.m. on June 21st just prior to the regular city council meeting, seconded by Hutchinson with all voting in favor.

The meeting adjourned at 10:10 p.m.

Our next meeting on June 21st would have on the agenda Resolution 94-29, appropriating funds for fiscal year 1994-1995, but on June 12th the *Uinta County Herald* came out with an article by reporter George Hammond-Kunke. The article was titled COUNCILMAN VRANISH AT ODDS WITH HERALD AD BILL, and appeared on the front page of the paper.

The Hammond-Kunke article began: *Evanston City Councilman Clarence Vranish took exception Wednesday night to an advertisement purchased by the city in the Uinta County Herald's Progress-Horizons 1994 edition.*

Vranish asked the council to amend the budget and not pay the $775 bill to the Herald because "of the message we're sending to the public. We either have too much money or we're not spending it wisely."

Mayor Dennis Ottley said the money spent "is part of economic development for this community."

On Thursday morning, Ottley said that Varnish's motion caught him by surprise, adding that "Vranish didn't even mention that a full-page story about Evanston accompanied the ad. Clarence showed only one side. We've been doing this for years. It's a way to promote our city," Ottley said, noting that the money comes from the mayor's contingency fund....

"I just don't like spending taxpayers' money that shouldn't be spent. [The ad] is no different than using my picture to gain me popularity with a name recognition type thing. My picture was part of it and I didn't like it," Vranish said. "We've got a really big problem with communication. This is the 10th budget coming up and this is the first one where the council did not see the budget until it was completed. The mayor had all the work done and then he gave it to us. We had virtually no work session on it," Vranish said.

The Herald article continued: "The ad was nothing more than promotion for the individuals pictured in it," he said.

"It's a waste of taxpayers' money. I hate to see the city advertise itself. I hate spending other people's money," Vranish said...

Uinta County Herald, May 27, 1994.

The full-page ad of the Uinta Herald's Annual Progress-Horizon edition that Councilman Clarence Vranish had a problem paying for.

Vranish said Ottley spent nearly $15,000 of contingency fund money the first six months of the year, and added $5,000 more to the fund....

❧

The *Herald's* article by Hammond-Kunke in the June 17th edition continued: *[Councilman] Hutchinson said: "Why hasn't this been discussed in a work session or budget meeting? I have a hard time with this. This election has already started. Let's talk about things pertinent to the city. This is a budget discussion and we're wasting time."*

Barnard said he understood Vranish's frustration, but has no problem with the ad. However, Barnard said, "There's little communication between the mayor's office and the council. That's the thing that bugs me more than anything."

My response to Barnard's statement is that we had five regular city council meetings, five work sessions, six work sheets with the proposed budget were presented to the council on April 29th, and Resolution 94-29 was presented to them on paper for their interest so they would know what the council/mayor's proposed budget was, and to give them plenty of time to amend the budget if so desired. We all also had the opportunity to attend the staff meetings when the employees worked on their requests for the department budgets, and they had the right to meet with City Treasurer Steve Widmer anytime they needed. There was no excuse for not participating in the budget process; unless they were absent from all the budget sessions or if they were asleep, in which case I could see where they might not know what the new proposed budget consisted of. This is the same system that we always used to obtain a balanced budget and the council always ended up voting in favor.

However, this being election year for the mayoral race may have had something to do with it, because it appeared that most of the council members were trying real hard to see that Councilman Will Davis beat me at the polls in November. Hell, I could even lose in the Primary Election. They should at least have waited until that was over before they decided to start campaigning against me.

As far as Councilman Barnard, the newest member on the council, saying, "There's little communication between the mayor's office and the council"—that is not at all true. If he felt that way it is his own fault, because I have always requested conversations with council members, time and time again. This is the first set of council members to ever accuse me of not communicating with them. And if that's the way they felt, it was them, not me, being unreasonable.

LETTERS TO THE EDITOR
Councilman Vranish says budget priorities are mayors, not the council's

Dear Editor:

To me, being on the City Council is a sacred trust with tremendous responsibility. Since the Mayor and Council are in continual contact with each other and the employees, we sometimes forget who we actually work for, and that's the quiet voter who hardly ever complains.

This is my tenth year on the City Council and this is the first year that the Council had absolutely no input in determining priorities and developing the budget. In fact, the Mayor kept the budget secret from the Council until he completed it in late April. The Council was not given much opportunity to work on the budget. We attempted to discuss it with the Mayor at a couple of scheduled work sessions and he became very defensive each time when questioned about any particular item. The Council requested a meeting with the City

Treasurer to discuss the budget. The Mayor denied that request with the comment that it would have been "Bad Government." Refusing Council access to City employees isn't new either. On more than one occasion they have been told by the Mayor that they aren't to be talking to the Council. I submit that, indeed, that is truly bad government.

The City has good dedicated employees but we are already employee rich and now we are asked to add two more. We bought new garbage trucks to make our operation more efficient, two drivers instead of nine employees, but other than retirement, we lost no one. Positions were created in the street and water departments to accommodate these employees.

Community Development wants to add a position for one temporary employee. That temporary employee has already been

with us for one year, currently at $6 per hour. Every 120 days we renewed his temporary status at $6/hr. and now we are asked to make him a permanent temporary at $10.50/hr. That's quite a salary increase. Next we will be asked to make that position permanent with full benefits.

Urban Renewal wants to hire a 1/2 time employee to perform secretarial services for $8,000. There is absolutely no reason that the current City staff couldn't provide that service.

In prior years, the Mayor and Council met to set goals for the coming year, that never happened this year. Subsequently, the priorities reflected in this budget are entirely the Mayors. Sure we discussed with him changes that we wanted made, but it didn't do much good. The Mayor has even set the Council up as bad guys concerning salary increases in the last few budgets. The Mayor and

Council as a group would come to a consensus as to the amount of the cost of living raise that would be given that year. Later the Mayor would tell the employees a differing amount that was always larger. If the Council stuck to the amount agreed upon, then we were the bad guys.

The budget just passed is short of revenue by more than 2 million dollars. That shortfall will be made up by using carryover and about 1 million dollars from our cash reserves.

This budget exhibits similarities to the Federal Budget, it spends our savings. The oil companies tell us that many reservoirs will be depleted in just a few years. The sensible approach would be to tighten our belt now and keep our expenditures in line with our revenue. This budget didn't accomplish that.

Clarence Vranish
Evanston City Council President

Uinta County Herald, July 1, 1994.

LETTERS TO THE EDITOR
Councilman Hutchinson says council had plenty of opportunity to be involved in budget process

Dear Editor:

I write in response to councilman Vranish's article in your July 5 newspaper. First of all, I want to say that Mr. Vranish's opinions are his own and do not reflect those of the entire city council. As for his remarks toward the budget, let me just say that the budget is a public concern. All of the proper public hearings and procedures according to law have

been met. The budget is at the city hall and all of the council members have copies if anyone would like to review it.

As to all the other accusations made by Mr. Vranish, I would just remind everyone that it's an election year. Please come to city hall or call and talk with the mayor and the other council members and the city staff and employees about the budget and the other

issues questioned by councilman Vranish — get the other side to these issues, please!!!

I commend Evanston Treasurer Steve Widmer and the mayor's office and the council and all the city departments for the hard work and effort that went into this year's fiscal budget for the city. It's a workable budget that I feel reflects the needs of the community and above all pro-

vides for the services that we have asked our city government to perform for all of us.

Councilman Vranish said that he felt left out of the budget process this year. There were plenty of opportunities to be involved, Clarence. If you felt left out, well, perhaps that was your choice.

Respectfully,
Tom Hutchinson
City Councilman, Ward III

Uinta County Herald, July 8, 1994.

Also, Councilman Vranish sent a Letter to the Editor to be published in the *Uinta County Herald* titled, COUNCILMAN VRANISH SAYS BUDGET PRIORITIES ARE MAYOR'S, NOT THE COUNCIL'S. He stated in his letter that the 1994-1995 fiscal year budget was only the "Mayor's Budget," and not the council's.

However, during the June 21st regular city council meeting, after completing other business, I called for a public hearing, conducted by City Attorney Dennis Boal, on the proposed budget which was to be acted on this same date. The Wyoming State Law requires a budget hearing for First Class Citizens to be held the third Tuesday in June at 8:00 p.m. The 1994-1995 budget proposed by the Evanston City Council had been officially published and posted for the public's interest according to law. This hearing was recorded and would be on file at City Hall.

City Treasurer Steve Widmer gave a run-down of the proposed budget, followed by a considerable amount of questions and discussion, mostly by members of the council. Widmer gave explanations and answers concerning the budget process.

Former Mayor Eugene Martin was present and asked several questions, mainly about the revenue. It appeared that Widmer answered his questions satisfactorily.

No one else, other than the former mayor and members of the City Council, was present to voice concerns and questions about the budget, and City Attorney Boal closed the hearing.

At this time Councilman Hutchinson introduced the following resolution:

RESOLUTION 94-29
A RESOLUTION PROVIDING INCOME NECESSARY
TO FINANCE THE BUDGET AND PROVIDE FOR AND
AUTHORIZE ANNUAL APPROPRIATION OF FUNDS FOR
FISCAL YEAR 1995.

Motion was made by Councilman Davis to adopt Resolution 94-29, seconded by Hutchinson, but during discussion, Councilman Davis made a motion to amend Resolution 94-29 as follows: *To create a new Section 12. The anticipated GAAP fund (a fund controlled through the Governor's office) revenues of $285,258.00, shall be used by the City of Evanston to construct athletic ball fields within the community. Add $2,000.00 to the Urban Renewal budget, add $500.00 to Capital Improvement for bicycle path signage.* Motion to amend was seconded by Wall with 6 votes in favor and 1 absent (Nelson). Motion to amend passed.

The vote on the main motion to adopt Resolution 94-29 as amended was 4 votes in favor, 2 votes against (Barnard and Vranish) and 1 absent (Nelson). Motion passed.

The 1994-1995 fiscal year budget was finally approved by the majority of the council and mayor in the amount of $12.7 million, including anticipated grants, loans and so on.

Prior to adjourning I polled the Staff and Council for comments and announcements.

The City Planner gave a brief report on the High Uinta Classic Bike Race and the Downtown Race held on June 18th and 19th. He thanked everyone involved for helping to put on, once again, a successful program and was looking forward to next year.

Councilman Barnard gave a short report on the status of the BEAR Project, and stated that much had already been accomplished this year, and they were looking at more donated funds and assistance from various sources to continue the project.

I complimented water department employee Deb Wagstaff for her success in completing and receiving her Certification Water Exam achievement.

The meeting adjourned at 10:08 p.m.

In response to the Letter to the Editor written by Councilman Clarence Vranish and published in the July 1st edition of the *Uinta County Herald* accusing the recently approved 1994-1995 budget as being only the "Mayor's Budget" and not the council members, Councilman Tom Hutchinson wrote a Letter to the Editor published in the July 8th issue of the *Uinta County Herald* titled, COUNCILMAN HUTCHINSON SAYS COUNCIL HAD PLENTY OF OPPORTUNITY TO BE INVOLVED IN BUDGET PROCESS.

Halfway through his letter he stated the following: *"I commend Evanston Treasurer Steven Widmer and mayor's office and the council and all the city departments for the hard work and effort that went into this year's fiscal budget for the city. It's a workable budget that I feel reflects the needs of the community and above all provides for the services that we have asked our city government to perform for us.*

"Councilman Vranish said that he felt left out of the budget process this year. There were plenty of opportunities to be involved, Clarence. If you felt left out, well, perhaps that was your choice."

Respectfully,
Tom Hutchinson
City Councilman, Ward III

I thanked Tom for setting things straight by writing the letter and really appreciated his support when the rest of the council members seemed to be so inconsistent.

⟿

The next regular city council meeting was held on July 13th, and with all council members present a quorum was declared. Following the initial business of taking roll call and approving minutes of the previous meeting and approving the payment of all outstanding bills, Councilman Nelson made a motion to approve a catering permit to J. and K. Edwards, Inc. for the Sagebrush Theater's Shakespearian Sampler on July 16th to be held at Depot Square. The motion was seconded by Barnard, with all voting in favor.

J. R. Dean invited everyone to "A Day at the BEAR" on July 23rd. During his presentation Dean also invited everyone to sponsor a duck in the Rubber Ducky Race for $25.00.

Leanne Johnson, representing the Uinta County Extension Office, requested that the City of Evanston waive the $100.00 deposit and 50 cent per mile fees for use of the city bus to transport 4-H participants to the State Fair in Douglas in late August. Councilman Davis followed with a motion for the City of Evanston to grant the waiver request, seconded by Nelson, with all voting in favor.

In new business, the council passed two ordinances on first reading: Ordinance 94-20, making it a crime for a person to conspire with another to commit a crime, and Ordinance 94-21, making it a crime for a person to counsel, encourage, command or procure another to commit a crime. Both ordinances were passed unanimously during all three readings and became law.

Councilman Barnard made a motion to authorize the Evanston Preservation Committee, a subcommittee under the Urban Renewal Agency and spearheaded by Agency Director Jim Davis, to make an archaeological dig on the City of Evanston's property on July 25th through July 29th in the vicinity where Old China Town once stood. The motion, seconded by Nelson, was passed unanimously.

Director Davis reported that the archaeological dig had been planned and discussed by the Preservation Committee for quite some time, and was encouraged by the Wyoming Historical Society, who offered their assistance and help. The project was funded through grants and volunteer assistance, some local, and was an attempt to discover artifacts and other items of interest from Old China Town.

Davis also announced that those volunteering to help and the general public are invited to attend a Chinese Feast at 6:00 p.m. on Friday, July 29th at the Beeman-Cashin Building, and that immediately following the feast, Dudley Gardner, an archeology instructor at Western Wyoming College, would give a presentation on early Chinese settlements in southwest Wyoming.

After acting on several new ordinances, Councilman Davis introduced Resolutions 94-33 and 94-34 that authorized the execution of contracts and memorandums to non-profit organizations and set up regulations to implement the placing and supervision of employees hired by the city, pursuant to the Evanston Youth At Work Program.

Both resolutions were adopted by motion and a second, passing by a unanimous vote.

Prior to adjournment, Councilman Davis made a motion to hold a work session on July 20th at 5:00 p.m., seconded by Hutchinson with all voting in favor.

Evanston's Urban Renewal Agency Director Jim Davis reported on the number of telephone calls that his department had received in response to an article published in *American Heritage Magazine* concerning the Tracks Across Wyoming project.

Councilman Vranish read a memo from City Engineer Brian Honey concerning a telephone conversation with Jim Montura of the Wyoming Highway Department, about the possibility of displaying signs prohibiting the use of engine compression brakes within the City of Evanston. After a short discussion, City Attorney Dennis Boal was instructed by the council to write a letter to the Wyoming Attorney General's office asserting the city's authority in the matter of these brakes disturbing the peace. Further action would be taken up after Boal's response from the Attorney General's office.

Councilman Davis announced a special walk for raising funds for the American Cancer Society would take place on July 22nd and 23rd at the Evanston Middle School football field.

The meeting adjourned at 8:35 p.m.

The second regular city council meeting held on July 27th was business as usual, with a lengthy agenda. Councilman Nelson, early in the meeting, made a motion to approve a malt beverage permit application submitted by Cowboy Joe's for the Beautification Committee's annual Volley Ball Tournament to be held at Depot Square on August 13th from 9:00 a.m. to 6:00 p.m. The motion was seconded by Wall and passed with 7 votes in favor.

I appointed Rick Lavery to fill a vacancy on the Parks and Recreation District Commission for a three-year term. Councilman Vranish made a motion to confirm the appointment, seconded by Davis, with all council members voting in favor.

The next item on the agenda was a motion by Councilman Davis to approve a malt beverage permit to the Evanston Cowboy Days

Committee for September 3rd and 4th from 4:00 p.m. to 1:00 a.m., and September 5th from 12:00 noon to 6:00 p.m. The motion was seconded by Nelson, with all voting in favor.

There had been discussion in the past concerning the sale of water to some of the ranchers in the area and City Attorney Boal had been directed to draw up a resolution for the possible sale. At this particular meeting, rancher Mike Sims was present to represent the ranchers in their request to purchase water from the reservoir. After more discussion concerning the subject Councilwoman Wall introduced the following resolution:

RESOLUTION 94-39
RESOLUTION OF THE CITY OF EVANSTON, WYOMING, AUTHORIZING THE SALE OF UP TO 2,500 ACRE FEET OF WATER FROM THE SULPHUR CREEK RESERVOIR TO UINTA COUNTY IRRIGATORS FOR THE 1994 IRRIGATION SEASON FOR THE SUM OF $5.00 PER ACRE FOOT.

Motion to adopt Resolution 94-39 was made by Nelson and seconded by Hutchinson, but during discussion on the motion, Councilman Davis and Councilman Vranish each made a motion to amend the main motion as follows: *Add a Section 3: No more than 100 feet of water shall be sold to each user and the City shall sell the water on a first come, first serve basis under supervision of the city engineer; plus adding Section 4: As a condition of each sale the City shall require that all water purchased shall be used on real property owned or leased by the purchaser.*
Both amendments passed with all voting in favor, plus the main motion to adopt Resolution 94-39 as amended passed unanimously.

Mr. George Dickerson made a request for the city to provide a bike path along the west side of Yellow Creek Road from the south end of the Twin Ridge Subdivision to the south end of Overthrust Road.

After some discussion Councilman Vranish made a motion for public works to proceed on this request for the bike path, seconded by Wall with all voting in favor.

Later in the meeting under new business, Councilman Davis introduced Resolution 94-37, a resolution giving the City of Evanston the authority to purchase 2 lots of real property with a large industrial building located in the Sunset Industrial Park for the use of the Parks and Recreation District and other city departments if needed.

I don't recall the price of the property, but the question of how the city was going to fund it did come up. However, I was in favor of the purchase and knew that the Recreation District was badly in need of more space. Therefore, the motion to adopt Resolution 94-37 was made by Councilman Nelson, seconded by Hutchinson, with all voting in favor.

The meeting adjourned at 9:00 p.m.

The Uinta County Economic Development Commission (UCEDC) had been working on promoting a company named Allsop, Inc. to locate in Evanston. County Director Ken Klinker and Evanston Community Development Director Paul Knopf had been working very hard to promote industry in Uinta County and Evanston. They both spent a lot of time trying to persuade Allsop to select Uinta County as their new location.

However, on August 4th County Director Klinker sent a memo to me stating the following:

Allsop, Inc., which has been considering a move to Wyoming for quite some time, has apparently decided to pursue a site in Laramie. However, we want to present the enclosed information to them in case the deal falls through in Laramie. We need you to sign the cover letter. Will you please take a look at this proposal and see if it is something you can endorse?

Please let me know what you think. Thanks.

Ken Klinker, Director

The information that Klinker had included in the packet prepared to send to Allsop, Inc. included the two-page cover letter, which I was very anxious to sign, and several pages of plats of various locations available in the Evanston area and drawings of their proposed site.

Klinker had added a Proposal Sheet stating that Uinta County Commissioners and the Evanston City Council had both endorsed their proposed new manufacturing and distribution facility in Evanston and submitted the following proposal:

1. *UCEDC will provide land in the Evanston Industrial Center #3, Lots 1-10, and Lot 1 of the Evanston Industrial Center, a total of 8.973 acres, at a cost of eight thousand dollars ($8,000) per acre. See the attached plat map and site plans.*

2. *A second 10.536 acre site is also available, but the owners have been unwilling to quote a price at this time. They will talk to interested buyers.*

3. *UCEDC will offer $50,000 to subsidize the purchase of either of these properties through September 15, 1994. After that date, we will have to re-evaluate our offer to see if the funds are still available.*

4. *The lots will be properly zoned for Allsop's manufacturing facility.*

5. *All amenities, including city water and sewer, paved roads, natural gas, and electricity will be available at the site boundaries.*

6. *All water and sewer hookup fees will be waived.*

7. *UCEDC will apply, on behalf of Allsop, Inc., for grants from the State of Wyoming to pay for new employee training.*

8. *The City of Evanston agrees to sponsor any applications for loans from state or federal sources necessary to finance construction of the new facility and to pay for relocation costs.*

9. *First National Bank in Evanston agrees to work with Bank One to provide a smooth transition of banking services.*

10. *UCEDC will apply for a grant from the State of Wyoming Local Organization Grant program to pay for a consultant to coordinate the move for Allsop, Inc. This grant is limited to $15,000 from the state.*

11. *Should Allsop, Inc. decide to purchase additional land to accommodate future growth, the City of Evanston agrees to accommodate their zoning needs in accordance with the City of Evanston zoning ordinance.*

12. *UCEDC will introduce Allsop, Inc. to personnel associated with the manufacturing engineering departments at Weber State University and Brigham Young University to help accommodate the need for university interaction and cooperation in the development of new products and manufacturing processes.*

I don't know what more a community could offer and stay within the boundaries of the Wyoming state laws, but although the proposal was approved by resolution by both the City of Evanston the County of Uinta, apparently Allsop, Inc. elected to locate in Laramie where the University of Wyoming is located.

However, although this was a big disappointment for Evanston, Paul Knopf and I continued to work hard with Klinker and UCEDC to attract commerce and industry to the area. I knew that there was no way we could afford to lose the Union Tank Car Company (UTCC).

The next regular city council meeting was held on August 10th with Councilman Vranish absent and another full agenda. Following the initial business to pay the bills and so on, I presented City Treasurer Steve Widmer an Award of Financial Reporting Achievement issued by the Government Finance Officers Association of the United States and Canada. I explained that this award had been given to the City of Evanston for the first time for its excellence in the Comprehensive Annual Financial Report for the fiscal year ending June 30, 1993. I congratulated Steve for his outstanding achievement and thanked him for his excellent work in getting the city financial reports in as required.

As the first item under public participation, Recycling Director Barry Constantine updated the city council on the Recycling Conference that would be held in Evanston on September 13th, 14th and 15th.

I commented how successful the recycling program had become and thanked Barry for his dedication to the program and in getting the Recycling Conference to be held in Evanston, especially because Evanston's recycling program is so relatively new.

Mr. Bill Grey, representing the Evanston Lions Club, suggested the City of Evanston allow a Fish Derby at the Sulphur Creek Reservoir to help raise funds for Cornea Transplant patients. He explained that this would be the first year for the Fish Derby and that the Lions Club hoped to make it annually.

After a short discussion Councilman Nelson made a motion to allow the use of Sulphur Creek Reservoir for a Fish Derby on February 11 and 12, 1995, seconded by Davis, with 6 votes in favor and 1 absent (Vranish).

Parke Ottley, accompanied by a group of citizens, approached the City of Evanston to participate in helping to pay for flood lights at the Evanston High School Football Field. Parke stated that the group would like the city to pay approximately half of the total estimate of $30,000, which would be $15,000.

Following Parke's and the group's explanation and request, Councilman Hutchinson made a motion that the City of Evanston contribute $15,000 towards paying for the lights, contingent upon Uinta County School District No. 1 agreeing to approve the project and their assurance that the district would pay for part of the funding. Motion was seconded by Barnard with 6 votes in favor and 1 vote absent (Vranish).

After several ordinance readings were acted upon, with all passing unanimously, we opened the new business segment of the meeting. Purchasing Agent Mike Lake presented a list of high bids on a number of pieces of used equipment that the city council had previously authorized for sale to the high bidder.

The list of items were old used vehicles, including five police cars, and other old equipment from various departments that were no longer useful to the city and were just taking up space. With Lake's suggestion that we sell this equipment through a bidding process, the council agreed to his suggestion.

After looking at the list and after a short discussion Councilman Hutchinson made a motion to award each item to the high bids as presented, seconded by Davis, with all council members present voting in favor.

Following new business, I presented a letter from Ken Klinker, Director of the Uinta County Economic Development Commission, thanking Evanston's assistant to the Planning Department, DuWayne Jacobsen for his work preparing aerial views and front views of lots available for Allsop, Inc. to set up in Evanston. I also expressed the city's appreciation for the very professional work Jacobsen had done for UCEDC.

Prior to adjourning I called for a work session to be held on August 31st. The meeting adjourned at 9:50 p.m.

The Purple Sage Golf Club was concerned about extending Evanston's 9-hole golf course to make it an 18-hole regulation-size course. It got back to me that the Golf Club was concerned about my thoughts on it and asked to have something from the mayor giving some kind of assurance. So I decided to write a letter to Chris Bauman, who was President of the Club at that time.

My letter stated that I was 100% in favor of the additional 9 holes to be added to the present golf course. By receiving the 265 acres from the Union Pacific Land Resources, whatever acreage is needed for extending the course would be available. I added in the letter that the main reason to acquire the land was to be able to retain the Union Tank Car Company and to create large acreage lots to encourage other industries to locate in Evanston. But I felt that an upgraded 18-hole golf course would also be something that would interest any industry that might consider Evanston for their locale. It was all about economic development for the betterment of our community, and I said as much in my letter to President Chris Bauman of the Golf Club.

Also on August 11th I got a thank you letter from the Uinta County School District's Activities Director Brad Jacobson for the city's support and funds to help make it possible for Evanston High School get lighting for their football field. I read the letter to the city council and made it known that it was great that the city and school district could work together to get things done for the community.

I had also announced in a city council meeting that the 5th Annual Mayor's Golf Tourney was to be held on August 12th at the Purple Sage Golf Course and that brunch would be served after the first nine holes were played, followed by cash awards made up of Evanston Chamber of Commerce "Chamber Bucks" given to the winners after the second nine holes were completed. I told the council that the committee reported that the program would be, once again, a big success.

On August 16th the Primary Election was over. I got the most votes with a total of 1072, Will Davis came in second with 875 votes, and Rick Sather was third with 729 votes. Garland Nelson got 267 votes and Russell Cook got 116 votes. The General Election would be between Will Davis and me.

I was quite happy with the results, but with the way the votes came in I was a long way from a close majority and felt my chances might be 50/50 at the best. I knew I was going to have a lot of problems getting re-elected because of the way the majority of the council was working against me. I try very hard not to knock my opponents. I always try to run on my own record, and although I hate to have to justify my actions, I do the best I can. But no matter what anyone thinks of my actions, I have always been honest and upfront and tried very hard to uphold the Oath of Office.

In the *Uinta County Herald* of August 17th I was interviewed by Hammond-Kunke. He quoted me saying, *"I feel great. I'm not surprised. I thought it would come in pretty close.*

"No, I wasn't surprised that (Sather) did that good. I figured he would get a lot of votes," Ottley said

Ottley said he feels the votes that went to Sather, Nelson and Cook would be split if it follows the same pattern of past Primary and General Elections.

"I look for it to be split pretty evenly. I've got to get out and work at it," Ottley said.

"I congratulate Will for doing as well as he did. I look forward to running a clean campaign against him in the upcoming election," Ottley said.

But, was I ever wrong!

Uinta County Herald, August 19, 1994.

Woman asks where Mayor Ottley was during work day

Dear Editor:

I would like to expand on the letter from Ronald Barnard to Ann Bell in Tuesday's paper. I would like to know where Mayor Ottley was when work day on Yellow Creek Road was held, to paint the fence he held up for months.

Where is Mayor Ottley with the landscaping that was promised for Yellow Creek Road. I hope the voters in the Twin Ridge area remember this come the general elections.

Shar Pullen
of Evanston

Friday, August 26, 1994   UINTA COUNTY HERALD

Mayor Ottley serves people in public relations

Dear Editor:

Now that the primary elections are over, I certainly hope some of the negative letters to you will stop for a while and we can return to some honest evaluation of our incumbent candidates and those running for office.

I take particular exception to the letter written by Shar Pullen asking where Evanston Mayor Dennis Ottley was during the painting of the Yellow Creek Road fence.

Perhaps I can answer that question for her. Perhaps he was attending almost all events at the Uinta County Fair.

Perhaps he was giving a welcome at the recent Wyoming Arts Council meeting.

Perhaps he was attending meetings pertaining to economic development for Evanston or he could have been meeting with members of the Bear Project, Beautification Committee, Chamber of Commerce or organizations to represent the city at their many functions.

I attend my fair share of events in Evanston and have seldom not seen the mayor and his wife, Sandy, in attendance.

I am totally amazed that they can spread themselves so thin for civic responsibilities and still have full-time jobs.

On the other side of the coin, I seldom see several members of the Evanston City Council at events even when they have received special invitations.

Before we throw stones at our dedicated public officials, let's make sure that we are not expressing our views from special interest only; and that we have all the facts.

I, for one, would like to express my appreciation to those public officials who do devote so much of their private life to supporting projects, events, and meetings. You are appreciated.

Denice Wheeler of Evanston.

Uinta County Herald, August 26, 1994

Councilwoman Jerry Wall wasted no time in helping Davis with his campaign. Just after the primary election, Wall organized a work party with the folks of Ward 2, whom she represented, and who resided in the neighborhood parallel to the east side of Yellow Creek Road. The work party was held on Tuesday, August 16th with volunteers from Ward 2 invited to participate. The volunteer group, set up by Wall, was to clean up the sidewalk area on the east side of Yellow Creek Road and repaint the street side of the fence which she had been talking about for several months, and which was badly in need of the work.

When she brought this project up in the meeting, the city council agreed to pay for the paint. As far as I can find, Wall never told us when this work detail was to come off. She may have let the city council members know in one of their secret meetings, but the date or time was never mentioned in any of our regular or special city council meetings, according to the minutes.

In the *Uinta County Herald* of August 19th, a Letter to the Editor was published from a Shar Pullen, one of the volunteers that resided in Ward 2. Her letter was titled: WOMAN ASKS WHERE MAYOR OTTLEY WAS DURING WORK DAY. She stated in her letter, *"I would like to know where Mayor Ottley was when work day on Yellow Creek Road was held, to paint the fence he held up for months."*

In the first place I had nothing to do with the project. This was a private fence and the city had no business even furnishing the paint for it, but we did. We had never helped any other residential group paint their fences. I knew the project was planned, but I had no idea when, and I had not been invited to attend.

However, Denice Wheeler, a long-time resident of Evanston and obviously a good friend to me, responded to Ms Pullen's letter by also writing a Letter to the Editor. Denice's letter was published in the *Herald* edition of August 26th and was titled, MAYOR OTTLEY SERVES PEOPLE IN PUBLIC RELATIONS. Her letter said in part, *"I take particular exception to the letter written by Shar Pullen asking where Evanston Mayor Dennis Ottley was during the painting of the Yellow Creek Road fence...*

Perhaps I can answer that question for her. Perhaps he was attending almost all events at the Uinta County Fair."

Perhaps he was giving a welcome at the recent Wyoming Arts Council meeting."

Denice added in her letter, *"I attend my share of events in Evanston and have seldom not seen the mayor and his wife, Sandy, in attendance...*

"On the other side of the coin, I seldom see several members of the Evanston City Council at events even when they have received special invitations."

Friday, August 26, 1994

UINTA COUNTY HERALD

COMMUNITY

SENIOR NEWS

Raffle tickets for handmade quilt on sale

The Seniors have had a busy time this past week. The last outdoor breakfast of the season was held Saturday morning at the Bear River State Park and more than 60 seniors and guests from Evanston and Bridger Valley enjoyed breakfast of juice, biscuits & gravy, scrambled eggs and hash browns. Delicious!

Everyone enjoys these cookouts so much and we are all dreading the thought that the summer season is about over.

An acknowledgment celebration took place with the unveiling of the new handmade quilt for the annual raffle.

A scrumptious roast beef dinner was served and the dedicated quilters were presented a handmade "quilter's heart" pin and many thanks.

The ladies who worked on the quilt along with the designers Bessie and Evelyn Belle were Maxine Goodwin, Fontella Kunz, Theora Jones, Gen Putnam, Agnes Whittaker and Beth Gerrard.

Saturday Aug. 26 two buses filled with 40 seniors will travel to Pickleville eat dinner and hiss and boo at the performance of the melodrama at the Pickleville Playhouse.

A reminder that the blood draw is scheduled at the Senior Center on Wednesday August 31 beginning at 6 a.m.

Breakfast will be served at the Center at 7 - 10 a.m. the cost is a regular meal donation.

The Center will be closed Labor Day but a celebration is planned with the Evanston seniors at noon on Sept. 2 at Brown Park.

On the menu is BBQ pork ribs and a special treat for all those who participate in the "hat day". Wear a hat which will depict the type of labor or jobs you have done or just a great hat....a surprise!

Menu for Aug. 26 - Sept. 2
Aug. 26 Ham & Swiss on rye/choc. chip cookie
Aug. 29 Hamburger/bun/cantaloupe
Aug. 30 Baked cod/carrot cake
Aug. 31 Baked ham/rice pudding
Sept. 1 Salads/rice pudding
Sept. 2 BBQ Pork/plums

Bessie and Evelyn Belle unveil the handmade quilt for the annual raffle. The two ladies designed the quilt and stitched it together with the help of Maxine Goodwin, Fontella Kunz, Theora Jones, Gen Putnam, Agnes Whittaker and Beth Gerrard.

Evanston Mayor Dennis Ottley purchases the first raffle ticket for the handmade quilt from Agnes Whittaker. Proceeds from the raffle go toward the senior's annual Golden Days Celebration.

Denice proved to be a good friend, although she had run against me for mayor in 1986. As far as I was concerned, she ran one of the cleanest campaigns against me that I had ever been through, and she also would have made a good mayor. Anyway, I really appreciated her taking the time and effort to respond to Pullen's letter.

The second regular city council meeting of the month was held on August 24th and with a full council I declared a quorum and called the meeting to order. Following the initial business I called for a public hearing to consider an application for a Community Development Block Grant from the Wyoming Investment Fund Committee to be used for the expansion of Union Tank Car Company.

City Attorney Dennis Boal was directed to be the hearing officer. Explanations were given by Ken Klinker, Uinta County Coordinator for Economic Development.

After comments and questions from the members of the city council, and with no one in attendance to voice any opposition, Boal closed the hearing.

Councilman Nelson introduced Resolution 94–43 pledging support for and giving authorization to proceed with obtaining a grant from the State of Wyoming Investment Fund Committee, through the Community Development Block Grant Float Loan Program, in the amount of $1,500,000 to be used for a loan to Union Tank Car Company for relocation and expansion of its Rail Car Repair Facility. Motion was made by Councilman Hutchinson to adopt Resolution 94–43, seconded by Nelson, with a unanimous vote in favor.

I was really happy to hear from UTCC's CEO Mr. Ken Fischl that they had definitely decided to stay in Evanston. They did request support and assistance from the City to obtain industrial development loans from the State of Wyoming, and they requested a reasonable agreement on the purchase price of whatever land they required for their plant site. This would be a parcel of land from the 265 acres of property that UPLR donated to the city.

After getting a unanimous vote from the council to support the Tank Company in obtaining loans from the State of Wyoming agencies, I felt much better. We still had a long way to go before the whole deal was finalized, but I felt really good knowing that the city council had finally decided that keeping the tank car company in Evanston was definitely the thing to do.

Also during the August 24th meeting Councilman Davis made a motion for Councilwoman Wall to be the voting delegate and Councilman Nelson to be the alternate delegate at the upcoming National League of Cities Conference, seconded by Hutchinson with all voting in favor.

Prior to adjournment I reminded everyone of the City Picnic on August 25th at Hamblin Park and that there would be a work session at City Hall on September 7th at 5:00 p.m.

The meeting adjourned at 10:00 p.m.

The special city council meeting on September 7th was to act on Resolution 94–48 and any other business that might come up.

Resolution 94–48 was introduced by Councilman Davis authorizing the City of Evanston to present an application to the Wyoming Farm Loan Board for a 50-50 loan in the total amount of $410,800 to be used for site preparation of the real property (75 of the 265 acres that the railroad land company had donated) now owned by the City of Evanston. Councilman Hutchinson moved to adopt Resolution 94–48, seconded by Davis, with 6 votes in favor and 1 absent (Vranish). The motion passed.

❧

The *Uinta County Herald* of September 9th had an article written by Hammond-Kunke stating: *Evanston Mayor Dennis Ottley pushed hard to get passage of the measure.*

"We need to get this [application as stated in Resolution 94-48] sent in before Sept. 21 to open bids. We need to do this groundwork this fall or we may lose out on it," Ottley said.

"It's been a bugger all summer to try and get this squared away. I feel a lot better about it now than I did two weeks ago, but we still have a lot of work to do," Ottley said.

Ottley pointed out that Gov. Mike Sullivan, Secretary of State Kathy Karpan and State Auditor Dave Ferrari support the project.

Ottley said the first initial phase (leveling the 75 acres needed) *of the project is a sacrifice to the city.*

"We need to level that area. The long-term benefits are there. A report the state put out shows the benefits. We need to get going on it. We need to pass the resolution and prepare a packet for the Farm Loan Board," Ottley said. "It's going to be quite a benefit to the future of Evanston."

Evanston Councilman Tom Hutchinson said the initial plan is "put together as well as it can be."

Evanston will only have to put up $260,800 for the project which will employ numerous railroad-type workers. The average pay will be about $9 per hour....

The bids for the excavating work will be voted on at the Sept. 21 meeting. Five bids for the job have been submitted. The lowest bid was from an Orem, Utah company.

Ottley said he hoped the [ground leveling] project could be completed within 30 days after the bid is awarded....

The $10 million building will include a completely new repair shop with cleaning, painting and sandblasting facilities. Ottley said the building could be ready by next summer.

Union Tank Car, located in East Chicago, Ill. is one of the largest tank car manufacturers in the world...

The bids for the land will be voted on at the Sept. 21 Evanston City Council meeting. There is a slight possibility that somebody other than Union Tank Car could bid on the 75 acres of land. However, there is a clause that will allow the city to reject or accept any bid.

⊷≋⊶

Hopefully there would be no other bids because that would just add chaos in trying to get the project completed. Also, the $9.00 per hour average wage wasn't too bad at that time. It was far above what minimum wage was in 1994.

Also during this special meeting, Councilman Nelson made a motion to reschedule the September 14th regular city council meeting to September 21st because of some conflicting issues, seconded by Davis, with 6 votes in favor and 1 absent (Vranish). The meeting adjourned at 8:45 p.m.

The rescheduled first regular city council meeting of the month was held on September 21st. With all council members present and declaring a quorum I called the meeting to order at 7:00 p.m.

During the meeting, under public participation, Councilman Nelson made a motion to accept the resignation of Police Officer Wayne Weston, seconded by Wall, with all voting in favor.

I made a statement and spoke of the city's appreciation to Officer Weston for his dedication to duty while serving on Evanston's Police Department, and wished him well in his future.

I continued by appointing Jane Henderson to the Public Service Advisory Board. Motion was made to confirm the appointment by Councilman Hutchinson, seconded by Davis, with all council members voting in favor.

Former Wyoming State Representative Janice Bodine was in attendance representing, Wyomingites for a Better Economy Today and Tomorrow (WYBETT). She made a presentation and showed a video that described some facts about gambling and how it had affected some surrounding areas.

Her presentation showed both pros and cons on a state or county having legalized gambling in their area. The Gaming Initiatives would be on the ballot during the upcoming General Election on November 8th.

Under New Business, Ordinance 94-22 was sponsored by Councilman Davis and introduced by Councilman Nelson as follows:

ORDINANCE 94-22
AN ORDINANCE OF THE CITY OF EVANSTON, WYOMING AMENDING SECTION 24-17 OF THE EVANSTON CITY CODE TO PLACE LIMITS AND REQUIREMENTS ON THE KEEPING OF DOMESTIC ANIMALS IN THE RURAL RESIDENTIAL AND AGRICULTURAL ZONES.

A number of citizens of the City of Evanston desiring to live within the city limits and keep domestic animals such as horses, ponies, donkeys, mules and llamas were in attendance in favor of the ordinance.

However, a much larger number of citizens residing within the limits of the city were concerned with the problems the keeping of such animals could cause, such as odors, insects, and dust.

Councilman Barnard made the motion to pass Ordinance 94-22 on first reading, seconded by Nelson.

During a lengthy discussion in which several citizens expressed themselves and there was much discussion of the ordinance, it was decided that a work session should be held to discuss this ordinance more and propose of some needed amendments before the second and third readings.

I then ceased any more discussion and called for the vote on the passing of Ordinance 94-22 on first reading. The motion passed with 6 votes in favor and 1 vote against (Vranish).

After a work session and several amendments were approved, the motion passed on the second reading by a vote of 6 votes in favor and 1 absent (Hutchinson).

When the vote came up to pass Ordinance 94-22 as amended on third and final reading during the October 26th regular city council meeting, motion was made by Councilman Barnard and seconded Davis with all voting in favor.

After another lengthy discussion I called for the vote with 1 vote in favor (Barnard), 5 votes against and 1 absent (Hutchinson). The procedure to make Ordinance 94-22 a code of the city failed on third and final reading.

Also under New Business, Councilman Nelson introduced Resolution 94-51 authorizing the City of Evanston to execute a contract for services with the Department of Commerce, Division of Economic and Community Development, to prepare an Industrial Park Development Plan.

This resolution would allow the city to obtain a $25,000 grant to be used to prepare an industrial park plan on the 265 acres of the railroad property that the City of Evanston now owned. The plan would also include the extension of the Purple Sage Golf Course to an eighteen-hole course.

Councilman Hutchinson made the motion to adopt Resolution 94-51, seconded by Davis, but Councilman Davis made a motion to table Resolution 94-51 until September 28th, seconded by Vranish, with all voting in favor.

Although I went along with the motion to table, I couldn't see any purpose for it unless some of the city council members just wanted to slow the project down. However, when Resolution 94-51 came off the table there was some additional discussion, and I thought some of the council members would be adding amendments, but there were none. I ended discussion and called for the vote on the tabled motion with 6 votes in favor and 1 absent (Hutchinson). The motion passed.

The bids came in for the groundwork for the Union Tank Car proposed site with Councilman Nelson making a motion to award the bid to the low bidder, Robinson Construction of Orem, Utah in the amount of $589,600, seconded by Hutchinson with 7 in favor.

Wyoming's State Farm Loan Board had approved the grant and the loan that Evanston had applied for, totaling $410,800 for site development of the property that would be used for the proposed Union Tank Car Company project. This meant that the City of Evanston would have to come up with the difference out of the present budget. The city had budget just over $200,000 for the project.

Also during the September 21st meeting a lengthy discussion was held concerning regulations of gaming establishments and cities, towns and counties preparing their areas by zoning, and other issues.

Councilwoman Jerry Wall had requested permission to read a statement concerning the gaming initiative. This statement is very lengthy so I will try to quote her on some of the more important highlights as follows:

"As the members of this body are aware, the Wyoming Association of Municipalities (WAM) membership stands in opposition to the gaming initiative that will appear on the November ballot...In June the membership of WAM renewed its opposition at the annual business meeting. Five of the seven members of this body were in attendance are well aware of the issues at hand. Following the business meeting, the Executive Board of WAM, of which I am a member, directed the staff to work with the WAM counsel and municipal

attorneys to develop some concrete proposals of ways that city governments can act to mitigate the impact of gaming on their communities, should the initiative be approved by the voters.

"First of all, I want to state that I really don't care if you are philosophically for or against gaming as an industry for the State of Wyoming or for our county...Whether or not widespread gaming becomes law will not be a decision of this body. The choice will be made on November 8 by the voters...Should the initiative be approved on November 8th, the voters of Uinta County will then face a county option election to decide if gaming will be approved in Uinta County...

"The central issue at hand for this Council is: Should the initiative be approved, are we going to have gaming on the terms of the gaming industry or on the terms of the community? Both opponents and proponents of gaming should want the problems handled in a quality manner. In my mind it is the difference between our city leaders being proactive or reactive. If we are proactive, we consider all of the possibilities and formulate a plan of action and solutions—we take an offensive stance. If we are reactive, we sit on our hands and wait to see what happens—then attempt to defend our community...

"First of all, even though the statewide vote will be followed by a county vote, the November 8 decision of the voters has the largest impact on our ability, as a city, to plan for our community. Prior to the general election, municipalities are allowed to legislate regulations regarding gaming establishments... The initiative states in Article 2, item (e)—and I quote—"The governing body of an incorporated city or town may not by ordinance or resolution prohibit the conduct of any gaming activity authorized by the electors under this chapter..."

"It is true that there would probably be a period of several months before any gaming would actually be established, due to the need to appoint and approve a commission, formulate rules and so forth. But, the initiative becomes law effective immediately upon certification of the Secretary of State that it was adopted by the electorate...

"November 8 is a critical date. I cannot stress this point enough. The WAM attorneys and several municipal attorneys feel that this date is so vital that should the initiative pass and should there be a lawsuit, those municipalities who passed ordinances dealing with zoning, parking and so on prior to

the General Election and the preemption will have legal standing and those municipalities who wait until after the General Election and the preemption will not have legal standing. Are you all willing to risk forfeiting the legal right to pass local regulation for this community?

In her statement Councilwoman Wall stated that all this was based on a "worst case scenario," and explained some of the big "ifs" of what might happen if we didn't take her advice. She also said that several polls have shown that the initiative will pass and just one poll indicates it will fail. Most of the polls I have seen and heard of had been the opposite. But her statement continued to read as follows:

"These are many of the reasons for action. What are the dangers of taking action now? You may feel that this will have some political repercussions, that the public will perceive that you are endorsing gaming for Evanston...

"I have great faith in the people of Evanston and believe that, when given the reasons for action, [they] will be supportive. Should they not understand? Well, I would remind you that we are all here to do our best for the community and not just what will help us each politically...WE MUST DO EVERY-THING WE CAN to insure that our community continues to be a good place for families, children and business. WE MUST NOT WAIT to see what happens. That is, excuse the term, too big a gamble for us to take...

"What if we do all of this and the initiative fails? Well, what if? What have we lost? We have lost some evenings we will need in order to accomplish this and we will have subjected ourselves to some very lively public debate. I, personally, am more than willing to give this extra time. As to the debate, no matter how emotional and intense, public debate on any issue is good...

"You are all aware that I have been talking to you about this for more than a year. I have been reluctant to make a motion because I may have some perceived conflicts, due to properties that my husband and I are involved in within the City. But, a motion has not come forth and time is running out...

Therefore, I make a motion that the Evanston City Council proceed with zoning, parking regulation, building and fire code requirements and any other local regulations that we deem necessary to insure the protection of this City should the gaming initiative pass on November 8. These provisions must be adopted in ordinance form prior to that date. This motion includes adoption of the schedule of meetings to accomplish this task. If I can get a second to the motion, I will explain the rationale of the meeting schedule.

Councilwoman Wall's motion was seconded by Councilman Hutchinson. Therefore I opened up the meeting for discussion.

Jerry Wall continued by explaining her schedule of meetings, which the council had no problems with, but there was an enormous amount of discussion of questions and comments from several citizens who were in attendance and from the city council members.

In argument against the motion, I stated that if the gaming initiative is passed by the voters there would still be plenty of time to regulate county option gambling by zoning, parking regulations, and so on. I stated that Councilwoman Wall was wrong in her statement that "the initiative becomes law effective immediately upon certification of the Secretary of State." I continued, "The truth is that Wyoming State Statute 22-24-123 states that, if the initiative, any initiative passes by the voters it does not become law until 90 days after the certification of the election by the Secretary of State. This gives Evanston City Council more than 90 days to get their regulations in order.

"I do not feel that this is the time to put the Planning and Zoning Commission, or the city council through this type of ordeal. If the initiative does not pass, then we have gone through a lot of wasted time and confusion causing a lot of hard feelings for nothing. This will be a real can of worms."

I also reminded them that the County of Uinta also has to go through an election if the initiative passes, giving the municipalities more time to act on any regulations. Although I felt it would be best to wait and I didn't want the citizens to get the idea that the Evanston City Council was endorsing the initiative, I thought the city should stay neutral through the election. However, I stated that I would not oppose the motion knowing that the council would probably vote unanimously in favor.

I then ended discussion and called for the vote on Councilwoman Wall's motion. The vote was, as I expected, unanimous with all 7 votes in favor.

Next, Councilman Barnard made a motion to direct the attorney to prepare a resolution stating that the Evanston City Council go on record as being opposed to the Gambling Initiative based on the W.A.M. conclusions, which would be in the resolution, seconded by Hutchinson. The vote was also unanimous, with all 7 voting in favor of Barnard's motion.

Prior to adjournment I called for a work session to be held on October 5th at 5:00 p.m. and adjourned the meeting at 10:45 p.m.

A day or two after the September 21st meeting City Attorney Dennis Boal put out a memorandum, mainly to Councilwoman Wall, based on her schedule, "Procedural Steps Required for Amending the Zoning Ordinance." The memo read:

There are four procedural steps which need to take place in order to amend the Zoning Ordinance.

1. *The City Council needs to make a request to the Planning and Zoning Commission, specifying the change the Council wants the Commission to consider. The ordinance actually requires someone on behalf of the Council to complete the P & Z form, setting forth the request, and submit it to the secretary of P & Z.*

2. *P & Z then schedules a public hearing and publishes a notice of the hearing 15 days in advance in a newspaper of general circulation.*

3. *P & Z holds a public hearing and based on the hearing submits a report to the Council with its recommendations.*

4. *Any change would have to be enacted through an ordinance passed by the City Council.*

A possible time frame for completing this process is set forth below:

  a. City Council requests P & Z action on September 21, 1994.

  b. Notice of Public Hearing is published in the newspaper on September 27, 1994.

c. *P & Z holds its public hearing and issues its written report on October 13, 14 or 17, 1994. This would have to be a special meeting.*

d. *The City Council would then consider the ordinance on three readings of October 19, 26, and November 2, 1994. The October 19th and November 2nd meetings would have to be special meetings.*

During discussion concerning the Gaming Initiative, I stated that the City of Evanston would still have 90 days after the Secretary of State certified the initiative if Wyoming voted in favor of it. After I made that statement Councilman Davis printed the following in the *Uinta County Herald* issue of September 23rd:

Regardless, Council Member Will Davis argued that the council should use the time it has.

"We're talking about the future of the City of Evanston for the next 100 years," he said. "I don't know if I want to decide that in 90 days."

His remarks were fine. He didn't want to wait and try to push the zoning and other regulations on gambling in 90 days, but he had just voted in favor of a motion that we would be deciding all that (zoning, parking, etc.) within less than 50 days. I guess he was thinking right (according to City Attorney Boal's memo) as the election would be on November 8th.

Also, Councilwoman Wall requested that Boal's memorandum be added to the minutes of the next meeting on September 28th.

⁓◈⁓

During the second regular city council meeting of the month, held on September 28th, I announced that the City of Evanston had received recognition for the community's successful participation in the American Automobile Association's (AAA) 1993 Pedestrian Protection Program. I read the letter of recognition from Triple-A Wyoming and displayed a beautiful plaque that accompanied the letter. I also commended the Police Department and the Public Works Street Department for their involvement in making our streets as safe for pedestrians as possible.

Under New Business, Councilman Davis introduced Resolution 94-52:

RESOLUTION 94-52
RESOLUTION OF THE CITY OF EVANSTON,
WYOMING, INDICATING ITS OPPOSITION TO THE
GAMBLING INITIATIVE WHICH WILL APPEAR ON THE
GENERAL ELECTION BALLOT ON NOVEMBER 8, 1994.

Section 1: *The Governing Body of the City of Evanston hereby opposes Initiative No. 2, legalizing local option gambling, in the form in which it is currently proposed.*

Section 2: *If the Gambling Initiative is passed, the Governing Body of the City of Evanston supports amending it to include the following provisions:*

(a) A municipal option.

(b) A gaming tax of 20% on net income with 75% of the proceeds to be distributed to local governments and the remaining 25% to state government.

Councilman Vranish made a motion to adopt Resolution 94-52, seconded by Davis, with 6 votes in favor and 1 absent (Hutchinson). The motion passed.

In the discussion, I stated that I would just as soon see the Evanston City Council remain neutral on Initiative No. 2, but I would go along with this resolution. I also announced that personally, I was opposed to the gaming initiative after reading a study put out by Robert Goodman, Director of the United States Gambling Study, provided by the Aspen Institute and the Ford Foundation. It was a very thorough study and pointed out many pros and cons concerning gambling.

During the meeting, Councilman Davis introduced Resolution 94-56, and Councilwoman Wall excused herself from the chambers because she felt that she had a conflict of interest.

Resolution 94-56 was to authorize the City of Evanston to execute an agreement with Uinta Engineering and Surveying, Inc., for engineering and surveying services, and management and testing services necessary for the Union Center Industrial Park Project.

Councilman Davis made a motion to adopt Resolution 94-56, seconded by Nelson, with 5 votes in favor, 1 abstaining (Wall) and 1 absent (Hutchinson). The motion passed.

Resolution 94-59, introduced by Councilman Barnard, was a similar resolution to 94-56. It also authorized the City to execute an agreement for the same services with Uinta Engineering and Surveying, Inc. for the Bear River Pathway Project. Motion was made by Councilman Vranish to adopt Resolution 94-59, seconded by Davis, with the same vote. The motion passed.

Councilman Nelson made a motion to authorize the mayor to write a letter of support to Mountain Regional Services concerning financial support from the Wyoming Community Development Authority (WCDA) for a housing loan, seconded by Davis with 3 yes votes (Davis, Nelson and me), 3 no votes (Barnard, Wall and Vranish) and 1 absent (Hutchinson). Motion failed with a tied vote.

I had received a letter from the Western Wyoming Resource Conservation & Development Area requesting that the City of Evanston waive the mileage and fuel costs and provide drivers for two buses for their annual tour of the Western Wyoming RC&D Area.

After a short discussion, Councilwoman Wall made a motion to waive the deposit and mileage required on city-owned buses for the Western Wyoming RC&D Area tour but the city was not to furnish drivers. Motion was seconded by Nelson, with all 6 votes in favor and 1 absent (Hutchinson). The motion passed.

I adjourned the meeting at 8:35 p.m., but first I reminded them that the 8th annual Support Your Community Week was scheduled for October 23rd through 29th and I hoped everyone would take part.

It had been a year ago that a Mr. John H. Harmer had first approached the City of Evanston about re-opening the Oxbow Refinery, located approximately 8 or 10 miles east of Evanston on the old Highway US 30 S. They approached the City of Evanston to extend city services to the site at the city's expense and were turned down by the city council, and they apparently never had the necessary funds to get it started, so it became a dead issue and never got back in operation.

However, just a few weeks before the 1994 General Election two gentlemen from Roosevelt, Utah came to my office to meet with me concerning the re-opening of the refinery. These gentlemen, Don Biggs and Allan Beck, whom I believe were affiliated with Mr. Harmer, talked to me for quite some time to explain that if they could get the federal government to agree to an economic development loan, they could no doubt get the refinery in operation.

During their visit they asked me if I would be willing to meet with Wyoming's Congressional delegation about the idea and get them to agree to support them for the federal funding they needed. If the delegation agreed, they could possibly get the refinery in operation sometime in 1995 or at the latest 1996.

After listening to them I felt that they were very sincere, and very anxious to get moving on the idea. Therefore, because the Republican Party was about to hold their Wyoming RPAC conference in Rock Springs in a few days, and all three Wyoming delegates would be there to speak, I told my Secretary Sharon Constantine to make arrangements for me to attend that conference.

So in a few days I drove to Rock Springs with information that Biggs and Beck had given me to pass on to the delegates. At this time Representative Craig Thomas was running for the Senate seat vacated by Malcolm Wallop.

When I got to the Convention Hall in Rock Springs and after hearing Senators Wallop and Simpson, and Representative Craig Thomas speak, I made arrangements to speak to each of them separately about the information I had given them concerning the refinery. All three treated me like a long lost friend and each assured me that they would support using any federal monies, loan or grant, that might be available for a project such as the refinery. They also told me to tell the refinery group that the sooner they got started, the sooner we could all act in support of it.

When I left Rock Springs, I was feeling pretty good and as soon as I got back to Evanston I got on the phone and explained to Briggs and Beck what occurred and how receptive Wyoming's Congressmen were. I told them that they should get this going immediately be-cause, being election year, there could be some changes.

Although I was out of office, the trip to Rock Springs must have paid off because the Oxbow Refinery re-opened and was operating ear-ly in the year of 1996 under a new name, "Silver Eagle Refinery," put-ting dozens of folks back to work. Mr. Don Biggs moved to Evanston and was the General Manager of the refinery for the next several years.

Most of the citizens of Evanston never knew the part I had taken to support the re-opening of the refinery. I didn't stop with Wyo-ming's Congressional delegates, I also made a few visits to Cheyenne to visit with Governor Mike Sullivan and other state officials, asking for their support and keeping them informed of where we were as far as getting the refinery back in operation. I contacted any official that I thought could help Evanston get the refinery going.

⁂

The *Uinta County Herald* of October 4th published an article written by the *Herald's* news editor George Hammond-Kunke, titled MAY-OR SAYS GAMBLING QUICK FIX. Mr. Hammond-Kunke had interviewed me prior to the article, which read as follows:

Four-time [sic.; I was only elected three times] Evanston Mayor Dennis Ottley is in opposition to the passage of casino gambling but if it is passed, he said he will work hard to see that it is put in effect fairly and that it is properly zoned.

"I'd rather see Evanston be an industrial town than a town with bars and casinos. When people talk about jobs for their kids, they don't mention being a card dealer in a casino," Ottley said.

"I've always been opposed to casino types of gambling. The reason I'm op-posed to it is because of how it affects the quality of life. It's not a good economic development move. It's just like a quick fix. It'll help the economy for a couple of years, but that's all. Some people will make some big bucks on a temporary basis, but a lot of other people will be hurt," Ottley said.

It might create a lot of tax dollars, but not enough to offset the increase in the amount of social services that will be more heavily needed and the domestic problems that will arise," Ottley said...

Most of the jobs are going to be lower-paying jobs, which will cause an increase to our social services," Ottley said. "We had a lot of domestic problems during the boom. Casino gambling will create a lot of temporary housing. Do we want people here who are on the move a lot? People may take offense to that, but it's a fact. It takes away from your quality of life.

"It seems like one vice follows another. If it's legalized, people will say that it's not a vice, but to me, it's still a vice. The worst types of elements will come to Evanston...

"The way we're doing it now is the best way to help the economy. Right now, Evanston is sitting probably as good as any town in the State of Wyoming," Ottley said.

The unemployment rate in Uinta County is just 5.9 percent, compared to what it was in Jan. of 1993, when it was at 8.6...

"We're on the right move. The economy is on the upswing. ESAM [a manufacturing company] just moved in here last spring, and Union Tank Car is on the move to hire people for next spring. When new businesses look at Evanston, they look at it for the quality of life," Ottley said...

"Our fiscal budget is in good shape because we've been fiscally responsible. The city's budget is in better shape and is more solvent than it has ever been," Ottley said... "People come to Evanston because we have a good educational program, recreation, and a lot of volunteerism," Ottley said.

"Personally, I don't think we need to start worrying about zoning the city this early. We've got plenty of time to do that," Ottley said...

"I don't want to see the downtown become a casino business. We've done a lot of good things with the downtown. We built a nice post office. We've done a lot of work with Depot Square...Casinos would take away from all of that effort," Ottley said.

Ottley has visited the cities of Wendover, Wells and Elko, Nev., in an effort to research the casino-ridden towns. He said the downtown areas in those three cities are "almost completely closed up. I just don't like what I've seen in those cities. I don't want to see that happen to Evanston.

"If you approve of gambling, you're prostituting your town. I'm definitely against Initiative No. 2 because it's so vague. It doesn't give the cities and towns much leeway...

"*I think most of the people of Evanston don't want gambling. But a lot could happen between now and the election,*" Ottley said, as the article concluded.

During the October 12th meeting and after all other business was acted on, prior to adjournment Councilman Barnard made a motion to authorize the mayor to write a letter to Wyoming's Partners for Parks, which is a statewide alliance, formed on behalf of Wyoming's state parks and historic sites. The City of Evanston had just recently become a member of the partnership alliance. The motion to write the letter was in support of putting Elk at Bear River State Park. Motion was seconded by Nelson, with 6 votes in favor and 1 absent (Hutchinson).

Evanston man calls Mayor, Weston hypocrites for gambling stance

Dear Editor:

When I read your paper today, October fourth edition, I could not believe my eyes. The first article was a letter to the editor from Herb Weston. I want to get this straight. Herb has the audacity to say he is against gambling.

He is the biggest current benefactor of gambling in the state. If gambling came he has the potential of being one of the biggest. He houses off track betting at the Weston Budget Inn and accepts lease money from the off track betting parlor. He sells rooms to gamblers from the Downs and takes their money in his two cafes and bars in Evanston. I will bet he is against selling alcohol too but I doubt if he would be willing to turn away that money either. Horse racing is the most addictive form of gambling. Herb, how much have you been offered on options on your properties if gambling comes to Evanston?

If the people buy his insistence that he is against gambling he must figure they are awful gullible or in the market for the Golden Gate Bridge. Herb, you can't have it both ways. You must be holding back the laughter when you tell people you are against gambling.

The other article that amazed me was the one where Dennis Ottley is so adamant against gambling. In his real estate business he has been accepting gambling options on property listed by his company.

Like Mr. Weston, Mayor Ottley's real estate business would boom if gaming were to come. He has been a big fan of the Downs. I see several pieces of property listed by ERA which is owned by Dennis Ottley. Dennis are you trying to tell us that you would not be a benefactor if gambling came to Evanston either directly by your listings or indirectly by the increase in market prices that gambling would bring? You have a conflict of interest if you sit in on the gambling proceedings because of the property you have listed. No wonder you are against having it downtown. Most of the commercial property you have listed is on the west end of town.

How can you make a rational decision if on one hand you will vote on zoning and on the other you sell what you zone?

Denny, if you believe that everything in Evanston is coming up roses you must not read the Casper paper where Uinta County has the highest unemployment in the state. Every summer the unemployment rate dips. Comparing January's rate to July's rate when the seasonal tourist economy is at its height is ludicrous. The reason people are moving to Evanston is to take advantage of the low wages, the more generous welfare benefits, and to retire because it is so much cheaper to live here.

More than half of the record number of kids attending schools qualify for free lunches and breakfasts. You need to call Rod Cable at the human resources building to understand that nearly one in three people in Uinta County receives government assistance to survive in Evanston.

Your $30,000 mayor salary plus what you make at your real estate firm must have blinded you to the suffering of others. You must not have walked the streets in downtown Evanston to see that we have a number of vacant buildings when you tout the ESAM jobs as good paying jobs. Gaming's lowest paying jobs are higher than the best jobs at ESAM.

Denny, how can you talk about downtown and property owners. You don't own any property in Evanston and have no idea how hard it is to own business property in Evanston. If you think that having 5,000 tourists a day in Evanston who gamble would not help business you're not thinking right.

The town of Deadwood had $5 million dollars in unanticipated gambling revenues the first year and did not have two million people living a hundred miles away on the Wasatch Front. I am sure you could find a way of spending that kind of money if you are mayor when gambling comes. Come on Denny and Herb, you cannot be that gullible or hypocritical to believe people will believe the information you're putting out.

Are either of you willing to turn back what you have already earned, give up what you are currently making, or forfeit what you have the potential of making in the future if gambling were to come to Evanston?

Donald B. Cook
of Evanston

Uinta County Herald, October 7, 1994.

I don't know if the letter had anything to do with the Wyoming Parks Commission's decision to house two bull elk at the Bear River State Park or not, but we did end up getting the elk.

I also displayed a Certificate of Achievement for Excellence in Financial Reporting plaque to the council, and thanked City Treasure Steve Widmer and his staff for the fine work they did in once again receiving such a great honor.

I once again reminded everyone of *Support Your Community Week* on October 23rd through the 29th and adjourned the meeting at 9:42 p.m.

⤜⤜⤜

October was getting hot and heavy with a lot of controversy throughout the City of Evanston because of Gambling Initiative No. 2 and Ordinance 94-26 and the city council's efforts in trying to cause me to lose the election, but I wasn't concerned about the election; I was only concerned with the future of Evanston and its economy. October, 1994 was probably, by far, my worst month ever, during the three terms I served Evanston as their mayor.

To make it worse, the *Uinta County Herald's* news editor George Hammond-Kunke wrote an article in the *Herald's* October 14th edition with the headline: CONTAMINATED SOIL THREATENS TO DERAIL UNION TANK CAR'S EXPANSION PLANS.

The article started: *The City of Evanston may have hit a major hurdle in its attempt to consummate a deal with Union Tank Car Company of Chicago. The company has put on hold a proposed deal after the discovery that the Evanston property is contaminated.*

In a letter to City Attorney Dennis Boal from Holland & Hart, Attorneys at Law from Cheyenne, Lawrence J. Wolfe wrote: "The preliminary results indicate significant soil contamination at levels well in excess of DEQ (Department of Environmental Quality) standards, as measured by total petroleum hydrocarbons. The groundwater results show high concentrations of several priority pollutants.

"We urge the city to immediately review this information and consult with appropriate environmental specialists. In light of the soil's contamination, we

would urge the city to consider shutting down further work on the site while the city analyzes the testing information, reviews its contractual obligations with Robinson Construction, and develops plans to address the environmental issues. It is probably in the interests of both the city and the contractor to avoid any actions that may cause a release of contaminants into the water, land or air. Once the city has received the testing information, it may have obligations to notify the appropriate state and federal environmental agencies."

This was the letter I spoke of that I held back from the council for a day earlier in the year, because I was afraid the majority of the council would back off on the deal with UTCC.

The *Herald* article continued: *Evanston City Engineer Brian Honey said REI consultants [environmental inspectors] were testing for volatile organic compounds, or heavy metals. But the tests were considered "preliminary and unsubstantial," according to REI spokesman Mike Caldwell.*

However, Evanston Mayor Dennis Ottley remains optimistic that the deal will not fall through.

"I want to make it clear that they [UTCC] still think they'll be able to go through with it at this point. We have not stopped the construction at this time. As far as we know, they're still very interested," Ottley said. "It's not dead by a long shot. We may have to do more cleaning up," Ottley said on Wednesday. "We're going to go ahead with leveling the property anyway.

"This is another one of those bridges we have to cross. Every time I turn around, something else comes up," Ottley said.

William Sinkler, safety director for Union Tank Car Company said: "I'm sure the company won't back out. We have a vested interest in Evanston."

Director of Communications for Union Tank Car in Chicago, William Durack said: "I have not been closely associated with all of this, but I'm sure we're still interested."

The public relations department for the firm in Chicago then said any statements to the press should be channeled through Mayor Ottley's office...

The groundbreaking ceremony was canceled last week. The study is sched-uled to be done early next week, possibly Monday, the *Herald* article con-cluded.

This article came out several weeks before Evanston received the letter in question, but one or more of the five council members that were doing underhanded things to affect my re-election, had given the letter to the *Herald* just to stir up more problems for me. Actually, it was old news and the area was in the process of getting cleaned up and leveled because the contamination, such as it was, was being taken care of.

During a special meeting on October 19th Ordinance 94-26 was sponsored by Councilwoman Wall and introduced by Councilman Nelson as follows:

ORDINANCE 94-26
AN ORDINANCE OF THE CITY OF EVANSTON, WY-
OMING AMENDING SECTIONS 24-14, 25-15 (b), 24-16
(b), 24-42 (b), 24-44 AND 24-105 OF THE ZONING ORDI-
NANCE OF CHAPTER 24 OF THE EVANSTON CITY CODE
TO PROVIDE FOR THE ZONING AND REGULATION OF
GAMING ESTABLISHMENTS.

City Attorney Dennis Boal explained the new ordinance, which was quite lengthy, and the council chambers were well attended with scores of citizens, some pro, some con.

As I said to start with, *We'll be opening up a real can of worms.* And I sure in hell was right on, because it didn't seem that we could make anyone happy through the lengthy discussions.

During this first reading there were suggestions to amend the ordinance before second reading. The biggest concern was to add a 1,000-foot requirement from churches, schools and other public properties. Councilman Davis made a motion to pass Ordinance 94-26 on first reading, seconded by Barnard. But Councilman Hutchinson made a motion to amend Ordinance 94-26 by a adding *"and 1,000 feet from all public districts,"* seconded by Wall. The vote on the amendment was 1 vote in favor (Hutchinson), 5 votes against (Wall, Nelson, Davis, Barnard and me) and 1 absent (Vranish). The motion to amend failed.

I called for the vote on the main motion made by Davis with the motion passing by 6 votes in favor and 1 absent (Vranish).

But City Planner Paul Knopf was still directed to prepare a 500-foot and a 1,000-foot overlay relating to public districts for the next city council meeting.

The next city council meeting was held on October 26th, and Ordinance 94-26 came up for second reading. Again the chambers were full with folks concerned with the ordinance regulating gambling, and again, some were pro and some were con. The biggest concern appeared to be the distance gambling establishments should be from public properties and approval of gambling in the downtown district.

Motion was made by Councilwoman Wall to pass Ordinance 94-26 on second reading, seconded by Barnard, with a lengthy discussion following.

Councilman Vranish made a motion to amend the ordinance to allow gaming from 9th Street to Harrison Drive (11th Street) on Front Street. The motion failed because of a lack of a second.

Councilwoman Wall made an amendment to the ordinance to allow the overlay, prepared by City Planner Knopf. The overlay added the 1,000-foot distance requirement from public properties in the Highway Business-Established (HB-E) zones only, seconded by Nelson, with 6 voting in favor and 1 absent (Hutchinson). The motion to amend passed.

Councilman Vranish made a motion to amend the ordinance to change the zoning map to include an area east of Overthrust Drive on the south side of Cheyenne Drive, but again his motion failed with 1 vote in favor (Vranish), 5 votes against and 1 absent (Hutchinson).

Councilman Davis made a motion to amend Ordinance 94-26 to state, *"a state permit is to be granted before a conditional use permit is to be granted,"* seconded by Wall. The motion passed with 4 votes in favor, 2 votes against (Vranish and me) and 1 absent (Hutchinson).

After I ceased discussion and called for the vote to pass Ordinance 94-26 on second reading as amended, the motion passed by 5 yes votes, 1 no vote (Vranish) and 1 absent (Hutchinson). During a special city council meeting on November 2nd, Ordinance 94-26 came up for third and final reading, again with a full house of concerned citizens.

Motion was made by Councilman Vranish to pass Ordinance 94-26 on third and final reading as amended, seconded by Nelson.

I opened up the floor for discussion. A lengthy discussion, like the other two meetings, went on with basically the same people. Everyone who wanted to have their say was given the opportunity to do so.

After hearing many comments, pro and con, from the public and council (basically the same comments that we had heard in the two previous meetings), Councilman Hutchinson made a motion to change much of the wording in the ordinance, seconded by Davis. This amendment passed with 6 votes in favor and 1 absent (Wall).

The vote on the main motion to pass Ordinance 94-26 on third and final reading as amended passed with 6 votes in favor and 1 absent (Wall).

After the passage of the ordinance a lot of folks left very unhappy, but some were also very happy. It's impossible to satisfy everyone on any ordinance, but boy, was I ever glad it was over. However, I still felt that it was unnecessary to go through this mess before election, because I didn't feel that the Gambling Initiative would pass. I felt that the folks in the State of Wyoming were way too conservative to pass such an initiative.

⤜⤛

Initiative No. 1 would also be on the ballot. This was an initiative to continue the assessment of 1 mill for the Lifelong Learning Center (presently Uinta BOCES #1 Education Center). This initiative was getting a lot of attention, but most were in favor of the initiative. I didn't believe there was any doubt that Initiative No. 1 would pass. I personally was in favor of it.

Lifelong Learning Center was a real asset to Uinta County. It gave the folks in Evanston and Uinta County the opportunity to gain credits in different occupations. The credits were provided by some of the area universities and colleges. It was a great benefit to those who wanted to better their education, and it gave them the opportunity to improve themselves in many ways.

I hoped that Initiative No. 1 passed.

⁓

The second regular city council meeting of the month was held during Support Your Community Week, and during the meeting we invited all winners of the "Why I Love Evanston" Essay Contest. I first introduced the teacher for each grade and had them call on their students to read their essays. There were approximately 63 students from kindergarten through the eighth grade of the six schools participating. Those present were the 1st, 2nd and 3rd place winners.

After the winners were called on to read their essay, City Planner Paul Knopf and Chamber of Commerce Director presented each participant with a certificate, and a ceramic cup to the 1st place winners.

In addition I followed up by presenting each participant with a "Fresh Air, Freedom and Fun" lapel pin and thanked all the students for their participation. As always, most of the essays were great.

After the essays were read, Evanston High School Cheerleaders Pania Tolman, Amy Horton, Melissa Williams, Kimber West and Jeni George gave several minutes of Evanston cheers before we opened up the meeting for business. First I thanked everyone who participated in Support Your Community Week and extended the city's appreciation for their part in helping the program once again be a big success.

I called for a five minute recess to give those leaving a chance to clear the chambers before re-opening the meeting for business.

During the same meeting I made some appointments to the City Beautification Committee. Kelli Furness, Pat Hadley and Jack Mathson had been recommended by the Urban Renewal Agency. Councilman Nelson made a motion to confirm the appointments, seconded by Davis, with 6 votes in favor and 1 absent (Hutchinson). The motion passed.

Recycling Coordinator Barry Constantine gave a comprehensive report on the recent State Recycling Convention recently held in Evanston. Barry stated that there were approximately 125 participants and only positive comments were received about Evanston's Recycling Center. He received an award and plaque from the state committee naming him as "Recycler of the Year." He displayed the award for everyone to see.

On behalf of the city, I congratulated him for receiving such a grand award and told him how proud we all were of him. I thanked him for his efforts in bringing the Recycling Convention to Evanston and his report that the convention was a big success. I also extended the city's appreciation to Barry for his good work in making the recycling program successful.

During this meeting, during the discussion on the second reading of Ordinance 94-26, Mr. Gale Curtis of the Evanston Historic Preservation Commission read the following statement for the record:

"The members and staff of the Evanston Historic Preservation Commission would like to commend the City Planning and Zoning Commission and the Community Development Department submitting the proposed zoning recommendations which would prohibit gaming in the Evanston Downtown Historic District. By vote of a quorum, the commission would like to enter this statement for the public record as being in full support of these recommendations. We would like to take this opportunity to remind the Mayor, the City Council and the community that Evanston's downtown area holds a distinct, significant honor of being listed on the National Register of Historic Places. The district represents not only Evanston's heritage, but in a much greater sense, it represents the heritage of main-street, small town America.

Many other small communities who have adopted gaming in their overall economic strategies have noted that gaming can result in significant impacts to the community. In some of these communities, important historic buildings and structures have been removed or altered to the point that the historic significance of the structure is diminished or even destroyed. Because of this issue, we would like to take advantage of this public forum to express our appreciation to the Planning and Zoning Commission and the Community Development Department for their insight and wisdom in helping to guard the public welfare against this type of loss. The commission feels that failure to promote a sense of community or sense of place will result in the great-

est loss of all. Evidently, the Planning and Zoning Commission shares the same concern because it has listed as item number four of the "Other Issues" page "Maintaining the City's sense of place within the region" as one of its considerations.

Each of us in this room should take a moment to remember that these are our memories we are talking about. It's <u>our</u> history. And, because of that, it's worth saving."

I thanked Mr. Curtis for his statement and assured him that I totally agree, and indicated that the city council members and a large majority of Evanston's citizenship also agree with him.

Prior to adjournment I thanked everyone for their good work during Support Your Community Week and reminded everyone of the General Election on November 8th. The meeting adjourned at 10:27 p.m.

During the Support Your Community Week banquet held on Friday, October 27th at the Legal Tender Restaurant, we had arranged the room with table and chairs for folks to eat and visit and set a head table at the top of the room reserved for Evanston City Council members and their spouses and representatives of the Evanston Chamber of Commerce. However, Councilman Tom Hutchinson and his wife LeAnn were the only ones that sat at the head table with Sandy and me, and members of the Chamber of Commerce. The other city council members and their spouses that attended sat at a table in the rear of the room quite some distance from the head table. At first I personally was embarrassed, but later on in the evening I was more embarrassed for those council members and thought what a childish thing to do. And they had all along tried to tell me that they always represented the citizens of Evanston. But it sure appeared to me, at that time, that it was much more important to them to show their disrespect towards me than it was to show their respect to those long-time city citizens, the volunteers that were being honored for their outstanding civic work in helping to make Evanston a better community to live in.

Those council members and their guests kept talking during the program, mostly whispering, but sometimes snickering and giggling like a bunch of kids, intentionally trying to disturb the program. I wanted to say something to them about their manners, but I didn't want to make an issue of it and hoped the folks present would just ignore them, and they did.

That evening we honored Dora and Clarence Bateman, Kilburn Porter and Ruthe Spencer. These folks had all been nominated by the public and had all been instrumental in making Evanston programs successful. Their involvement was tremendous and outstanding. The awards were presented by me and the Chamber. It was a real honor to be involved in presenting the awards to some of the city's most outstanding citizens for their patriotism, their volunteerism and for their love of community.

In my comments I thanked the Evanston Chamber of Commerce for their co-sponsorship in making Support Your Community Week once again a successful program and that I hope to see it continue on for many years. It's a program that brings folks together, and that is very important to our economy and welfare.

Also during that special week we held the 4th Annual Mayor's Prayer Breakfast on the morning of October 25th with the Honorable Tom Mealey, Uinta County Court Judge, giving the Mayor's Prayer Breakfast Message. His message was based on "Fellowship," and America's four freedoms: "Freedom of Speech," "Freedom of Religion," Freedom from Want," and "Freedom from Fear." A great message!

With approximately 100 in attendance, I felt the prayer breakfast was once again a big success. But the fact that most of the city council members did not attend was no surprise to me because I knew it didn't fit their agenda. However, I was a bit disappointed because I felt they owed it to those in attendance to be there no matter how they felt about me. Also they needed the message on "Fellowship."

Mayor's Prayer Breakfast

The honorable Uinta County Judge Thomas Mealey addresses a crowd of about 100 people during the Mayor's Prayer Breakfast Tuesday morning at Lotty's. The 4th Annual Prayer Breakfast was part of the "Support Your Community Week" activities. Judge Mealey addressed the audience on America's four freedoms: Freedom of Speech, Freedom of Religion, Freedom from Want, and Freedom from Fear.

Uinta County Herald, October 18, 1994.

During the special city council meeting of November 2nd, and after the third and final reading of Ordinance 94–26 (the gaming ordinance which was passed), Urban Renewal Director Jim Davis gave a short report on the agency's activities which would be featured in a monthly magazine called *Preservation Wyoming*. He also reported that the dig at the Old China Town site had been successful and they had found dozens of artifacts that would be on display in the Chinese Joss House at Depot Square. He also gave a good report on Tracks Across Wyoming and how successful it had become.

⨎⨎⨎

A few weeks before the election an admirer of mine sent me a letter wishing me luck in the upcoming election. With that letter was an old quote that stated the following:

"YOU HAVE BECOME A TRULY PUBLIC PERSON, SO YOU WILL BE ATTACKED, MALIGNED AND SLANDERED, IN YOUR PROFESSIONAL LIFE, AND IN YOUR PERSONAL LIFE AS WELL. NEVER REPLY TO YOUR CRITICS!!! NEVER EXPLAIN, NO MATTER WHAT YOU'VE SAID OR DONE!!!!! IF YOU ATTEMPT TO DEFEND YOURSELF, YOU WILL KEEP ALIVE A CONTROVERSY. AS THE FRENCH SAY, SPEECH IS SILVER, BUT SILENCE IS GOLDEN!!!!!!!!

PRIME MINISTER GLADSTONE

ENGLAND

1880-1885 & 1892-1894

I don't know if that quotation was the way to go or not, but in my 1982 election against Gene Martin, which was also a tough election, I never did defend myself. I got cussed out by some of my constituents for not defending myself and I still got beat, so I thought I ought to defend myself, to a point, during this election, because there were so many lies, innuendos and underhanded tactics thrown against me by city council members.

⨎⨎⨎

For several meetings Councilwoman Wall and other council members had wanted the Evanston City Council to go on record as being in support of the gambling Initiative No. 2, but I had pleaded with them to stay neutral on the issue, although they did adopt Resolution 94–52 during the September 28th meeting in opposition to the gaming initiative. Why? I don't know.

During this period I was put through a lot of hell and the council members were having their secret meetings working on their agenda to get me out of office. It seemed like the only council member that was with me was Tom Hutchinson, but Wall, Davis, Vranish, Nelson and Barnard were all in favor of the City of Evanston endorsing the Initiative No. 2.

LETTERS TO THE EDITOR

Woman says 'it's time for citizens to reclaim Mayor's seat'

Dear Editor:

Yes, it is election time. It seemed to get an early start at city hall this year. The budget process was very curious. The mayor concealed and then strong-armed his version of a budget he described as "very good." The truth is, the city of Evanston overspent its annual revenues to the tune of $1.3 million last year under Mayor Ottley's watchful eyes. The mayor dipped into our dwindling city savings to cover the shortfall.

The mayor has been feuding with the city council on just about every issue since the great budget debate. He's privately running the Union Tank Car show (which taxpayers are now obligated to sup-port to the tune of $1.1 million). He's publicly opposed the Council on zoning for gaming (which might be our only control over gaming if it passes). He's claimed credit for the ESAM jobs (which seems odd because our full-time Mayor/Realtor almost killed the ESAM deal when he found out they didn't want to buy property from him).

It's so bad that 5 out of 6 city council members are openly supporting the mayor's opponent hoping to prevent a 5th term for Evanston's "strong man."

All 6 members of the council have privately stated that "it's time for a change in the mayor's office." There's got to be a reason for 6 out of 6 people working so close to the mayor's office to appeal to voters for a change.

During the primaries, Mayor Ottley tactlessly referred to Will Davis as "the guy who wants to take my office." That statement is quite revealing. Guess what Mayor Ottley, it's not YOUR office and Evanston is not YOUR city. It's OUR CITY and OUR MAYOR'S OFFICE. You seem to have forgotten who you represent and who pays your $30,000 salary.

We're tired of the dictatorship. We're tired of you shutting out our city council representatives. We're tired of your secrecy with information that should be public. We're tired of conflicting real estate dealings. We're tired of your threats against city employees and depart-ment heads and your questioning of their loyalty when they do anything which might hinder your re-election campaign. We're tired of your re-election media blitz being funded with our tax dollars, including the "free" tickets you hand out purchased with our tax dollars.

If you think I'm exaggerating the problem, give your city councilman a call. Ask any one of them how the mayor is running the city. It will be enlightening. We want OUR city back, and we can reclaim it on November 8th. It truly is time for a change.

Marion Comstock
of Evanston

See Letters on page A5

Uinta County Herald, October 18, 1994.

UINTA COUNTY HERALD   Friday, October 21, 1994

OPINION

Councilman: Evanston has crisis in leadership

As city council members, we should be in a position of providing information to the public rather than learning about city business from the newspaper. But none of us on the council could answer questions about "significant" contamination problems on the Union Tank Car project when reporters asked last Thursday. In fact, if it hadn't been for an anonymous tip and a good job of investigation by the Herald, we probably still wouldn't know about the Union Tank Car letter. "Ottley-Gate" broke it wide open.

Mayor Ottley had a copy of the Union Tank Car letter on Wednesday before the council meeting. He decided to hide the information from the Council at the very time we were deciding whether to make a $205,000 commitment to the project. Well, this time he got caught.

All of us on the council are fed up with the mayor's tyranny at city hall. You have seven elected officials to run your city — one mayor and six city council members. Unfortunately, the mayor does all he can to make it a one-man show. He excludes the council from important city business and meetings. He screens correspondence and hides information from your city council members or delays access to that information. He decides for us how much we should or shouldn't know and when we should know it.

You need to realize that Mayor Ottley has been doing everything he can to restrict information to your city council members. That makes your council members mad, but more importantly, it dilutes your representation as citizens of Evanston.

Fortunately (or unfortunately) I'm the only council member who has the luxury of speaking out publicly without reprisal because I'm a lame duck in Council. Please spend some time talking to your own city council representatives privately. This has gone on long enough and the public has got to know about it so it can be stopped this election. The Union Tank Car letter is just one example, but it is a clear example. Consider the specific events and draw your own conclusion:

October 5, around noon: A public groundbreaking ceremony involving Governor Sullivan, Mayor Ottley, and Union Tank Car is hurriedly arranged. Mayor Ottley rushes out invitations to local dignitaries. The mayor frantically arranges a last minute newspaper ad. No one but the mayor knows anything about the groundbreaking event, but it's shaping up to be a great campaign headline.

October 5, around 4 p.m.: Within hours, the groundbreaking event is canceled. The newspaper ad is canceled, but invitations have already been mailed out.

October 6: Union Tank Car hires REI consultants to conduct environmental tests on the proposed site of the railcar repair facility.

October 11, afternoon: Union Tank Car receives preliminary results indicating "significant" contamination problems. Mayor Ottley is notified by phone.

October 12, 10:29 a.m.: Union Tank Car sends a fax letter to the city attorney. The letter states "preliminary results indicate significant soil contamination at levels well in excess of DEQ standards" and that "groundwater results show high concentrations of several priority pollutants."

October 12, noon: A copy of the faxed letter is delivered to Mayor Ottley.

October 12, 7 p.m.: City Council meets. Mayor Ottley chooses to keep the Union Tank Car letter a secret. Not one member of the council is informed of the contamination problems. With no knowledge of the letter, City Council approves participation on the project which commits the city to repayment of a $205,000 loan.

October 13, 1 p.m.: Evanston's own "deep throat" drops an anonymous tip to the Uinta County Herald. Investigative reporters press for answers on the Union Tank Car project. The story breaks wide open. With the heat on, Mayor Ottley finally makes copies of the Union Tank Car letter available to the City Council and to the Herald.

I know that the mayor will be very upset about my speaking out about the Union Tank Car fiasco, but... the real issue is not one of politics. The real issue is one of integrity and leadership. The mayor fell short on both counts when he did not share the information with the Council.

Ron Barnard
Evanston City Councilman

UINTA COUNTY HERALD

Friday, October 21, 1994

LETTERS TO THE EDITOR

Woman defends mayor, asks for truth in campaign

Dear Editor:

I am writing this letter to the people of Evanston to set a couple of things straight on the editorials written by Donald Cook and Marion Comstock. I will only comment on the things that I am certain about so be assured that the information in this letter will be true fact and not second-hand gossip.

1. REAL ESTATE/GAMBLING

To give you a brief description of a real estate transaction, when you make an offer to purchase a piece of property with your chosen real estate agent, you are required to put down earnest money.

The listing office holds this earnest money until the sale is or is not completed. Referring to Donald Cook's letter, Dennis Ottley does have listed several commercial buildings/lots in which gambling prospects may be interested. As a realtor, he has a duty to his seller to do his part in selling the sellers property. Dennis has taken earnest money on property from other real estate companies here in Evanston that have been working with gambling prospects, but he has not been involved with the buyers that are wanting to purchase property for the purpose of gambling.

At this time, Dennis is not even holding any earnest money for gambling investors. This is not hypocritical behavior as previously stated.

2. COUNCIL MEETINGS ETC.

I do know that the council members have to approve all budgets, ordinances, city laws, city policies etc., and especially where and how much money is spent on which projects.

The mayor, as Chief Executive of the City of Evanston, has only one vote in these council meetings and the other 6 council members cast their votes also. The mayor cannot override the majority vote or spend money if it's not approved by other members. Since I am not on the council (and neither is Ms. Comstock) I will just throw this out to Evanston for thought: Could it be that Mayor Ottley has not been given a fair shake on this 1.3 million dollars spent? I'll bet this money was spent wisely to the benefit of the Evanston community and certainly with the approval of the council. Think of all the good things that happened this year such as the Joss House, Bear River State Park and all the road work, a lot has been going on. These things don't just happen.

Let's be positive about this campaign and not resort to repeating things we're not certain about that have come second-hand. Let's hear the truth! I'm sure that's what you would get if you asked Mayor Ottley about anything that has to do with the City of Evanston.

Traci Gomez
of Evanston

Tuesday, October 25, 1994

UINTA COUNTY HERALD

OPINION

Woman responds to Barnard letter, says councilman should have spoken up sooner

Dear Editor:

I usually try to stay out of politics, because as someone who chooses not to run for office, I can't understand why people will set themselves up for ridicule every time an election rolls around. It seems to me, that in an election year, if folks can't really find a fire, all they can do is try to blow enough smoke to make people believe there is one. With that in mind, I wanted to respond to Ron Barnard, and address a few points he made in last week's editorial.

First, let me mention what was referred to as "Ottley-gate." (Nice touch, Ron. That will appeal to the emotionalism of the reader!) Ron, you related a series of events that were pieces of a very interesting story. Not the whole story, but obviously some interesting tidbits. Let me tell you how I think "the truth" works. If two observers see a man running down the street, observer one might believe the man is running away from something. Observer two might think the man is late for something. If you ask the man who's running, you might find that he just plain loves to run! Now, Ron, if people want to know why a man does something, they can certainly ask the observers. But I think I would start by asking the man himself. That is, if I really want to know!

The second point that concerned me was your insinuation that the council members would have something different to say "privately" than they would publicly. You mentioned your "lame duck" status being the reason for your speaking up. I would hope that the person I vote for as council member wouldn't wait until he is a lame duck to stand up for something. I would hope that person would have the backbone to say what they thought respectfully, in the presence of those affected by it. When people require secrecy to say things, I become suspicious that their truth wouldn't shine so brightly in the light of day. Someone can be very convincing if he can select for sharing only the information that suits his agenda.

Ron, you suggested that the mayor tries to run things singlehandedly. You and I both know that the job is much too big for that to happen. I know how many hours of commitment are required by both the council and the mayor, to keep the city running efficiently. As a final thought, I think the city of Evanston is in great shape! And I thank the mayor and the city council for their hard work in making it that way.

As a member of the city council, Ron, if you don't want to take your share of the credit for that - I guess that's up to you!

Kerri Ottley
of Evanston

Tuesday, October 25, 1994

UINTA COUNTY HERALD

OPINION

Mayor Ottley responds to letters of criticism

After reading two letters in recent issues of the Uinta County Herald attacking me and my integrity I feel that I should not let these letters go unanswered. These letters are not only incorrect, but in most cases downright lies. The first letter I will respond to is the letter written by Mr. Don Cook and published on Friday, October 7, 1994.

Mr. Cook:

First of all, you either did not read the entire article on my comments I made in the Herald dated October 4, 1994, or you did not comprehend what the article said. I did not state that I was adamant against gambling. I said that I was opposed to casino type gambling in Evanston. Whether or not you believe it, there is a large difference.

Second, Uinta Realty, my real estate firm, has very little property listed that would benefit from gambling. But then this is none of your business unless you are interested in purchasing some.

And third, yes, I read the Casper Star Tribune, and if you have read the October 14, 1994 issue with an article on the front page titled "Report: State Enjoys Solid Growth In Jobs", you would know that the economy is on the upswing. Furthermore, the figures I used in my comments were taken from Mr. Rob Cable's records, and from the most recent Wyoming State Data Center bulletin dated June, 1994.

Mr. Cook, I would recommend that you check out your facts and understand what you read before you jump to any conclusions. You are always welcome to call me.

Remember, I have a right as well as an obligation to the people I represent to express my opinion and concerns on any and all issues that may affect our community. People in Evanston deserve that.

The second letter I refer to was published in the Herald on Tuesday, Oct. 18, signed by a Marion Comstock. This letter was not only entirely wrong, but was full of innuendos and vicious and slanderous lies by a person that I am not even acquainted with. Therefore, I am submitting the following letter in response to her.

Mrs. Comstock:

First I want to point out to you the type of government the City of Evanston has. We have what is known as a strong Mayor/Council type system. The mayor acts, by law, as the chief executive and administrator of the city. All rules, policies, laws, as well as all resolutions, ordinances and budgets are passed and acted upon by the governing body of the city. This body is made up of a mayor and six city council members. The mayor has but one vote on all business. Therefore, I cannot imagine how you can claim that I am strong-arming the council members, unless of course they let me.

You called me a dictator, you referred to me as Evanston's strongman. I don't know for sure who is feeding the information to you, but you say there are at least five members on the council that are opposing me in my reelection as Mayor. If this is true I am glad that I am a strong mayor, because obviously none of these five have any leadership strength. As a matter of fact I must intimidate these people to the point that they cannot even perform the duties that they were sworn under oath to. This is their weakness, not mine.

Mrs. Comstock, if I were a city council member — and I was for 12 years — whether or not I was against the incumbent mayor I would not be such a coward that I would have to have someone such as you speak for me. But, I don't believe the five or six members are using you in this manner. I do believe that two or three of them are using you, but if you are so gullible to believe his or her lies, then I guess you are comfortable with being used as a goat.

If you really want to know the truth of what goes on in the City, please call me or my staff or both. We will be glad to talk to you.

Dennis J. Ottley, Mayor
City of Evanston

During the past meetings I had done everything I could think of to prevent the council from publicly endorsing the gaming initiative. I spent hours looking up state laws, trying to find a way to stop them. I did everything possible and requested City Attorney Dennis Boal to try to find a way, but he said there was nothing I could do, short of trying to use my veto power, but I knew that would not work because with two-thirds vote they could overrule my veto. With 5 council members definitely going along with Wall, I knew there was no sense in even trying to veto. All I could do by this time was to try and encourage them to stay neutral.

There is nothing in any of the minutes indicating that a motion or resolution was made for the Evanston City Council to go on record as being supportive of the gambling Initiative No. 2, so I guess the council didn't get their way.

During recent meetings there was a lot of whispering going on. Some of the council members would hold their hand over their mouth and whisper things back and forth. It was mostly councilmembers Wall and Vranish, who were sitting side by side. Sometimes it was councilmembers Nelson and Davis, who were also sitting next to each other. I knew it was going on and I just ignored them, trying to keep the meeting from being disturbed. There were Letters to the Editor in the *Uinta County Herald* about it, so I knew that the folks in attendance noticed it.

My wife Sandy was in attendance during one of those meetings and told me afterwards, "I was so mad that I was going to ask Jerry Wall just what she and Vranish were whispering about, but I didn't want to disturb the meeting any more than it already was, plus I didn't want to make a big issue of it." I appreciated that, but later on Sandy told me she wished she had said something at the time.

⸺◈⸺

During the last two weeks of October and the first week of November, just before the General Election, the Uinta County Herald was covered with Letters to the Editor, some favoring me but most of them opposing me. In fact, there was one letter from a woman that had just lived in Evanston a few months. That woman was Mrs. Marion Comstock, a mother-in-law to Dan Yates, Chairman of the Evanston Planning and Zoning Commission. Yates was a supporter of the Davis/Wall team, but I didn't think he or whoever would stoop so low as to use an elderly woman I had never even met, and who had just moved to Evanston, for the purpose of writing a letter with so many innuendos, vicious and slanderous lies. After reading that letter by Mrs. Comstock, I thought to myself, *Just how low would a person go to win an election?* You'd have to be a pretty sick person to use someone like Mrs. Comstock to get what you want, a person that in no way could know what was going on.

I really felt sorry for Mrs. Comstock for letting her son-in-law use her to write vicious lies and untruths about someone she had never met. Something like that should never happen. I only hoped Dan Yates had a conscience.

For proof of what I'm saying, I have posted most of the "Letters to the Editor" and "Guest Editorials" in this book concerning the mayor's race and the gaming Initiative No. 2 for the reader's information. This 1994 Mayoral Election was much worse than the Mayoral Election in 1986 between Gene Martin and me, and that one was bad enough.

It's a shame that some folks running for election can't just run on their own record and future plans and let the votes go wherever. But there must not have been anything Councilman Will Davis had to run on, except a six-month plan of promises that were already being taking care of. You'd think that after being on the Evanston City Council for eight years that Davis would have some kind of record to run on, but in his case there wasn't much. These last few years he had done nothing but let Councilwoman Wall intimidate him.

In *Uinta County Herald's* issue of November 8th, election day, *Herald* Reporter David Carkhuff quoted Councilman Craig Nelson of Ward 3 as saying that the pre-election uproar between mayoral candidates was part of politics.

"I think when it's all over, whoever's in there, we'll be able to set our differences aside and go back to Work," Nelson said.

I don't know why Nelson would say that the uproar was part of politics. I had never run for re-election where I defended myself; maybe I should have in the 1982 election against Martin, but I'm just not good at it because I never felt that I needed to. While in office I felt that I had upheld the Oath of Office and always had the best interest of the citizens in mind, and if anyone could ever show me where I'm wrong, speak up, if you have the courage.

It was now November 9th and the election was over. I lost the election. I was somewhat disappointed, but relieved. Will Davis got 2,191 votes and Evanston received a new mayor. I receive 1,997 votes. Other City of Evanston election results were the following: in Ward 1, vacated by Will Davis, Mark D. Baca (837 votes) beat out Kim West (545 votes); in Ward 2, Bruce R. Barnard (988 votes) beat Joe Adams (516 votes). Ron Barnard, outgoing council member didn't run again. And in Ward 3, unopposed Craig Nelson won with 826 votes and 241 write-ins. Evanston would have a new mayor and two new city council members in January, 1995.

However, I was very happy to see Uinta County vote the gaming Initiative No. 2 down with a vote of 5425 votes against and 2115 votes in favor. The initiative lost in Uinta County by more than 2 to 1. And in the State of Wyoming, Initiative No. 2 was beaten by a vote of almost 3 to 1. I felt that it was a good day for both Evanston and Wyoming, to see the gaming Initiative No. 2 losing by such a margin.

OPINION

City engineer disagrees with Councilman Barnard's letter

Dear Editor,

Mr. Ron Barnard presented guest editorial comments about what he considers to be Mayor Ottley's attempt to cover up reports of contamination in relation to work being done to reclaim the old gravel pit located west of the Roundhouse. Due to personal involvement I disagree with Councilman Barnard. I know that Mayor Ottley has made NO attempt to cover up nor has he withheld information in any attempt to mislead the City Council.

Officials of Union Tank Car (UTC Company) for several years, have expressed a desire to expand their railroad car repair operation presently located within the Roundhouse. Representatives of UTC have sought between 55 and 75 acres for this expansion. The only site available in Evanston as well as the logical site for expansion is the mined-out gravel pit area immediately west of the Roundhouse. The obvious task in order to accommodate this move is to fill in the gravel pit.

The Mayor, City Council and City Staff have been working for months to accomplish that task and as part of the effort the City has hired a local engineering firm to oversee the project and to prepare plans and specifications for work to be done. The City also hired an environmental consulting firm from Salt Lake City to perform a Phase I Environmental Site Assessment. That report was completed in June, 1994 and the report identified a reclaimed oil well site, an existing oil well, a concrete/asphalt dump area, an old Union Pacific dump site plus various other common such as drum storage and above ground tanks containing diesel fuel, all of which present a potential for environmental liabilities, meaning possible site contamination.

The engineering work has proceeded in good faith and full communication with the Wyoming Department of Environmental Quality (DEQ). The reported environmentally sensitive areas have been avoided in the construction planning, except for the concrete/asphalt dump. The construction plans call for these dumped materials to be sifted and sorted to remove materials unsuitable for construction fill such as large concrete chunks, metals, wood and of course contaminants, should any be found during the sifting process.

As the City proceeded to fill the gravel pit, UTC desired to have a Phase II Environmental Audit performed at the site. The letter that Mr. Barnard references was written to alert the City of preliminary findings of that Phase II Audit. As Mr. Barnard stated, the preliminary results indicate soil contaminants. This in and of itself wasn't the greatest alarming factor. The main concern was verified in the letter as UTC "would urge the City to consider shutting down further work on the site while the City analyzes the testing information." The ensuing discussion between Mayor and Staff was not centered upon contaminants or no contaminants. It was centered upon the financial, legal and contractual consequences of shutting down the contractor.

This event occurred only hours before the October 12th City Council meeting. The information was said to be preliminary and unverified. This was further proved by phone calls to UTC. Mayor Ottley asked staff personnel if we needed to present this matter during the Council Meeting, the staff response was that we should wait until we have verified information, substantial in nature to warrant a discussion regarding shutting down the work. These discussions are common to staff work, as to when we have sufficient and reliable data to present to the City Council. The Mayor alerted the Council the very next day, the City received additional information the day after the Council meeting and the additional information since then.

Our Engineers have asked the contractor to work in other areas until the contamination problem can be fully evaluated. With this approach we have been successful in progressing the work while seeking assistance with environmental issues.

I say we did not cover up nor hide the information. We were dealing with the issues we felt were most pressing and of immediate consequence to the City of Evanston.

Brian Honey
Evanston City Engineer

Councilman Vranish accuses mayor of underhanded working practices

Dear Editor,

Mayor Ottley, your response to Marion Comstock's letter was really hitting below the belt. Your statement that her "letter was full of innuendoes and vicious and slanderous lies" is in itself, in fact, I called Marion Comstock and told her that her letter was "totally accurate" and I commend her for having the courage to speak out. For several years, have attended your council meetings and told me that they have also received threats of harm personally from the Mayor and his wife. So much for free speech.

In Mayor Ottley's public lambasting of Mr. Cook and Mrs. Comstock, the mayor failed to talk of facts but instead resorted to personal insults.

Let's also about some facts. This year Mayor Ottley developed the budget in secret without council input. We weren't allowed to see it until late April when he was done. Mayor Ottley severely restricted the time that we were "allowed" to discuss the budget. The Council asked the Mayor to have the city treasurer available to discuss the budget with us. Mayor Ottley refused our lawful request.

Evanston came within hours of losing ESAM to another town. When ESAM wasn't interested in any of the properties that Mayor Ottley had listed, he dropped them like a hot potato, but they were determined to locate here and made an option to purchase on a suitable building they had located. Then, they heard stories of problems with the sewer line and of freezing water pipes, they couldn't find out from the city where the main sewer line was located, and combined with their perception of saying the heck with it and leaving town. Will Davis, Craig Nelson and heard about their difficulties and intervened in their behalf. The city crews came over and assisted with the location of the sewer and water lines and their fears were addressed. We agreed to fund the leveling and graveling of a parking lot for them and two days later the council approved the budget funds. We spent $10,000 which created 50 to 100 jobs. So I had a trade considering what Union Tank is going to cost. The Mayor was furious - trust he because the council was weak and without leadership qualities.

I leadership and knack when the Mayor said, "As a matter of fact I must intimidate these people (council) to the point that they cannot even perform the duties that they were sworn under oath to. That is their weakness, not mine."

This statement demonstrates his contempt for the Council! My personal perception is that the Mayor tolerates us only because the law requires him to do so.

Mayor, you use city vehicles for personal and business use. Many times you have threatened employees with loss of their job for talking to the council, do you have something to hide? You keep memos and letters from us and you selectively censor what information you want to share with us. I have spoken to you about these on several occasions. The net result was that now you consider me your enemy when all I really wanted was to have you stop doing these things because they make you and the city look bad.

It's not a question about you, Mayor, it's a question about what's good for the city. The council hasn't wanted to get on the podium and publicly embarrass you because we want to politically continue to work together and get projects done, but your actions have pushed a wedge between you and the council to the point where the interests of the city are now beginning to suffer.

Mayor, in the past, I have told you on many occasions that I had the utmost respect and admiration for your leadership and ability to make correct decisions. I don't know if the power of being mayor has intoxicated and corrupted you or what, but you have demonstrated that you will do anything, including lying to keep your office. I feel sorry for you and for the city and anguish that you have brought upon yourself and those around you.

Clarence Vranish
City Council President

UINTA COUNTY HERALD
Friday, October 28, 1994

OPINION

GUEST EDITORIAL

Citizen asks for answers from council members

I had written a letter to you which dealt with real issues involving the upcoming election. After reading Ron Barnard's entry in the Friday, October 21st edition of your fine publication, I tore my previous letter up. Mr. Barnard's disgusting brand of local politics has made discussion of real election issues impossible.

Many of your readers know that I am not a true blue Mayor Dennis Ottley supporter. I have publicly opposed him on a great many issues, both with letters to your Newspaper, and by speaking as a citizen at City Council meetings. But, I have never questioned his honor as a public servant or his ability to perform the job (that's right, its a job) of being our Mayor. Mr. Barnard's invention, Ottley-Gate has uncovered a real threat to the standards with which our local government maintains its business — and it has nothing to do with anything that Mayor Ottley has done. I see what appears to be an organized malicious effort to smudge the reputation of a man in the name of politics!

The voters of Evanston should not be misled by Mr. Barnard's interpretation of events surrounding the Union Tank Car deal. I have some questions regarding each and every Councilperson's actions in that regard. You see, I interpret those events quite differently.

Councilpeople, has anyone or anything prevented you from becoming every bit as involved as our Mayor in these goings on? Do the Citizens of Evanston expect that you cannot perform your elected tasks without being spoon fed information by our Mayor?

What Mr. Barnard (and his group — I'll get to that later) portrays as a scandal, I see as an example of laziness and even ineptitude on the part of Mr. Barnard and any other Councilperson who voted on the Union Tank Car project participation without being informed.

Am I to believe that if Mr. Barnard himself were as involved as he could have been in the project, that he wouldn't have been informed of the contamination situation at the same time as our City Attorney and Mayor? Deep Throat my puttute!

Did our Mayor, or anyone else really prevent you from doing your job, Mr. Barnard? You'd better think carefully, consider all the implications before answering that, Sir. If you or any other member of City Council has been ineffective there is a simple probability that the fault is your own.

Ten years from now, the contamination will be remembered, if at all, as an insignificant delay in the implementation of a project which yields continual benefits to our community. The actual substance of Mr. Barnard's complaint is null. What about his motivation? Recently in this publication, I've read letters accusing that Mayor Ottley has attempted to use his elected office for personal gain. Now, I'm just the kind of person who checks on such assertions. What do I know? They could be true. They are not!

None of these claims check out, even vaguely. I hereby call anyone who continues to purvey such garbage a liar! Why are these slanderous accusations made at election time? Something smells. Citizens, something positively stinks here.

Editor, I propose you have your folks do some real investigative reporting. Twice in the Uinta County Herald, I've read that seven members of our City Council are fed up with our Mayor. Do they all think he's dishonest? Do they all think he's trying to dominate our government? How would we as readers know? None of them besides Mr. Barnard have said a darned thing. Mr. Barnard says they are afraid of retribution, so they won't say anything. Well, I expect them to say something. I expect to read statements from each of them regarding this whole mess. If not, then tell us who refused comment.

Councilpeople, we didn't elect you to be intimidated. I simply cannot believe that you're all in on this. The only retribution you know you can expect will be from the voters if you continue to let others speak for you. Please comment when contacted by the press. If not contacted, issue a statement. There is some group among you who are conspiring to wrongfully tarnish the reputation of a man who has served this community honorably for many years. If some of you know that's wrong, that there are better ways of winning elections, say so. Will Davis, you are the Mayor's opponent, I don't want to think that you've sanctioned any of these filthy political techniques. Let us all know what is going on here.

The only real complaint against Mayor Ottley amounts to those whining that he continually disagrees with City Council. As I wrote earlier, I often disagree with our Mayor. I've been frustrated by his stand on major issues. Still, I believe that he has conducted the day-to-day job of Mayor with superb competence and with the utmost of integrity. Certainly now, after all of this, I intend to vote that he continue.

Voters, if you let this organized barrage convince you that we need a Mayor and City Council who are in continual agreement, then I propose we cancel City Council meetings. If they are all of one mind, then attendance by more than one would appear to be a social outing. They could do that sort of thing on their own time.

Jeff Morris
of Evanston

UINTA COUNTY HERALD   Friday, October 28, 1994

Mayor Ottley fires back at Councilman Barnard's letter

Dear Editor:

In reading your guest editorial in the Uinta County Herald of the Friday, Oct. 21, 1994 issue titled "Councilman Evanston Has Crisis In leadership" by Ron Barnard, Evanston City Councilman, I find it erroneous and somewhat amusing.

Erroneous? His dates and times are for the most part incorrect. It was the Union Tank Car Company that requested the ground breaking ceremony and set the date, not I. When U.T.C.C. called and informed me that they hadn't got any results from their phase II environmental study and that Gov. Mike Sullivan and others could not make the Oct. 12, 1994 date, we all mutually agreed that the ceremony should be canceled. If Mr. Barnard knew and understood what was going on he would know that the information concerning the soil contamination was given to Uinta Engineering and Surveying, Inc. immediately so they could check into the report. This is the engineering firm that the City of Evanston contracted to oversee the project. U.E.S.I. has sent these reports into the Wyoming Department of Environmental Quality. As soon as these reports are returned to them we will contact everyone concerned.

Mr. Barnard, why would I, or how could I, keep something like what you claim a secret? I am, believe it or not, glad we found the problems early so that we can correct them as the project progresses.

Amusing, humorous? When I read the editorial it was like it came out of a Jack Webb Dragnet series. I didn't know we had such a great super sleuth on the City Council, but obviously we do.

"Ottley-Gate", boy that does have a ring to it. Maybe, just maybe, the national press will capitalize off of it and give Evanston the same amount of press the "Watergate" received back in the 1970s.

Yes, Mr. Barnard you are a "lame duck", but I don't know for sure that you are speaking for the entire council. Three of the members of the council, Clarence Vranish, Tom Hutchinson and Craig Nelson, have come into my office to discuss the matter rather than write to the paper. You seldom come into my office to discuss matters and when you do you don't shut up long enough to listen.

Evanston's own "Deep-Throat"? Another amusing touch. I don't know for sure who "Deep-Throat" is, but anyone that writes an anonymous letter and doesn't have the courage to sign it cannot be much of a person. Thank God the Uinta County Herald has a policy not to print such letters. It's great to know that someone has ethics.

It seems to me that you, Mr. Barnard could be a little more original in your story. At any rate don't compare others to yourself. You are right about one thing. I was upset and disappointed. Disappointed, because I feel that the City of Evanston deserves better and more mature leadership on the council.

Dennis J. Ottley
Evanston Mayor

Mayorial candidate Davis says his election will end feud

Editor:

I have been reading and contemplating the news in the Uinta County Herald with mixed emotions. No one likes to see "pent-up emotions and concerns" aired in a public forum where feelings can be hurt deeply. However, when the issues involve public funds and public offices, the people have a right to know what is going on in city hall.

Now everyone is aware of the feuding between the Mayor's office and the City Council. We've disagreed over the city budget, over information sharing on economic development projects (Oxbow, Job Corps, Union Tank Car), over whether to zone for gaming, and the topics go on. We find ourselves bickering, pointing fingers, walking out of meetings, and arguing over who's at fault—the Mayor or the Council. It is not much fun for us and it certainly is not productive.

The fact is, we do have problems between the Mayor and Council. There just isn't enough trust and cooperation between us. It is not a good way to run the city, and it seems to be getting worse, not better. That's why I decided to run for Mayor.

We need to rebuild trust, cooperation and teamwork in city government.

I have laid out a six-month plan to restore trust and cooperation between the Mayor's office and the council. I believe I have the support of the current council members to achieve that goal. It is time to change the way your city is governed. It will be your choice to make that change on November 8th. The choice will be a clear one, a new approach to city governance or 4 more years of the same thing.

I would appreciate your support and your vote on Nov. 8.

Will Davis, Evanston Councilman
Candidate for Mayor

City planner wants to set record straight

Dear Editor:

In response to Mrs. Comstock's Letter to the Editor of October 18th, wherein she claimed that Mayor Ottley has threatened the jobs of City Department Heads, I wish to set the record straight. Mrs. Comstock should note that there are six City Department Heads appointed by the Mayor with the consent of the City Council. These Department Heads include the City Clerk, City Treasurer, City Attorney, City Engineer/Director of Public Works, Community Development Director, and Chief of Police. In talking with each of these individuals, none have indicated that they have had their jobs threatened by Mayor Ottley.

Also, Mrs. Comstock should be aware that non-appointed City employees are hired by Department Managers on a performance review basis. Any termination of an employee, must follow guidelines as outlined in the City Personnel Manual. It is not the Mayor's prerogative to hire and fire these employees at will.

Paul Knopf
Community Development Director

OPINION

Woman says Mayor Ottley's leadership has brought positive impact to Evanston

Dear Editor:

The City of Evanston is truly fortunate to have Dennis Ottley as our Mayor. He is a strong leader who is committed to the well-being of the citizens of Evanston and to the future of the community.

Through my volunteer efforts I have watched Mayor Ottley as a leader, and it has been because of his leadership that many excellent things have occurred which have positively impacted the community.

Mayor Ottley is a man of integrity who has always placed the needs of the community first. He has never compromised his commitment to community

excellence nor his pursuit to improve quality of life for the people of Evanston. In the years that Dennis Ottley has been our Mayor, I have had the opportunity to volunteer on several city committees.

Depot Square continues to develop, offering downtown beautification, a place for community events and a real sense of community pride.

A Historical Preservation Commission is in place, showing pride in our heritage and the value of saving it. The BEAR Project provides recreational opportunity for all, and restored habitat for wildlife.

The pride of Evanston continues

with the City's Tree Planting Program, offered to residential and business customers.

The Recycling Program was started and is moving ahead under the leadership of Mayor Ottley.

Economic development efforts have resulted in jobs for citizens. Housing construction is up, and the business sector continues to improve.

The attitude of the citizens is healthy

with a positive outlook for the future. Visitors continually remark about the progressive feeling of the community and wonderful overall appearance.

Volunteerism and community pride are alive and well as demonstrated by last week's celebration of Support Your Community Week.

Mayor Ottley has, of course, not done all these things without the help of the City Council. However, the Mayor has

provided the leadership and enthusiasm to accomplish these tasks. It seems to me that Mayor Ottley has done much for Evanston.

I, for one, am proud of my community and look forward to continued future improvements, under the careful leadership of Mayor Ottley.

Cheryl Loveham
of Evanston.

Five councilmembers endorse Davis for mayor

Citizens of Evanston:

You've heard about the problems between the Mayor and the City Council. There's little trust and cooperation between us and it's not a good way to run the city.

Mayor Ottley has told the Council "You work for me." In reality, the Mayor should realize that we all work for the people of Evanston.

The Mayor says with six out of seven votes, the Council could out-vote him on every issue. This may be true, but do the citizens of Evanston want the Mayor

and City Council to fight on every single issue? It's also difficult to decide issues when information is kept secret from the Council (as it has been on Union Tank, Job Corps, and others).

Mayor Ottley has said we need a "strong" Mayor to compensate for what he perceives as a weak Council. We feel that a healthy City Government includes a strong Council and Mayor working together in a spirit of openness, honest debate and teamwork.

It's time for a positive change. It's time to end the fighting and to focus on

the needs of Evanston's citizens. Will Davis has presented a plan to accomplish that. Will has laid out a six-month plan to restore teamwork, cooperation, and trust in City Government.

The choice for Evanston's Mayor over the next four years is yours. We are supporting Will Davis and his plan to restore positive leadership in Evanston. Whatever your choice, we encourage you to cast your vote next Tuesday, Nov. 8.

City Council members: Will Davis,
Ron Barnard, Jerry Wall, Clarence
Vranish and Craig Nelson.

Councilman Hutchinson remains neutral in mayor's race

Dear Editor:

Some citizens might be wondering why my name is absent from the letter to the editor from the rest of the City Council.

When the campaign started, I told both Mayor Ottley and Will Davis I would not endorse either one of them I

believe they both have good leadership abilities, but being a councilman, I don't feel it is proper for me to give an endorsement.

I want to make a plea to the rest of the council that we need to remember to agree to disagree. And no matter how the election turns out, we still have

a city to run, keeping the citizens' best interests in mind.

I ask the candidates to keep that in mind after the election and go on to do what we were elected to do.

Tom Hutchinson
City Councilman, Ward III

LETTERS TO THE EDITOR

Evanston city employee disappointed in conduct of candidates; says play nice or go home

Dear Editor:

For the past few weeks the letter to the editor have become more and more vicious and outlandish.

This is not a letter to state who I am supporting, who should win an election, or which political issues should be argued about. I am writing to express my disappointment in the council members who have used this section of your paper to publicly dishonor the Mayor of Evanston. I agree completely with Mr. Morris who stated that "if we need a Mayor and Council who are in continual agreement, then I propose we cancel council meetings."

Obviously if there has been problems between some council members regarding city business.

He has never made me feel uncomfortable when I have disagreed with him and I know of no one who has been threatened with their jobs. That is a strong allegation and one that Mr. Vranish most likely heard second hand.

As an employee at City Hall, I do know that Mayor Ottley will always discuss with me anything that is on my mind, and any questions I have had and the Mayor, they should have discussed the issues in a dignified fashion among themselves, not by talking in a public forum two weeks prior to election.

In regard to the letter written by Will Davis, candidate for mayor, what timing! Just after the unfavorable letters of Mayor Ottley are published he puts a campaign ad in the Letters to the Editor section.

I am disappointed. I expected our

Shanda Fife
of Evanston

Mayor's son tells Davis camp to deal in issues, not sling mud

Dear Editor:

The campaign is winding down and Will Davis has yet to deal with any issues in this campaign. Apparently his plan is to wait until close to the end and have others level charges that can't be defended because lies are very hard to defend.

He has allowed other councilmen to tell lies and innuendos. Since he has not condemned it I assume he condones it. He has allowed others to control his campaign. I wonder if he will allow others to control his office, should he get elected.

His apparent spokesmen (and I might add cry babies) Vranish, Wall and Barnard, have set the tone of his campaign. It is a campaign of deceit and disingenuousness that has reached an all time low in Evanston politics. I would expect no more from the latter three but I had hoped that Davis had more character than that. I guess politics can make monsters of all of us if we let it. It is apparent that any change Davis would make would be a change for the worse.

Let's let these purveyors of untruths and hurlers of mud know that this is not the kind of politics we want in Evanston. Let's keep some character and integrity in City Hall. Reelect Dennis Ottley for Mayor.

Kandy Ottley
of Evanston

Councilman Davis' daughter says father is honest, hard working and represents change

Dear Editor:

I am writing in response to Vicki Norwood's letter asking how Will Davis will have time to be mayor. I know that since I am his daughter that my opinion may seem a bit bias, but I am no different than a daughter-in-law or an employee of a candidate writing, and I assure you that I am writing this on my own; no one has "put me up to it."

Anyway, I feel that since I am Will Davis' daughter I know first hand just how much time he does put in down at city hall and how concerned he is over city issues. He is always setting time aside for city meetings and functions. I do not know how you could say you never see council members- more specifically my father-at city events. He attends many of them. I know that he is a very dedicated city councilman as are the other council members.

My father is the most honest man I know and he is the best choice for the mayor of Evanston. It is time that we the people of Evanston, think about what's best for our city and not be so afraid of change. On Tuesday, Nov. 8 we can vote for four more years of the same thing or we can vote for a positive change for Evanston. I know that I am voting for a change!

Jackie Davis
of Evanston

Neighborhood thanks Ottley, Davis

Dear Editor:

We, the area residents of 330 Hansen Ave., wish to express our thanks to Mayor Dennis Ottley and Councilman Will Davis for taking time out of their busy schedules to arrange for and attend the meeting with Mr. John Holderegger where our concerns with the MRSI Group Home were discussed.

We appreciate their efforts in letting us know that an individual's rights are still important in Evanston, Wyoming. We would encourage others to get involved and become more informed, because it is not just a neighborhood issue, but a community one. Again, our thanks to our city officials for listening to our concerns.

Area Residents of 330 Hansen

Letters to the Editor, *Uinta County Herald,* November 4, 1994.

Wyoming also had a new governor, Jim Geringer, Republican, who beat out Kathy Karpan, Democrat, in the state-wide election.

The three questions on the ballot affecting Uinta County, the 2% Lodging Tax, the Lifelong Learning Mill Levy and the Fire Prevention District Levy all won hands down, which was great.

The first regular meeting of November was held on the 9th with all council members in attendance except Councilwoman Wall who was excused.

As I opened up the meeting I first recognized Boy Scout Leader Dave Bennett and had him introduce the Boy Scouts that were in attendance to fulfill their Merit Badge requirements. Leader Bennett introduced Branson Bennett and Todd Smith from Troop 75.

I welcomed the scouts at the meeting and told them that they were welcome to take part in the meeting if there was anything that might concern them. I also presented each with an Evanston "Fresh Air, Freedom and Fun" promotional pin.

Following the approval of the agenda I congratulated Mayor-elect Will Davis for his win, and Councilman Nelson of Ward 3 for his. And although they were not in attendance, I congratulated the two new city council members, Mark Baca of Ward 1 and Bruce Barnard of Ward 2 for their wins.

I then appointed Spencer Goodro, introduced by Chief Dennis Harvey, as Evanston's Animal Control Officer. Motion was made by Councilman Hutchinson to confirm the appointment, seconded by Nelson, with 5 votes in favor and 1 absent (Wall). The motion passed.

At this time, Mark Baca arrived at the meeting and I introduced him as Councilman-elect for Ward 1, and I congratulated him for his win in the election.

Under New Business, Councilman Davis introduced Resolution 94-65, amending the budget resolution for the 1994-1995 fiscal year to provide a fee for Microbrewery Permits. This resolution would set an annual fee of $500.00 for a license or permit to be charged by the city for all microbrewery licenses.

Councilman Nelson made the motion to adopt Resolution 94-65, seconded by Ron Barnard, with all voting in favor.

I announced that there would be a work session on November 16th at 5:00 p.m., and that the two new council members were welcome to attend.

Councilman Nelson followed with a motion that the next regular city council meeting be held on November 23rd as scheduled and that there be only one regular meeting during the month of December on December 14th. Motion was seconded by Hutchinson, with 6 votes in favor and 1 absent (Wall). The motion passed.

In polling the staff and council members, City Engineer Brian Honey gave a very positive report on the testing of the ground in which the Union Tank Car Company was to build their new facility. Honey stated that all reports had come in with no significant problems, and Mr. Ken Fischl, CEO of UTCC, had indicated that their plans to build in Evanston were still a go. Great news!

Director of the Urban Renewal Agency Jim Davis reported that the Historic Preservation Committee would be holding a public meeting on November 17th at 7:00 p.m. at City Hall.

I announced that the City of Evanston had been honored, along with Uinta County, for declaring all city and county buildings as smoke-free facilities. Jackie Cushing of the State Nursing Service and Ruth Nickerson, R.N. of Uinta County Health presented the City of Evanston and Uinta County the Tobacco Free Challenge Award plaque during the November County Commission meeting. Along with Commissioners Pat Mulhall and Paul Barnard, I was at the commission meeting when the plaque was presented. The award was only one of two presented in the State of Wyoming this year.

After two hours of general business was taken care of, a discussion took place concerning the traffic lights at the Wyoming State Hospital underpass off ramps on Front Street (State Highway 150 S). The Wyoming Department of Transportation had made a request that the traffic lights be removed because they felt they were no longer needed and they were too costly to maintain.

After a short discussion, Councilman Vranish made a motion to support WDOT's decision to remove the lights, seconded by Nelson. Motion passed by 6 votes in favor and 1 absent (Barnard).

On December 2nd Sandy and I were invited to a surprise appreciation luncheon at City Hall by the Evanston city employees. They all greeted us with a lot of appreciation for all we had done for them during my tenure as a member of the Evanston City Council and as their mayor for 12 years, and Sandy as Evanston's First Lady.

After the luncheon, Sharon Constantine and others presented Sandy and me with tickets to the upcoming National Finals Rodeo in Las Vegas. They were season tickets of Luke Lym, a former rodeo performer, provided by Luke's son-in-law David Albrecht, a city employee, for a one-day performance.

Sandy and I went to Las Vegas and had a lot of fun, and we finally got to see a great rodeo at the University of Nevada Las Vegas Thomas Mack Arena, put on by the National Finals Rodeo. And with both Sandy and me being great rodeo buffs, we really enjoyed the show, and we had great seats.

Tobacco Free Challenge Award

Jackie Cushing of the State Nursing Service (third from left) and Ruth Nickerson of Uinta County Public Health present Uinta County Commissioners Pat Mulhall (far left) and Paul Barnard (far right) and Evanston Mayor Dennis Ottley with the Tobacco Free Challenge Award. The award was presented to the officials for their support in helping make Uinta County and Evanston City offices smoke free. The award was only one of two presented in Wyoming this year.

Uinta County Herald, November 4, 1994.

A sincere thanks to all the people of Evanston who have helped and supported my campaign.

It has been an honor and privilege to serve the people of Evanston as Mayor for 12 years. Evanston is truly a great place to live, work and play. Best wishes to our new Mayor, Will Davis, and our newly elected city council members. Continue to move forward for a bright future in Evanston.

Paid for by the **DENNIS J. OTTLEY FOR MAYOR** Committee

Uinta County Herald, November 9, 1994.

Letters to the Editor of *Uinta County Herald*, November 11, 1994.

Evanston man says thanks are in order for Mayor Ottley

Dear Editor:

Now that the election is over I think some apologies are in order. There have been several discrediting "Letters to the Editor" toward Mayor Dennis Ottley.

I have known Dennis for 35 years. He has done more for the city of Evanston than any other man. He has brought businesses and work to Evanston, has always been involved in civic affairs and sat on many different committees, as has his wife Sandy.

More than anything, he has been a friend to people, especially young people. He and his brother Bob ran the Evanston truck terminal during the 60s and a great percentage of the high school boys worked for them at one time or other. He was one of the founding fathers of Little League Football. He organized and trained the Evanston Boxing Team and gave many kids the opportunity to gain confidence and better themselves. Much of the funding for this came out of his own pocket. He has given many people the opportunity for a new start.

He must have done something right. People have elected him to the office of Mayor three times.

Let's give the Mayor a vote of thanks for all he has done for us.

Bruce Tueller
of Evanston

Letters to the Editor of Uinta County Herald of the November 11, 1994 and November 15, 1994 issues

Citizen ashamed of how city campaigns were conducted

Dear Editor:

I am ashamed of the mud-slinging candidates we were left to vote for. And I am ashamed of some of my neighbors and friends who have also resorted to slinging mud in retaliation. With all the mud left on the streets of Evanston now that the election is over, who will clean it up? Our new mayor, our departing mayor, the city council, any of our elected officials? Or will it just be left up to the citizens to do?

Yes, it is a privilege and our democratic right to vote, but is it any wonder why, in many elections, we can't get decent voter turnout? Who should we vote for? The one who throws the first handful of mud or the one who retaliates by throwing back? Children! The majority of you have acted like children! When will you learn when enough is enough? Tell me this, who wins? The one with the muddiest hands or the one who is covered most in mud?

Tom Hutchinson is to be commended for remaining neutral of the mayoral candidates. But how tacky it was, not just for the city council to endorse a candidate, but to do it in the manner in which Will Davis, Ron Barnard, Jerry Wall, Clarence Vranish and Craig Nelson did was not right. How dare you, as our elected officials, speak for us. And that's just what you did. We elected you to be our voice for what is right for our city and not to take a stand, where us as a whole, do not stand together.

I do hope, as most of the fine citizens of Evanston do, that in the next election we can all stick to the issues of the campaign and stop the demented behavior to which you as politicians have become accustomed. Behavior like this is to be expected (though I'm not sure why) at the federal level, but do we really need it shoved in our faces here at home?

As an employee of a establishment which works closely with the city, I request my name be withheld as I don't want anyone thinking my personal views reflect that of the establishment where I work.

Name withheld

Letters to the Editor, *Uinta County Herald*, November 15, 1994.

On December 14th I opened the last and only city council meeting of the month with all members of the council present, except for Ron Barnard who was excused. During the meeting I announced that Marie Hicks, one of my greatest constituents, wished to resign from the Evanston Housing Authority Board. Councilwoman Wall made the motion to accept her resignation, seconded by Nelson. Motion passed with 6 votes in favor and 1 absent (Barnard). I sent Marie a letter of appreciation for her long-time involvement on the Board, and the other committees and commissions she had served on.

I made the appointment of Morris "Tuff" Samuelson to the Evanston Housing Authority Board. Motion was made by Councilman Nelson to confirm the appointment of Samuelson to the Housing Authority Board, seconded by Hutchinson. Motion passed with 6 votes in favor and 1 absent (Barnard).

Councilman Davis made a motion to allow the Evanston Police Benevolent Association to have their Shop With a Cop Program parade coming up soon in the Spirit of Christmas, seconded by Wall.

Detective J. R. Dean, representing the Association, gave an explanation of the program and stated that there would be approximately 160 children involved.

I called for a vote on the motion with all voting in favor.

Terry McCarthy also requested a parade permit for a 5K fitness run on New Year's Day. Councilwoman Wall made the motion to allow the permit, seconded by Hutchinson, with all voting in favor.

After all business was taken care of, I reminded everyone of the Annual City Christmas Party on Friday night at 6:00 p.m., and adjourned the meeting at 8:40 p.m.

During the Christmas Party, I thanked all the employees for the great opportunity to attend the National Finals Rodeo in Las Vegas and told them of the wonderful time we had. I told of the fun we had just spending a day in Las Vegas and how much we enjoyed the best rodeo we had ever been to, and we had been to a number of them.

I then thanked them for all their services to the community and said, *You folks are the backbone of the city and Sandy and I wish you all the best in the future. You will be missed,* and I wished them all a very Merry

Christmas and a happy holiday season, and then we all sat down and had a nice dinner. It was a nice evening.

Although the employees all treated Sandy and me well, the existing members of the city council weren't as friendly, except Tom Hutchinson—but that was okay because we didn't expect much from them, anyway.

1994 ended up as a prosperous year for Evanston and the State of Wyoming, as far as I was concerned, especially after Union Pacific Resources donated the 265 acres to Evanston, and getting the final word that Union Tank Car Company would be breaking ground as soon as weather permitted, and the fact that the Gaming Initiative No. 2 was defeated by a state vote of almost 3 to 1.

Also, I was very proud that Evanston had had such a tremendous amount of volunteerism throughout the community to make all the programs and projects so successful. When this happens it not only helps the economy, but also makes for a respectable and loved community.

No matter how I felt about the members of the city council, I felt good that once again Evanston had had another great year. I want to thank City Councilman Hutchinson for all his help and for the respect he gave to his Oath of Office.

"The Positive Thinker sees the Invisible,

feels the intangible and
achieves the impossible."

By Winston Churchill

CHAPTER 29

1995, FINAL ACT....Well I lost, and I will no longer be Mayor of Evanston. It was a loss I expected and a loss that will end up in my favor, I'm sure. As President Ronald Reagan once said, "Both politicians and diapers need to be changed often for the same reason."

Ever since the November General Election, as time went on, I felt much better and even glad that I had lost the election. Now I could concentrate on my business and finally work at making a decent living. However, I'm still upset with the dirty underhanded politics the five council members used. I felt that each one of them should now apologize, but I didn't think any of them would, but I may be wrong in time. Since the election, not one of them had met with me one on one. The only time they met with me was when a group event or a meeting was going on.

But I did have one more meeting to open up and give my State of the City address, and that was on January 11, 1995.

Roll was called by City Clerk Don Welling, declaring that City Councilmembers Tom Hutchinson, Craig Nelson, Jerry Wall, Ronald Barnard and Will Davis were all present, but Councilman Vranish apparently had been excused because he was absent. When Welling declared that we had a quorum, I then called the meeting to order at 7:00 p.m. and welcomed everyone there.

As it was the first meeting of the year a new mayor and two new city council members, Mark Baca of Ward 1 and Bruce Barnard of Ward 2, were about to be sworn in. But first I asked for motions to approve the agenda, approval of the minutes of the previous meeting and a motion to approve payment on all outstanding bills. All were approved.

Because of the transitional change of elected officials to be sworn in during this meeting, there was a full house of folks in attendance. As outgoing mayor, my family, of course, was in attendance, plus some of my friends and constituents. This made me proud.

After general business was taken care of I presented Marie Hicks with an engraved silver tray, and expressed our thanks and appreciation to her dedication to the city for serving on the Evanston Housing Authority Board for the past 15 years. I announced that Marie was one of the original participants who made it possible for Evanston to have such a program.

To me, Marie was a great lady and one of Evanston's most dedicated long-term citizens who had been involved in numerous programs in the city over the years. I considered her a good friend to Sandy and me, and if we ever needed anything from her, including her advice, she was always there to help.

Gerry Bolger, Director of the Evanston Housing Authority also presented Marie with a decorative clock and thanked her for her service to the Board since he had become Director of the Housing Authority.

I then left the Mayor's bench and stepped down to the main floor and went to the public's podium to give my State of the City address. I placed the podium in a position where I could look both at the City Council and the public. I wanted to be in a position that when I mentioned a person in my speech I could look at him or her as I spoke.

My State of the City address was quite lengthy, but it seemed like this particular year I had a lot to talk about. My address was as follows:

Ladies and Gentlemen,

As I leave the office of mayor, looking back over the past eight years, I feel very proud of what has happened and what we have achieved. In this period of time we have made the City of Evanston the most livable community in the State of Wyoming. Time and time again over the years and in recent months visitors from all over the world have commented on how amazed they were at what a remarkable, clean and enjoyable city we have. When Sandy and I walk away this evening, leaving this building, we will walk away with our heads high and be very proud of our performance as Mayor and First Lady.

This community, the City of Evanston is, no doubt, an All-American City. We should all be very proud of our accomplishments and achievements over the past years. I could stand up here all night and talk of these accomplishments, but I'm sure you are already very much aware of them.

However, Sandy and I do want to thank all of those who really are the ones responsible in making Evanston what it is today. Without the loyalty, the cooperation, the friendship and hard work of the staff and employees, from those who served on the City Boards, Commissions and Committees giving their free time, and from all the volunteers throughout the community, this could not have happened. This is what really has made this community. It is not just me or you; it is the participation and hard work of all.

Today Evanston has the finest and most up-to-date infrastructure: water, sewer, streets, schools, hospital, recreation facilities etc. etc., than any other community in the State of Wyoming of equivalent size. Today Evanston is one of the fastest growing communities in the state, and has one of the lowest unemployment rates. With the exception of the boom days of the late 1970s and early 1980s, Evanston's economy is better than it has been for over 20 years. We also have one of the lowest crime rates in the State of Wyoming.

We have strived for and successfully achieved a very high quality of life in Evanston. Evanston is a community where people can raise a family without too much worry. This is something we should all feel very good about. This is something, among everything else, that will help sell this community to industry. If that's what we want!

I have been in city government for 24 years and have never seen this city in a more solvent financial position than it is today. We have shown excellent fiscal responsibility over the years with a budget that is in great shape.

Ladies and Gentlemen, during my annual address that I gave last year at this time, I spoke of the character of this community. How the community's character is judged is by how the leaders of the community conduct themselves. I spoke on strength in leadership. I spoke on courage, on vision, on integrity and confidence. I spoke on the value of well-being and contentment. I spoke on aspiration and love. But, obviously and unfortunately most of the members of city council were either not listening or they just didn't give a damn.

The past two years, five members of this council have taken it on them-selves to have their own agenda, not informing me or, to my knowledge, any of the staff. Their agenda was to downgrade any efforts I was trying to achieve as your mayor. This was an agenda of nothing but whispering and cheap backroom politics. Rather than assist me and the staff in accomplishing the objectives and goals of this city, these members implemented, through their conspiring and their scheming, one of the most underhanded campaigns this community has ever witnessed.

During this past election I have been accused of being the most notorious S.O.B. in the country. I was accused of being an egomaniac, a tyrant, a dicta-tor, a liar and a thief. I guess I was accused of most everything short of murder. How they missed that I have no idea. I had been accused of threatening my staff and other employees with their jobs if they spoke with any of the council members. I assure you this was not true.

These five members went far <u>beyond fair comment</u> in their campaign to defeat me. To do what was right and best for the people of Evanston was far removed from any of their plans that would interfere with their conspiracy to get rid of me, not to elect anyone else in particular, but to get rid of me. They want a mayor they can dominate. A mayor they can intimidate. Not a strong mayor who wants to do what is best for you, the people. This group went so far as to use a woman, a naïve woman, practically a stranger to Evanston, to sign and send a letter to the editor of our local newspaper stating nothing but a lot of slanderous lies, half-truths, and innuendos of my performance as your mayor.

This same group instigated an anonymous letter to the Uinta County Herald claiming there was a lot of contamination at the city project we call the Union Center, which there is some. They did this intentionally to make me look bad, and then our lame-duck council member wrote an editorial to the newspaper accusing me of tyranny, of withholding information from them and the public and other lies and half-truths.

This anonymous letter and editorial could very easily have destroyed this entire project, a project that, to my knowledge, is the largest and most promising economic move the City of Evanston has ever undertaken to bring diversity to our economy and create jobs.

But, this action doesn't surprise me, because some of these members have been trying to sabotage and destroy everything that I have been trying to do for quite some time. With what has happened, as much as I would like to, it is awful hard for me to give much credit to this council for our accomplishments and achievements these past two years.

However, I do want to thank Mr. Hutchinson for his part. I sincerely appreciate him for having the courage and strength to come in and talk to me whenever he had a question and for being his own person and not a follower. With him being the only one left on the council with the experience and leadership ability to perform as president of the council, which this board will be electing tonight, for what it is worth I would like to recommend him for this position. A mayor needs a president of the council that will assist him and communicate with him, someone that will help him in managing the city. I haven't had a president of the council for the past two years, or at least not one that would help me.

Ladies and Gentlemen, what I have said the past few minutes may appear to you as being sour grapes or just bad sportsmanship on my part for losing the election. Well, I'll assure you that losing the election does not bother me. I actually feel relieved. I have been mayor and on this council for quite some time. I'm sure that there are a lot of people that felt like Evanston needed a change. What really bothers me is being beat by a group that was so worried about losing the election that they felt they had to resort to such low underhanded tactics in order to win.

Ladies and Gentlemen, to set the record straight I have never, and I mean never, intentionally lied to the people of Evanston, or to the staff, the employees, or to anyone on the Evanston City Council. I have never intentionally held back information of any type from anyone, regardless of their position in this city.

I have done everything possible to get these council members to take part in the projects. I have held work sessions that they did nothing but complain about, asking for their involvement and input on the projects that we were undertaking, and asking for their input on this past year's budget. I have tried to make all these members a part of what I was doing. During the work sessions, they couldn't even agree among themselves. I have introduced them at every function that we attended. As a matter of fact, last spring at the Renewal Ball, I introduced Mrs. Wall as being the only lady on the Evanston City Council. But, in her arrogant way, she yelled out "I'm no lady." Folks, I guess that was the only time in the past two years that Jerry Wall and I have agreed on anything. (When I said that I was looking straight at her, but she had her head down).

I could stand up here all night and tell you things about these five council members, but I don't have the time and I sure don't want to lower myself to their standards. I guess what makes me really upset, and somewhat angry, is that every one of them knows what they've done. They know they lied and cheated. They know they were wrong—or do they? Isn't there any such thing as ethics and morals left in this society? Don't people have any principles? Is there no such thing as fellowship? It is a shame. A real shame!

Again, I want to thank my staff: Sharon Constantine, Brian Honey, Paul Knopf, Oop Hansen, Chief Dennis Harvey, Steve Widmer, Don Welling and Dennis Boal. I want to thank Dennis Poppinga, Jim Davis, Judge John Phillips, Gerry Bolger, and all the others who have helped us in obtaining our goals and objectives over the years. I don't think I could have asked for a better bunch of people. These are the real heroes of Evanston, these are the people who deserve the credit.

Sandy and I both will always remember you for your loyalty and honesty to us. We will cherish your friendship over the years and hope it continues.

To you, Tom, and the newly elected council members, Bruce and Mark, I can only say that I hope sincerely that you can instill the strength, the integrity and the courage that it will take to give this governmental body the class and character they'll need. I hope that you three at least can give this body the ingredients that it will take to serve the public to their best interest.

Ladies and Gentlemen, if anyone has any doubts of what I have talked about tonight, please feel free to call me sometime and I will be glad to discuss it with you, any of you.

Evanston is a great place to live, to raise a family, to love and enjoy. Don't let dishonesty, weakness in government, or adverse politics ruin this community. Evanston is a community with character, a community of pride, and of love and caring. Let's try to keep it that way." At this time I turned my eyes on City Clerk Welling and said, *Mr. Welling, are you prepared to proceed with the swearing-in ceremony?* He answered, *Yes Mr. Mayor, I am ready.* I said, *Please proceed.*

As Welling was preparing for the swearing in ceremony, I picked up my papers from the podium and walked out of the chambers with my wife, my family and my friends following. As we walked out in the hall, I heard Councilman Ron Barnard shout out, *Jerry Wall is a lady.* I thought to myself, *What an idiot.* And after the way Wall and Nelson treated him during the W.A.M. Convention in Sheridan last year. What a joke!

The next day, someone either called me or came to my office to let me know that Mayor Will Davis had presented Sandy and me with a beautiful milk-white figurine of two eagles flying. He made the presentation just after we left and said he thought the eagles flying together represented the way Sandy and I worked together, and that I was supposed to go to City Hall and receive it. Hell, I wasn't about to go get it. I told the person, *What's he trying to do, soothe his conscience? As far as I'm concerned I wasn't about to receive anything from that mayor or council. If I accepted any gift from that bunch it would look like I was forgiving them for what they did to me and said about me. No, I don't want anything to do with them.*

I thought of a quote that I once heard that went something like this: *"Time does not make any lies become truth,"* and it would a long time before Sandy or I would ever forget all the lies that were directed at us during the time I was mayor or a member of the city council.

They say never carry a grudge, but sometimes it's hard not to. For a long time I have had a plaque on the wall of my office with a quote that read, *"Honesty is not the best policy, it's the only policy."* I had that plaque on my mayor's office wall for 3 terms (12 years) as mayor, and I'm sure that if anyone was ever in my office they would have had to notice it. I believed in it very intensely.

In reading the minutes of the January 11th meeting I saw this: *"Mayor Davis acknowledged and thanked Mayor Ottley for leaving the City in a sound financial condition and stated that we must build upon what we have been left."* What a turnaround!

Just as I suspected, Councilwoman Jerry Wall was elected as President of the Council. Well, at least Davis would have someone to tell him what to do, which had been the case the past two years.

My last meeting to open was now over, over with a lot of bitterness, a lot of hard feelings and resentment. Although, Sandy and I were both very bitter, we also felt relieved, contented and very much relaxed. We felt free from an experience of hate, lies and responsibilities.

We will miss the members of the staff, the employees, all the folks who were willing to serve on various boards, commissions and committees, and all the others who were willing to help in any way possible. And I will never forget the mayors I served under when I was on the city council, and all the city council members that gave me so much help during the first 10 years of my mayoralty.

But now I can go to work at Uinta Realty, Inc. and start running my business as I should have been running it. It will feel great getting back to having only my real estate office to worry about and spending all my time making money for myself, for a change.

The end of one life, the beginning of a new life...

SPECIAL NOTICE

POINT OF INFORMATION

This story included almost all meetings, from the time I was elected to the Evanston City Council in January, 1967 and Evanston's Mayor in January, 1979. There was much more business, old and new, conducted than indicated in this story, titled "Evanston, Wyoming." This was business that I didn't feel was necessary to mention. Most business not mentioned was acted on <u>in</u> <u>favor</u> unanimously or by a majority. Therefore, I felt that if I had added all that took place in the <u>regular</u> and <u>special</u> meetings, it would have added too much to the story, which I believe would have been much more boring to the reader.

Thank you,
Dennis J Ottley, Author

EPILOGUE

I really enjoyed my time in City Government, except for the last two years, and I'm sure I would have enjoyed it then if it hadn't been for one city council member who was causing all the problems. I feel that if the four members had been stronger and had a mind of their own, we all could have and would have gotten a whole lot more accomplished. I feel that those four members would have worked with me to do was right for the public's best interest. I believe the four members would have been much more cooperative and much firmer in their beliefs and principals, but apparently they chose to let the one council member intimidate and control them, just because she had a grudge to hold.

Evanston needs strong leadership from the top and not a <u>yes</u> person. The mayor needs members from the council that will uphold the Oath of Office that they swore by when elected. There is a reason every elected person is required to take and swear by that Oath.

It wasn't very long into 1995 before the city council decided to come up with a new flag. They didn't seem to appreciate the flag that the City of Evanston had already adopted by Resolution 92-14 during their February 26, 1992 city council meeting.

We had a flag company design the flag with the Wyoming Cowboy and the official City of Evanston Seal in gold placed in the middle of the cowboy, and Evanston's promotional logo, "Fresh Air, Freedom and Fun" added. The flag was solid white with the cowboy and logo in red and blue, making the flag Red, White and Blue, with the gold City Seal. It was a flag of real class.

I have got to agree that their new flag is also beautiful, but they had voted on the previous flag by Resolution and I can't see why they changed it, unless it was to spite me, but it didn't bother me much.

They apparently didn't want anything to remind them of my administration. It was too late to change the official City of Evanston Seal, because it was embedded all over town in buildings and monuments. It would have been much too expensive for them to change that, but I bet they thought about it.

This administration also discontinued the Support Your Community Week program. That was a shame because the program was getting bigger and more popular than ever after eight years running. It was a program that helped the economy because of the involvement of all the citizens taking part in it. It was one of the best programs Evanston ever had getting local folks involved. Folks of all ages participated and volunteered to make the program a big success each year. It also helped the economy by bringing people, local and visitors, to either participate or as spectators. It was a shame to discontinue it.

One other change they made, which was on my agenda for years, was the new design of the police cars. But it was so far down on my agenda that I thought there were many more important items in the budget to consider. I didn't have anything against the all-white car with the wording of "Evanston Police" and "To Serve and Protect" on each of them. I actually thought they looked pretty classy, but I do like their new police car design even more. I think they look more like police cars with the new design, so I would have been in favor of that change.

I don't know why Mayor Davis and the city council decided to take their Retreat to Rock Springs this year. We had always held it in one of the motels in Evanston to help the economy. A Retreat is supposed to be a meeting of the mayor and council by themselves with no disturbance, but in this case all department heads were also invited, and according to Councilwoman Wall's report they had 100% of the department heads in attendance. That took a lot of leadership out of Evanston for the day and had to be very costly. Why they took it out of town I don't understand, especially after Mayor Davis had been so adamant about shopping in town.

I recall a Letter to the Editor that Councilman Davis wrote, which was published in April of 1994, climbing all over the First Security

Bank (presently Wells Fargo) for purchasing a contractor from our neighboring state of Utah to do their spring landscaping.

However, the incident of the Retreat being held in Rock Springs really upset my wife, Sandy. She, still being quite upset about the election, wrote a Letter to the Editor condemning the council for taking their business out of town, especially after Mayor Davis's recent article in the paper titled, *"Supporting ourselves begins by shopping locally."*

Uinta County Herald edition March 3, 1995

Free tuition

Richard Meyer, right, executive director with the Lifelong Learning Center, presents Dennis and Sandy Ottley with a lifetime tuition waiver for credit-free classes at the center in appreciation of their service to Evanston.

Letter to the Editor of Uinta County Herald of March 7, 1995 by Evanston's former First Lady Sandy Ottley

Buy local? Mayor Davis, council called on out-of-town retreat

Dear Editor:

I am quite confused concerning the guest editorial written by Mayor Will Davis, which was in the Herald issue of March 3, 1995.

His article was titled, "Supporting ourselves begins by shopping locally."

I'm confused when he stressed that we (the citizens of Evanston and Uinta County) should shop at home because when we purchase items in Utah or even Rock Springs, those dollars are used in those areas to help their economy, their youth activities, road repairs, etc., and then he wrote "the city council and city department heads met and established some goals to guide our efforts in the future."

What I don't understand is if he wants us, the citizens, to shop at home, why did the mayor, six council members and eight or so department heads have a so called retreat at a motel in Rock Springs on Feb. 17 and 18, 1995?

This was an overnight trip and had to cost the taxpayers of Evanston $3,000 or $4,000. They claim the reason was so they would not be disturbed and could have their privacy.

Hold on! I am sure that the local motel and/or restaurant owners would make sure that they were not disturbed if this money had been spent in Uinta County, or are meals not part of the mayor's shop at home plan? Is his philosophy 'do as I say, not what we do?"

Sandy L. Ottley
of Evanston

Letters to the Editor, *Uinta Country Herald*, March 7, 1995, by Evanston's former first lady, Sandy Ottley.

She got accused of "sour grapes" and "bad sportsmanship", but it was the truth, and she thought that the folks of Evanston wanted the truth. They say that truth always prevails.

But at any rate, on the morning after the last meeting I opened on January 11, 1995, I went to work at my real estate office and began to concentrate only on Uinta Realty, Inc. I no longer had the worry about what was happening in the City of Evanston.

With the help of my Secretary and Sales Associate, Traci Gomez and Bert Slavens, also Sale Associate, Uinta Realty, Inc. began to get real busy and become one of Evanston's busiest and largest agencies.

In March of 1995 Pastor Richard Meyer, Executive Director with Life Long Learning Center, presented Sandy and me with a lifetime tuition waiver for classes at the Center in appreciation for the service we had given Evanston over the years.

It was a great honor from a great person and a good friend. Although we were very appreciative of the certificate, we never used it.

In spring of 1995 the Evanston City Council decided to do the Yellow Creek Road landscaping. I guess Wall and Vranish were anxious to uphold their campaign promise. Even though we had budgeted for it and that doing the east side of Yellow Creek Road was fine, I felt that they should have waited on the west side, which is in Ward 1 (Vranish's Ward), until they first got the high power overhead line underground. There were monies budgeted for the project of burying the overhead line under Community Development: EUC in the amount of $50,000.

It was too bad that Vranish and the mayor hadn't had the line buried first, because now the city would have the problem with trees growing into the lines, causing problems like those the city had on the northwesterly side of Harrison Drive.

Two great things happened that year that I was really happy about: the first was the grand opening of Union Tank Car Company's new plant. I was very glad to get a personal invitation from CEO Ken Fischl, who was present at the grand opening. During his speech in opening the facility, and it was a beautiful plant, Fischl named me, out of all the folks present, and said "Your former Mayor Dennis Ottley is the man you all need to give credit to for this plant becoming a reality. He is the guy that you all should thank." I was really glad that I came and really glad to hear him make that statement.

The second thing that made me feel good was the announcement that the Silver Eagle Refining Company would be opening up in 1996 at full production. The Uinta County Economic Development Board assisted in getting the refinery back in operation again. Apparently, they had found federal funding to assist them in the re-opening of the old Oxbow Refinery.

After hearing this I once again met Don Biggs, who would be the General Manager and told him I would like to think that my visits and conversations with Wyoming's Congressional Delegation last year, at least, helped somewhat. But it was great news and I couldn't wait until they got the facility in operation.

The one thing that really disappointed me with the city was, not too long after the new administration went in, they closed the shop and ended the city's recycling program. This was a big disappointment because it was going along so well when I left office.

It was years before they got it going again, but it wasn't because of the city, it was because of the local citizens who were recycling advocates. They formed a committee, turned into a nonprofit corporation, and got the city to participate by leasing them a building. This corporation is still active with a big following of participants. It's a great program and saves thousands on our solid waste landfill.

It was about a year or so after I went out of office when Councilman Clarence Vranish came to my real estate office and asked me if he could talk to me. I said yes and told him to have a seat at my desk.

He said he wanted to apologize to me for the way he and others treated me during the election and how wrong they were. He admitted that they were way out of line. He also stated that he thought I had been the best mayor of Evanston that he had any knowledge of and thanked me for my service.

I didn't know what he had in mind, at the time, but I did appreciate his apology and his visit, something that I wasn't expecting. He's the only one of the five council members that said any more than "Hi" since the election.

In the *Uinta County Herald* of September 29, 1998, Clarence Vranish, no longer a member of the Evanston City Council, published a Letter to the Editor explaining my part in obtaining the 265 acres from Union Pacific Resources and being successful in keeping Union Tank Car Company in Evanston.

Again, I had no idea why, or what his reasoning was, but I could guess. However, whatever reason he had was appreciated because what he said in his letter was true.

Like they say, *the truth always comes out.*

[handwritten: does he want our support? or what Ha Ha,]

LETTERS

Evanston's Union Center the vision of a prescient leader and example

Dear Editor:

When we celebrate the accomplishments of today, we often forget those who deserve the praise and credit for a job well done, which actually served as the foundation and cornerstone of those accomplishments for which we now take credit.

In 1992 and 1993, the City of Evanston received title to 265 acres that was donated by Union Pacific Land Resources.

This was due to the efforts and vision of one man, Mayor Dennis Ottley.

Mayor Ottley also felt that the name "Union Center" would continually remind future generations of the very generous donation offered by Union Pacific, thereby promoting and ensuring the future economic success of the Evanston community.

At the grand opening celebration, Union Tank Car Company President Ken Fischl praised the visit to their Chicago headquarters paid by Mayor Ottley, Dennis Boal and council member Tom Hutchinson as being the one single event that convinced them to build their new facility in the Union Center Complex in Evanston.

Thanks to his vision of the future and the endless hours spent in pursuit of that vision by Evanston Mayor Dennis Ottley, Evanston today has an industrial center in which we can take tremendous pride and which will adequately serve as a cornerstone for Evanston's future and ensure our community's economic vitality for many years to come.

On behalf of the citizens of Evanston, I want to thank Mayor Dennis Ottley for his vision and for a job well done. Thank you.

Clarence Vranish
Evanston City Council

Letters to the Editor, *Uinta Country Herald*, September 29, 1998, by former City Councilman Clarence Varnish.

Although I feel very relieved from city politics, I feel that I was a good mayor and upheld my Oath of Office, always keeping the citizens' best interests in mind. Regardless of others' opinions, I am very proud of my performance as your leader of the community of Evanston, Wyoming, and I thank the folks of Evanston for that opportunity to serve.

"Fear is a reaction, Courage is a decision"
by
Winston Churchill

P. S. For over 40 years I had practically lived on *Rolaids*. Why? I don't know, unless it was because of being in business and in local politics all that time. I used to eat *Rolaids* like candy during that time, but since I got beat in my last election I have not bought a *Rolaid* since. No more heartburn. I am feeling great!

ACKNOWLEDGMENTS

This book would never have been written if it hadn't been for a number of people who had assisted me in remembering some of the events and occurrences mentioned in the book, and making minutes of meetings and other materials available to me. In showing my appreciation I wish to name those folks.

First of all, I would like to thank my wife Sandy for all her support and encouragement she gave me to help me through this book. There were many times when I was ready to quit, but with her encouragement and her editing, I was able to get it finished.

I also wish to thank Maryl Thompson, Receptionist and Administrative Assistant of my real estate agency, Uinta Realty, Inc., for all the assistance she gave me in using my computer. When I had a computer problem, she was always on hand to help me through it, as did Tonya Dennis, Associate Broker in the office, who also assisted me on the computer when necessary.

Also, I want to thank the Executive Assistant to the Mayor of Evanston and Deputy City Clerk Nancy Stevenson for her time and hard work in providing me with 16 years of copies of the minutes of all the official meetings of the Evanston City Council during my tenure as Mayor of Evanston, 1979-1983 and 1987-1995, plus the term of Mayor Gene Martin, 1983-1987.

Other folks I wish to thank and show appreciation to are Shelly and Deann Horne of Creative Ink Images for their assistance in preparing the book cover; and Former City Engineer Brian Honey for information he provided me concerning the Sulphur Creek Dam Project and many other projects that were constructed during my term as Mayor. Brian was City Engineer under me for my last eight years in office. Thanks are also due to City Attorney Dennis Boal for straightening me out on a few matters. Dennis was my City Attorney also during my final eight years of my term as mayor. Thanks also to retired Urban Renewal Agency Director Jim Davis for providing me with information for my book; and former City Councilmember Tom Hutchinson for the information and input that he provided me. Other city employees that I wish to thank are Paul Knopf, former city planner, Public Works Superintendent Allan "Oop" Hansen and Engineering Tech Bob Liechty for their input to my story.

I also want to thank the Uinta County Library in Evanston for the use of their equipment, the Uinta County Museum in Evanston and the Evanston Chamber of Commerce for materials provided me to be used in my book; and the *Uinta County Herald* for giving me the opportunity to look through many of their old newspapers.

I appreciate all those named above for the completion of this book *"Evanston, Wyoming…Boom-Bust-Politics"*.

However, I want to let you, the reader, know that almost all of the material used in this story was from my personal collection of photos, newspaper clippings, letters, etc., and from the actual minutes of the Evanston meetings during the period from 1967 to 1995. But some material is also from my own memory and from talking to some of those folks I mentioned above.

Thank You…
April 25, 2018

ABOUT THE BOOK

EVANSTON, WYOMING, is a story about one man's experience as a city official and about an old railroad tent city, "Hell on Wheels," that grew to become an amazing small community in southwestern Wyoming. It was a community that had gone through many boom/bust periods, yet survived through the hard times as well as the good times by having a good strong base of loving citizens.

This story is also a tale of a city official who served Evanston as a three-term city council member and a three-term mayor, and how it affected his life and family; plus the hell he went through trying to keep the community together through the toughest boom period in Wyoming history.

The book gives a full accounting of small town dirty politics of untruths, innuendoes and right-down vicious lies, and how it could have split the city. But this mayor, who was dedicated to the people and driven by his love for his community, was able to keep the economy strong and the community united.

ABOUT THE AUTHOR

Born January 28, 1932 in Salt Lake City, Utah, Dennis ended up in Evanston, Wyoming. He quit high school and joined the 141st Tank Battalion of the Wyoming National Guard.

When the Korean War started in 1950, his unit was called to active duty in September, but he and his wife, Sandy got married on July 26, 1950 before he left for active duty, and to serve time in Korea.

Dennis and Sandy settled in Evanston, where he served three 4-year terms as a member of the Evanston city council and three 4-year terms as mayor. Dennis retired at the age of 81 from his real estate agency, and after raising four sons and over 68 years of marriage, he and his wife Sandy still reside in Evanston.

www.ingramcontent.com/pod-product-compliance
Lightning Source LLC
Chambersburg PA
CBHW030410100426
42812CB00028B/2903/J